The Air Traffic System

Second Edition

A Commonsense Guide

The Air Traffic System

Second Edition

A Commonsense Guide

Milovan S. Brenlove

Iowa State Press
A Blackwell Publishing Company

MILOVAN S. BRENLOVE, of Bedford, New Hampshire, is an adjunct professor at Daniel Webster College in Nashua, New Hampshire, a flight instructor, and a freelance writer.

© 1987 Iowa State University Press
© 2003 Iowa State Press
A Blackwell Publishing Company
All rights reserved

Iowa State Press
2121 State Avenue, Ames, Iowa 50014

Orders: 1-800-862-6657
Office: 1-515-292-0140
Fax: 1-515-292-3348
Web site: www.iowastatepress.com

♾ Printed on acid-free paper in the United States of America

Second edition, 2003

Library of Congress Cataloging-in-Publication Data

Brenlove, Milovan S.
  The air traffic system : a commonsense guide / Milovan S. Brenlove.—
2nd ed.
    p. cm.
  Includes index.
   ISBN 0-8138-2960-7 (alk. paper)
   1. Air traffic control. I. Title
   TL725.3.T7 B665 2003
   6.136'6—dc21   2002155123

The last digit is the print number: 9 8 7 6 5 4 3 2 1

CONTENTS

DEDICATION

To Amanda and Rachael. The unending joy you have brought to my life is greater than any gift I could ever hope to receive.

WHEN I FIRST DECIDED to write this book, I believed my somewhat unique position of being both a pilot and an air traffic controller afforded me an equally unique perspective on the air traffic system. Now, twenty-plus years later, my perspective has shifted more toward that of a pilot and educator while the air traffic system I wrote about has undergone significant transformation. Still, as I knew then, my experiences as a pilot had helped me to become a better controller, and I knew that my experiences as a controller had made my life as a pilot a whole lot easier. Today, that belief continues to hold true for me.

I also knew then that too many general aviation pilots didn't know as much about the air traffic system as they should. So I thought I'd try to give them a hand at figuring out a system that, in spite of the fact that it existed to help them, seemed to be creating as many problems as it solved. Only later did I learn that more than a few air carrier pilots, steeped in the ways of the world of instrument flight, likewise wanted more information about how best to use the air traffic control (ATC) system for their own personal flying.

At that time, there weren't any publications that provided a simple, understandable, commonsense approach to using that air traffic system. There were government publications and a number of pamphlets and circulars that addressed one topic or another, but nothing that put it all into an easy-to-read and easy-to-use format for pilots. Hence, in 1987, the first edition of *The Air Traffic System, A Commonsense Guide* was born at Iowa State University Press.

Since those first copies of *The Air Traffic System* rolled off the presses, much has changed in our world of flying. In keeping with the international order of things, the airspace in the United States underwent a comprehensive reclassification. Gone are the TCAs, ARSAs, and the PCA that many of us grew up with. In their place are the likes of A, B, and C airspace. The then-wave of the navigational future, the microwave landing system (MLS), turned out to be little more than a ripple, swamped by the new kid on the block, GPS, the global positioning system. Even signage at the local airports had to change with the times. But while technology and change have run rampant throughout aviation, the real news is that much has remained unchanged with respect to the pilot/controller relationship.

The real heart of the ATC system is the pilots and the controllers who work with it on a daily basis. While most do an extremely good job of making that system work very well, because of the increased complexities of our present-day world, newcomers and many pilots educated in the old ways of using the ATC system have a lot more to comprehend than ever before.

Having spent the last fourteen years as a professor in a collegiate aviation program teaching both pilot and air traffic control students the art of participating in the pilot/controller relationship, my worldview may have changed a bit from the days when being a controller was my primary occupation. But the underlying premise that first prompted me to write this book has stayed the same. Beginning and experienced pilots alike have a lot to learn about the system that was developed to assist them. Since controllers heavily depend upon pilots to understand and fulfill their role in using the ATC system, to journey into that arena lacking the necessary knowledge is to ask for problems that don't need to exist.

So where do we start? We start by boiling down all the rules, regulations, and procedures to the essence of their existence. When it comes down to it, whether you are an IFR pilot flying professionally or a VFR pilot out for personal pleasure, everything within the ATC system exists for the purpose of getting you from Point A to Point B as efficiently as possible, without hitting the ground, obstructions, or other aircraft. As an aside, although a very important aside, as much as possible the ATC system also exists to assist pilots in avoiding weather conditions that may prove hazardous in flight. Simply stated, controllers are there to help you obtain the most from all the technology and procedures that have been developed for your use.

Step number two in the process is that, to avail yourself of everything possible from the ATC system and the controllers who staff it, you have to ask about everything that does not make sense to you. Experienced pilots ask questions about anything, any time a doubt exists. If, after the second run-through with a controller some questions still exist, they ask again. In recent years, most of the major incidents and accidents that have occurred in aviation have not been the result of mechanical failure or some other uncontrollable event but rather have resulted from miscommunication or misunderstanding between pilots and controllers.

To ask the right questions, you have to have some idea of what the right answers should be. All too often pilots, particularly those who are relatively new to flying, plod along blindly hoping either that the correct answer to a question will appear to them out of the blue (no pun intended) or that the controller, who never makes a mistake, will discern that the person at the other end of the mike didn't quite understand the instructions he (or she) just received. Unfortunately, neither of those events is likely to occur.

Throughout my years of teaching pilots how to better function within the IFR environment, one of the most significant points I urged them to remember was never to allow controllers, regardless of how well informed or well intentioned they may be, to lead them through a flight without constantly challenging (though not necessarily always on the frequency) their instructions. To do so is to give up the authority that should only reside in the cockpit. It can be done, but never without compromising the checks-and-balances safety valve built into the system.

The only way to correctly assess and effectively challenge what is happening or is about to happen is to know what is supposed to happen. And the only way to know what is supposed to happen is to have a solid foundation of knowledge from which to draw conclusions. While this book is not meant to be a substitute for a sound program of instruction and a good deal of self-study, it will give you the knowledge that my experiences as an air traffic controller, a pilot, and an instructor have given me throughout the years. Each of my roles in aviation has yielded a slightly different perspective on flying and a wealth of piloting experience from which to draw.

Over the years I have watched as thousands of pilots acted and reacted within the air traffic system. I learned as experienced pilots successfully used time-tested procedures to solve their problems and as novice pilots stumbled through common problems with a new sense of determination. Over the past fourteen years, I learned what goes on in the cockpit and in the minds of students trying to cope with high workloads while simultaneously trying to fit into a complex, dynamic environment. These experiences have enabled me to develop some ideas that have made my personal flying easier and more enjoyable. My hope is to share those ideas with you in the pages ahead.

Most of us will never become professional pilots, but we can become confident, safety-conscious airmen. As more people discover the fun of flying and learn the value of a "personal aircraft" for business and pleasure, the one sky we all have to share continues to get more and more crowded. We owe it to ourselves, our passengers, and our fellow pilots to develop our individual skills and knowledge to the highest degree possible.

I have come to believe that the problems don't lie with the logic of learning as much as possible about the ATC system or even learning as many of the Federal Aviation Regulations (FARs) as possible—as convoluted as they may seem. Rather it's that the rules, regulations, and procedures, if learned without a structure to put them in, tend to get all mixed up when combined with the task of flying a fast-moving airplane through a constricted chunk of airspace, while listening to a fast-paced controller joining into the mix. Most of the time this happens because the rules themselves do not really teach you what to expect. But if you can develop a normal progression of events to follow, and if you can learn how to use both the advantages and the limitations of the air traffic system to your benefit, then the entire problem becomes much easier to solve.

I hope that when you finish reading this book you will have more insight into why certain procedures and regulations exist. I also hope you will have gained enough knowledge and experience to save time, avoid common problems, and increase your flying safety. As you diligently add the hours to your logbook, the day will come when you will look back and wonder what all the confusion was about. You even may have added a few controllers to your list of friends. After all, in America anything is possible.

Defining Terms

The definitions and expanded descriptions of most of the specific terms relating to equipment, procedures, rules, and regulations that have been referred to throughout this book can be found in the Pilot/Controller Glossary. This document has been incorporated as an appendix into both the *Aeronautical Information Manual* and the *Air Traffic Control Manual*, published yearly by the U.S. government. I believe that no other single document contributes more to improving the effectiveness of the pilot/controller partnership. By providing the same definitions and descriptions to both pilots and air traffic controllers, the Pilot/Controller Glossary establishes a common foundation of knowledge from which participants may expand their understanding of the basic principles and elements that make up the procedures by which the air traffic system functions. It is the one glossary that every pilot and controller should read from start to finish.

Acknowledgments

Despite the fact that my name alone appears on this book, there are a number of people who have, in significant ways, helped to make it happen. I would like to take a moment to thank some of them.

First and foremost I would like to thank my wife, Charlotte, for her patience and support through it all. Her willingness to leave me to my thoughts and writing made a difficult task so much easier. I also want to thank Steve Kantola, a special friend who took most of the tower and approach control photographs in this edition and helped me get past the hurdles so I could spend valuable time at Pittsburgh Tower. Similar thanks go to Pete Pasquale for obtaining authorization for my visit to Boston Center, not an easy task in these post-September 11 days. Finally, I want to thank a number of people from Iowa State Press. Special thanks to Dave Rosenbaum for planting the seed for a revised edition and believing it was a worthwhile project. Thanks, too, to Tad Ringo for so effectively shepherding this project through its various stages. Last, but certainly not least, thanks to Carol Kromminga for her editing of my manuscript. To all those other folks behind the scenes who helped to make a pile of pages into a book that I am proud to have my name on, thank you too.

The Air Traffic System

Second Edition

A Commonsense Guide

Control Positions:
Where Are They?

IN THE FIRST DAYS OF MY FLYING LIFE, even after I had been an air traffic controller for some time, it struck me that whenever I talked to a controller over the radio, it seemed as though the voice booming back at me was some disembodied entity emanating from who knew where. So it seemed likely that if I felt that way, knowing what I did about the ATC system, other pilots with little or no knowledge of where that voice was coming from would feel even more confused and intimidated. Where was this person who was talking to me on the radio? How did this man or woman know who and where I was? How did this person relate to the next person I was going to talk to?

The answers to those and similar questions, however, are a good beginning for exploring the labyrinth that is the home for controllers. In the process of those discussions, an invaluable tool that can help make sense of the seemingly chaotic order is *visualization*. Experience as a controller, flight instructor, and pilot has confirmed for me that one of the easiest ways to pull together a host of disconnected elements and put them into an easily remembered, functional model is to create a mental picture of what seems to be an abstract concept.

Learning about the air traffic control (ATC) system is no different. Even if you have never been in a control tower, radar room (TRACON), or an en route center, you can use your imagination to create one. Most of us have seen a control tower at one time or another so that one is fairly easy, at least from the outside. Most radar rooms are located somewhere close to the tower—although the trend is toward regional TRACONs located almost anywhere—and are in a darkened room with no windows. En route centers, like the regional TRACONs, are found in larger windowless buildings, also located almost anywhere, regardless of their proximity to an airport.

The next step in the visualization process, and one that is worth practicing before every flight, is to mentally fly the entire trip before ever setting foot into an airplane. What person will I talk to first? What will that person say? After that, then what? Put the subjects, people, and rules into a logical, practical sequence. When the ATC system and the controllers who serve it are considered step-by-step, rather than as a whole, much of what seems confusing at the outset actually falls into a very understandable and usable sequence.

The best way to put all the pieces of the puzzle together is to develop an understanding of exactly which controller is where and who and how close her colleagues are. A lot of needless confusion stems from the fact that many pilots do not understand which controller is talking to them or how one controller's job relates to another's. But it is worth noting that, regardless of where a controller happens to be located, if she needs to talk to the next controller down the line, she almost always has a quick and easy avenue for communication. Controllers heavily rely on the timely exchange of flight information among themselves. So, once a pilot is "in the system," he seldom needs to be concerned about whether or not the next controller knows he is coming.

To create sense and order out of the confusion, it helps to identify the various elements and controllers you would be likely to encounter if you were to fly out of a major airport. Since smaller airports often combine two or more control positions onto one radio frequency, using a large airport simply ensures that the various responsibilities of each controller won't get lost in the shuffle. Large airport or small, the procedures are the same. It is just a matter of how many frequency changes you make and how many different people you talk to. But enough of generalities, it's time to examine those controller positions and how they will affect your main objective, getting out of the blocks and on your way.

ATIS

The *Automatic Terminal Information Service (ATIS)*, though not really a position manned by controllers, since many are now computer-generated and not "manned" at all, is the source of a lot of valuable information for pilots and should be the first frequency a pilot listens to. Since every controlled airport doesn't necessarily have an ATIS available, it's wise to check either a sectional chart (the ATIS frequency or frequencies are listed just beneath the tower frequency) or the U.S. government's *Airport/Facility Directory (A/FD)* (the frequency or frequencies are listed under "communications") to determine both the existence of an ATIS and how many different ATISs there are.

To keep the ATIS message as short as possible, most of the major airports have one ATIS for arriving aircraft and another for departing aircraft. Once the correct frequency is tuned in, a pilot need only listen to the recording and write down the information he believes is most important.

The ATIS is a continuously broadcast recorded message that contains information that is essential for pilots flying into or out of an airport. This includes current weather conditions at the airport, the runway or runways in use, the instrument approaches in use, runway or taxiway closures, construction, or anything else that could affect the safety of your flight. The ATIS is updated every hour, or sooner if new or unexpected conditions warrant the need for a change. As a matter of practice, that usually means that about five to ten minutes before every hour a new ATIS will be recorded. If you plan to depart or arrive within that time frame, it would be best to wait until a few minutes after the hour to check the ATIS. If waiting isn't possible, then you should expect to return to the ATIS frequency for the new information. Often, if time permits, controllers will just broadcast any significant changes, but either way, getting the latest information is something that should not be ignored.

Each updated recording is identified by a different letter of the alphabet. For example, if the 14:00 UTC ATIS recording is information A (or Alpha, as it is known in the phonetic alphabet), then, assuming no unexpected conditions or changes in the interim, the 15:00 UTC recording would be information B (Bravo), and so on after that.

The ATIS serves several purposes. First, it relieves controllers of the tedious and often time-consuming task of relaying the same information to every pilot they talk to. In the process of providing that relief, it frees up the frequency for both pilots and controllers to use it for more time-critical communications. Second, the ATIS provides pilots with the opportunity to obtain common but vital information at their own pace. Since the recording repeats itself about every thirty to forty-five seconds, if you miss something the first time around, you only have to wait a few seconds to hear the information again.

Although there are no regulations that make it mandatory for pilots to listen to the ATIS broadcast, there is a rule that requires that at least one controller ensures that every pilot has received the information contained in that broadcast. Consequently, if you, the pilot, do not listen to the ATIS and then advise the controller that you have not listened, the controller must then make up for your omission. Not surprising, most controllers aren't overjoyed at having to take time away from more important concerns to repeat information that a pilot could have obtained in a less-disruptive way. You can buck the system and ask the controller to give you your own personal broadcast or you can be considerate and professional and listen to the ATIS. If you choose the former, it can truly become a situation of "pay me now or pay me later" when it comes to playing the rest of the game. Regardless, since the controller needs to know whether or not you have the information, the best way to accomplish that task is, whenever you first talk to a controller at a different facility (i.e., Boston Approach vs. Bradley Approach), advise her that you have received the ATIS information.

On a practical note, when you do get ready to listen to the ATIS, pick a time to do it when you will be free from interruptions and can concentrate on listening. When getting ready to depart, it can be a good idea to listen to the ATIS even before starting your engine. That way, if there are traffic or weather delays that could impede your departure, you can find out without having wasted any fuel. Although those delays most often affect only pilots planning an instrument flight, occasionally even the VFR pilots may be subject to a delay.

If you are arriving at an airport with an approach control, listen to the ATIS before you contact the approach controller. If you will initially contact the tower, then, likewise, listen to the ATIS prior to that initial contact. Even if you have been receiving advisories from another facility and the controller there advises you to contact the approach controller for your destination airport, the time to listen to the ATIS is still before you call the approach controller. While it is unwise to stay "between frequencies" for an extended period of time, taking a minute or so to listen to the ATIS without having to keep one ear on the broadcast and the other on the approach frequency is preferable to immediately going to approach control and then possibly missing important information on one frequency or the other.

The phraseology for telling the controller you have listened to the ATIS is simple: "Boston Approach, Mooney 801 Delta Whiskey inbound with information Alpha." Or, "Manchester Ground, Cessna 1234 Charlie taxi for takeoff with information Alpha."

ATIS was developed to assist pilots by making important information available in a convenient, easy-to-use format. It was also developed to significantly reduce the controllers' workload. Always using that tool makes it a win-win situation for everyone.

Clearance Delivery

The next step on the way out of the ATC maze is the clearance delivery position. This one also can be utilized before engine start-up (fig. 1.1). While larger airports have a specific radio frequency dedicated to clearance delivery (also available in the *Airport/Facility Directory*), at most smaller airports, clearance delivery and ground control are combined on the ground control frequency. Regardless of whether there is a specific frequency for clearance delivery or whether the responsibility for that position is combined with ground control, your actions and responses do not have to be any different.

Next consider if you even need an Air Traffic Clearance to begin your flight, keeping in mind that many pilots confuse an Air Traffic Clearance with an ATC instruction. The Pilot/Controller Glossary in the *Aeronautical Information Manual* (AIM) defines Air Traffic Clearance as "an authorization by air traffic control for the purpose of preventing collision between known aircraft, for an aircraft to proceed under specified traffic conditions within controlled airspace." Whereas the Pilot/Controller Glossary defines ATC Instruc-

Fɪɢ. 1.1. The clearance delivery controller issues an IFR/VFR clearance to aircraft awaiting departure.

tions as "directives issued by air traffic control for the purpose of requiring a pilot to take specific actions; e.g., 'Turn left heading two five zero,' 'Go around,' 'Clear the runway.'" It is possible and often likely that a VFR pilot is able to depart a controlled airport without having received an Air Traffic Clearance, but it is all but impossible to do so without having received at least one or two ATC instructions.

So, when do you need to contact clearance delivery for a clearance? For the pilot planning to depart on an instrument clearance, the answer is simple. He always needs to contact clearance delivery to obtain an IFR clearance. Although recent advances provide many air carrier and corporate pilots the ability to obtain their IFR clearances electronically, for the time being most general aviation pilots still have to use the radio to accomplish the same thing.

For the pilot planning to depart an airport VFR, it isn't quite as routine. Saving many of the specifics of airspace requirements for later chapters, a good rule of thumb is that if a separate clearance delivery frequency exists, it is probably an indication that a VFR pilot will need some type of clearance to depart the airport. Add to that rule the idea that, if your departure will take you through Class B or Class C airspace or a TRSA (Terminal Radar Service Area), then some type of clearance will usually be required. But if ever a doubt exists as to whether or not a clearance is required, the simplest solution is to contact the clearance delivery controller and ask.

Most often the clearance delivery controller is located in the tower. Although the controller assigned to that position does not actually separate airplanes, it is still as important as any other control position in the tower. The clearance he issues to a VFR pilot could include an initial heading to fly or an altitude to maintain. In the case of the instrument pilot, the clearance most likely will include routing all the way to the destination airport with the implicit authorization that, should the pilot ever lose radio communication capability, he may continue to his destination via the route and altitude issued in that clearance. So, whether IFR or VFR, a mutually correct understanding of any clearance is essential for every pilot and controller.

Making sure the clearance has been correctly received is an important responsibility for the pilot, so be ready to listen and write before contacting the clearance delivery controller. You do not want to miss something because you were fumbling around for a pencil and paper as the clearance was being issued. Since almost every clearance is issued in a standard format, many pilots develop their own form based upon that format and essentially end up just filling in the blanks as opposed to having to write the entire clearance. Regardless of whether you are IFR or VFR, get into the habit of writing down the important parts of the clearance and then reading them back to the controller. That gives you the advantage of having a ready reference for later use and also of having someone confirm that you have copied down the correct information.

Occasionally though, especially when clearance delivery and ground control are combined, you may be authorized to start your taxi and told to "stand by" for your clearance. Then, almost inevitably, somewhere along the taxi route the controller contacts you and advises, "I have your clearance, advise ready to copy." At that point, your response should be nothing other than, "Stand by." Too many pilots have the misimpression that they need to start copying their clearances immediately, all too often at the risk of running off of a taxiway or into another airplane in the process. It is completely acceptable to either ask the controller if you may stop where you are to copy the clearance or just advise her that, upon reaching the run-up area, you will contact her for your clearance. Just because you don't need your hands to steer an airplane on the ground doesn't mean you don't need your eyes and brain to determine where you are going. When it is convenient for you, your clearance will still be available. There is no need to rush.

One item you will almost always be given as part of your clearance is a *departure control frequency*. Particularly for the inexperienced pilot, this frequency and when to use it create varying degrees of confusion. For now, just make a mental note that it is usually assigned by the clearance delivery controller. In a few pages, what to do with it should eliminate that confusion.

Whether a pilot is planning to fly on an instrument clearance or depart the airport VFR determines how much information the clearance delivery controller has ahead of time. For the IFR pilot, the flight plan he filed, either with a flight service specialist or through some electronic means, is ultimately fed into the air traffic computer belonging to the en route center that is responsible for the airspace through which he will initially depart. Exactly which en route center that is, for the purpose of correct distribution, is of no real consequence to the pilot filing the flight plan.

NGF05E	0722	AGC	+AGC073 HOMEE JST300 JST+			
BE55/I	P1545		AGC JST V12 PTW V143***HYA			
739	90		OANGEL FLIGHT			

Fig. 1.2. A computer-generated flight progress strip awaits the IFR pilot at the departure airport.

The flight plan is automatically routed to the en route center about two hours before the pilot's proposed departure time and then is sent to the appropriate airport about thirty minutes prior to the planned departure. There, it is printed out on a piece of paper, or the electronic equivalent, called a *flight progress strip* (fig. 1.2). Printed on that strip is all the information a controller needs to effectively provide service for an IFR pilot. As indicated in figure 1.2, the aircraft identification, type aircraft and equipment, requested altitude, and route of flight as well as the proposed departure time and assigned transponder code are all available for the controller.

Of the points for the IFR pilot to consider, the first is that, depending upon how saturated the ATC system is on any given day, there can be a fifteen- to thirty-minute delay from the time the flight plan is filed until it is received at the departure airport. The second is that, on a normal day, an IFR flight plan is only kept on file for two hours after the pilot's proposed departure time. If a pilot anticipates a delay longer than two hours, he should file a revised departure time. Otherwise, when it comes time to pick up his clearance, that clearance will have already disappeared to the world of never-never land.

For the pilot who wants to depart an airport on a VFR clearance, the procedures are a little bit different. Even though a VFR pilot may have filed a VFR flight plan with flight service, the clearance delivery controller will have nothing on file regarding that flight plan. A VFR flight plan primarily is used for search-and-rescue in the event a pilot is determined to be overdue at his destination.

Consequently, instead of clearance delivery having a printed flight strip on hand for the VFR pilot, she will, instead, formulate a clearance based upon the information the pilot gives her over the radio. Once the clearance is developed, the controller then must handwrite it on a blank flight progress strip (fig. 1.3). Though not associated with the clearance delivery procedure, the same process of handwriting a strip also holds true when a VFR pilot contacts a controller for clearance into, as well as out of, the airspace. In either case, controllers do a lot of their planning based upon the information contained

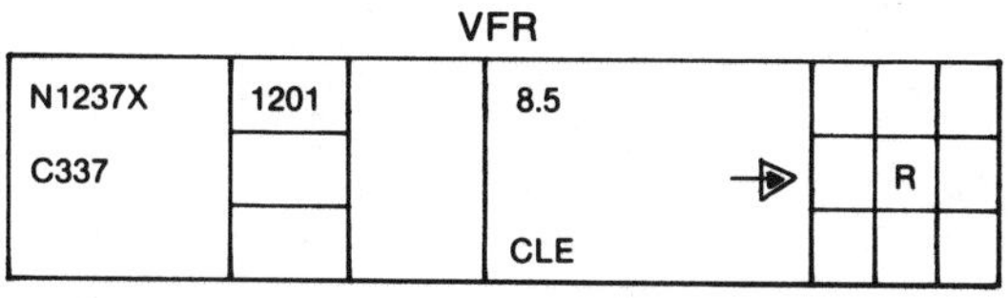

			VFR				
N1237X	1201		8.5				
C337					→▷	R	
			CLE				

Fig. 1.3. A flight progress strip provides the controller with all the necessary handwritten information about a VFR pilot.

COM3027	7454	A1547	IFR				
T/CRJ2/F	PYRAT						
151	WISKE		PIT				

FIG. 1.4. An IFR arrival strip provides advance information for controllers.

on the flight strips. If a pilot decides to change anything with respect to that information, he always needs to inform the controller of the change.

Whether IFR or VFR, either physically or by electronic duplication, the flight progress strip associated with your flight plan will be passed along to every controller who will be working with you along your route (fig. 1.4). This action accomplishes two things. First, it gives each controller advance notice that your flight will be passing through her airspace. That advance notice gives the controller the opportunity to take whatever action may be necessary to adjust or rearrange her traffic flow to accommodate your airplane. Second, since the controller has your flight strip before you even contact her, it eliminates the need for you to repeat the information you gave the first controller to every other controller down the line. All that information you gave clearance delivery about your direction of flight, destination, and altitude precedes you with every other controller you will talk to. So repeating everything every time you make a frequency change is not just an exercise in futility, it becomes a needless use of frequency time that could best be used in any number of different ways.

The whole idea behind having a clearance delivery position is to reduce, as much as possible, needless frequency congestion on the active control frequencies. Do not defeat its purpose by giving every subsequent controller you talk with the same five-minute dissertation you gave clearance delivery on initial contact. Rest assured, any time a controller needs more information, he will ask for it.

Ground Control

Once the preliminaries and the paperwork have been completed with the clearance delivery controller, it is time to get the show on the road and start taxiing. Since you are still sitting on the ground, it is only logical that the next person you should contact is the ground controller. But all is not quite as simple as might be hoped. Although at the smaller airports there is almost always only one ground controller responsible for the entire airport, at the major airports there are often two and occasionally even three different ground controllers. In order to find out which controller is the correct one for you, you may have to either consult the *Airport/Facility Directory* or listen to the departure ATIS for your instructions. If those options fail and you know ahead of time that the correct frequency for ground is just beyond your grasp, ask the clearance delivery controller during your preflight chat. It's not an unheard of request.

Keep in mind when talking to ground control, if ever there were a job that made a controller feel like a traffic cop, it would be ground control. Though the responsibilities may vary slightly from airport to airport, basically the ground controller's job is to control the movement of all the airplanes and the vehicles on that part of the airport known as the *movement area* (fig. 1.5). The movement area always includes taxiways, but it can also include various portions of the ramp area. Normally, any time a pilot wants to move his airplane beyond the parking area designated by a set of dashed and solid yellow lines (the solid line side indicates a nonmovement area), he must first receive approval from the ground controller.

Ground control may sound like one of the easiest jobs a controller may be asked to perform, but that is not necessarily the case. Try to picture one policeman being responsible for fifteen or twenty intersections, none of which have traffic lights, stop signs, or any other indication of who should be given the right-of-way. Add to that the fact that the same policeman has to talk repeatedly to whoever is responsible for any adjacent highways (those being the runways) and you can understand some of the issues a ground controller might face. Finally, there exists the very real possibility that many pilots tend to be a little less alert while operating on the ground.

So from where does the ground controller direct this intricate ballet of movement? She does so from the tower where she can visually keep track of the airplanes under her control. Although some of the country's larger airports have surface radar to assist the controller, it is mainly used at night or during periods of reduced visibility. Most of the time the ground controller works her craft by looking out the tower windows, with or without a pair of

FIG. 1.5. The ground controller is responsible for all aircraft movement to and from the runway.

binoculars, depending upon how far away the traffic is and how advanced in years the eyes of the beholder are. The ground controller's position in the tower cab is usually right next to the tower controller.

CONTROLLER COORDINATION

It is worth a few moments of slight digression here to mention some of the behind-the-scenes work that controllers do. Although in this case it applies to the ground and tower controllers, the basic process is true for all controllers and it is called *coordination*, discussing with one another the movement of traffic between or among their respective areas of responsibility.

One of the most basic and fundamental tenets of air traffic control is that one controller never allows an aircraft to enter another controller's area of jurisdiction without *first* having received approval to do so. While there are several methods by which that approval may be obtained, each requires some form of coordination. If I had to ballpark a percentage of the time that a controller spends talking on the frequency, it would be about 30 to 40 percent. Much of her remaining time is spent coordinating with someone about something in an effort to more effectively move the traffic.

The ground controller is no exception. Every time a pilot has to cross an active runway, the ground controller must obtain approval from the tower controller. Whenever a pilot is taxied down a runway, active or not, the ground controller must coordinate. The same holds true for vehicles, which, at one time or another at almost any airport, frequently outnumber the aircraft that are moving around. Sometimes, if the person working the tower position is too busy or too preoccupied with her own traffic to talk to the ground controller, a pilot on the ground may be delayed when, to him, there doesn't seem to be a justifiable reason. Rest assured, safety is the reason.

RUNWAY INCURSIONS

Over the past decade *runway incursions* have been and continue to be a source of real concern for the entire aviation community. A runway incursion is when there is a close call or a collision between aircraft or aircraft and vehicles on a runway that was supposed to have been occupied by one arrival or departure aircraft. Although these incursions occur at uncontrolled as well as controlled airports, when they happen at the latter, often the problem started with someone missing something in the communication loop with the ground controller.

With a few commonsense practices, every pilot should be able to reduce or eliminate his risk of becoming another runway incursion statistic. For starters, before making the initial call to ground control, double-check and make sure you are indeed ready to taxi. Particularly when one or more aircraft of the same or similar type request taxi instructions around the same time, a lot of needless confusion can be created when one pilot calls "Ready to taxi," and then sits on the ramp for another five or ten minutes. If an unanticipated delay occurs, let the controller know as soon as possible. When you are then ready to go, call again and request to taxi. Keep in mind that smaller registration numbers combined with parking ramps often being half a mile or so from the tower can make it all but impossible for the ground controller to tell one Cessna or Piper from another.

When you do finally contact the ground controller, tell her exactly where you are on the airport. She can begin to locate you and then decide on the most efficient path to get you to the correct active runway. In any case, do not leave the nonmovement area until you get the official go-ahead. To do otherwise could put you nose-to-nose with someone much bigger than you, in which case the "Golden-Tow Award" will be delivered to you as you are "tugged" back to start.

If you happen to be a stranger to the airport, several suggestions can help to keep you out of harm's way (fig. 1.6). One is to pick up one of the publications that provide "taxi charts" for the larger airports. They give a bird's-eye view of the airport with each taxiway labeled more clearly. But even with that in your lap, it would be wise to let your secret out and tell ground control that you are not familiar with the airport and you would like *progressive taxi instructions* to the active runway. The controller will give you step-by-step directions as you move along, and she will also give you a little more of her attention, particularly at those points where confusion might arise.

The request for progressive taxi instructions isn't unusual. Many professional pilots make it whenever they are unsure. Some who didn't ask, paid dearly for their reticence. With procedures that make some taxiways "occasionally runways" and vice versa, it is just too easy to get confused. Do not needlessly put yourself in a potentially dangerous situation. Getting pilots safely to the correct runway is the ground controller's job, so give her a chance to do it correctly.

Fig. 1.6. With so many runways and taxiways, asking for progressive taxi instructions can help eliminate confusion.

Once under way, there are a number of suggestions you can follow to make the journey safer. Remember that the instructions "taxi to the active runway" no longer authorize you to cross any *active runway* at any time without specific authorization. While it may seem like overkill to some pilots and controllers, my personal recommendation when crossing any runway at any controlled airport is that pilots ask for verification *prior* to crossing the runway. A simple "Confirm Cessna 2 Delta Whiskey is cleared to cross runway 28 Left at Bravo" is all that's needed. If you receive a snippy reply (which you most likely will not) that you were already cleared across, ignore it. You are much more likely to be injured by flying debris than that person up in the tower. Besides, my own experience is that 99 percent of the professionals do it, so why shouldn't you?

When you get the confirmation to go ahead, just as mom used to tell you, look both ways before crossing. It's still good advice. Most important, whenever any doubt exists about anything at all, ask for clarification!

The good news is that, by the time a pilot gets to the active runway, one of the more difficult parts of the trip is behind him and contact with the ground controller should be just about finished. For propeller-driven aircraft, it is expected that a run-up will be a routine part of the pretakeoff procedure and advising ground control of that fact is not necessary. But it is important to monitor the ground controller's frequency during the process. It is not necessary for a pilot to advise ground control when the pilot changes to the tower frequency, and most likely ground control will not remind him to do so. The accepted procedure is, when a pilot is ready to go, he will initiate a call to the tower controller to let her know.

The only common exception to that procedure is when there are more than one or two pilots waiting in line for takeoff. Then, rather than each pilot in line telling the tower controller he is ready to go, everyone will be advised to *monitor* the tower frequency. Monitor means that each pilot will switch to the tower frequency, but will, instead of checking in on the frequency, just listen for the tower controller to initiate communications with the pilot when it is his turn. One caution though, should you find yourself in the number-one position at the runway and you have not received a transmission from the tower, it's time to make a call and speak up. Somewhere, someone goofed.

It may not seem like it when you're sitting on the ground far away from that glass room in the sky, but that ground controller has all the tools she needs to help you get where you are going. With a little help and consideration from you, she will do her job correctly every time.

Local Control

When a pilot completes the preflight necessities, the next person in line to help get him going is the tower controller, or as she is referred to within the FAA, the local controller. The local controller is always found in the tower cab and her job is to separate and/or sequence all the aircraft operating within the local vicinity of the airport (fig. 1.7).

FIG. 1.7. The local controller is responsible for separating all traffic using the active runways.

SEPARATION VERSUS SEQUENCING

The difference between separating or sequencing aircraft is significant and needs to be understood. My own experience with students and discussions with other controllers have led me to understand that, all too frequently, pilots believe they are being provided separation when in fact they are only being sequenced.

When a controller is required to provide separation between aircraft, she is required by regulations to keep those aircraft a designated distance apart. For example, standard lateral separation between two IFR aircraft is three miles. When a controller is only sequencing aircraft, her job is to regulate which aircraft follows which. The responsibility for keeping those aircraft separated falls upon the pilots involved, not the controller.

If you are operating as a VFR pilot, whenever you are flying into or out of an airport or when you are staying in the traffic pattern, you are being sequenced not separated from the rest of the traffic in the local area. When you are advised to "report a one-mile left base leg" or "follow the traffic abeam the tower on a downwind," it is your responsibility to comply with those instructions. When you are instructed to look for traffic to follow and then you are advised to follow that traffic, you are the one who must maintain a safe distance from that traffic. For sure, the local controller will also be looking to ensure you and everyone else are following her instructions, but maintaining a safe distance from any other traffic in the area is still your responsibility.

If you are operating as an IFR pilot but flying into or out of an airport where VFR aircraft are also operating, there is little difference. Your IFR clearance affords you the required separation from other IFR aircraft, but it means nothing with respect to separation from VFR aircraft flying around the airport. You will be sequenced with those VFR pilots, but the responsibility for maintaining safe separation lies on your shoulders.

Where the local controller does provide separation is on the runways. It is her job to ensure that airplanes inbound for landing are provided with the required separation from any other airplanes landing or taking off from the same runway. Although there are instances when two airplanes may be on the same runway at the same time, the separation standards by which that may be accomplished are tightly regulated and followed.

It is also the local controller's job to ensure that aircraft waiting for take-off or aircraft operating within the traffic pattern—such as those practicing touch-and-goes—are not unnecessarily delayed. Although not a hard-and-fast requirement, a local controller's priorities are generally that aircraft inbound for landing receive first priority, aircraft waiting to depart get second priority, and aircraft practicing in the pattern get third priority. That's why occasionally, if other traffic starts to receive excessive delays, pilots practicing in the pattern are advised to (1) depart the pattern until traffic thins out, or (2) make full-stop landings, get in line with others awaiting departure, and take their share of the delay. The idea is that no one group of pilots should have to absorb all the delays while the others operate unrestricted.

It is worth noting that when a local controller is working with an approach control that sequences aircraft that are arriving at an airport—as is most often the case with airports within Class B or Class C airspace—the local controller's flexibility for adjusting the arrival flow is significantly less than her counterpart working at a smaller airport. The result is that, often, aircraft waiting to depart or aircraft operating in the pattern may seem to be the ones who suffer more delays. Ultimately, every pilot flying within a busy area receives the most efficient service the ATC system can offer.

Regardless of whether a local controller works at a large airport or a small one, she bases the majority of her instructions and decisions on what she sees out the window (figs. 1.8, 1.9). Although visual cuing may not seem very scientific or precise, the truth is that an experienced controller can provide maximum utilization of runways when she can visually separate the inbound and outbound traffic. During instrument weather when the ceiling and visibility are low, either the local controller, if radar is available as a separation tool in the tower, or the approach controller, if it is not, must provide greater separation standards for aircraft landing and taking off from an airport. The required increased separation standards can significantly reduce the rate at which aircraft can be moved into or out of an airport. Thus, we have at least a partial explanation of why IFR weather often increases delays for anyone using the ATC system.

Regardless of whether she is working in IFR or VFR weather conditions, the local controller has to know when there is room to get a departure out before the next inbound arrives and when there isn't. The judgment and tim-

FIG. 1.8. The control tower provides the ground and local controllers with a bird's-eye view of the airport.

ing needed to do that job effectively do not come overnight. It often takes years of watching and working with pilots before the entire process becomes second nature.

FIG. 1.9. The local controller looks out the window and uses his radarscope to safely separate arriving and departing planes.

So, it is important for pilots to remember that, because so much of the local controller's job is based upon judgment and not precise parameters, occasionally errors will occur. Usually the result is that a pilot on final approach ends up having to execute a go-around. As long as everyone involved stays alert for that possibility, it becomes an inconvenience instead of an incident.

Additionally, in an effort to reduce the likelihood of runway incursions, at a few airports the FAA is testing a program called *Airport Movement Area Safety System*, or *AMASS* (fig. 1.10). This system, operating in conjunction with the radar used to detect aircraft and vehicle movement on the ground, alerts the local controller any time it senses a conflict between an inbound aircraft and a vehicle or another aircraft on the runway. When it does detect a problem, it issues an aural warning instructing the local controller to issue a go-around to the inbound aircraft. The good news is that it is one more tool to help reduce the likelihood of a runway incursion. The bad news is that, even if the impending situation is recognized and being resolved, once the warning is issued, the local controller is mandated by regulation to send the aircraft around.

It is also helpful to remember that, when it comes to a local controller exercising her judgment with respect to separating arrivals and departures, her decisions usually have been proven correct. This is not because a controller is smarter than a pilot (a discussion that like religion and politics always is best avoided regardless of which side of the issue is defended), it is

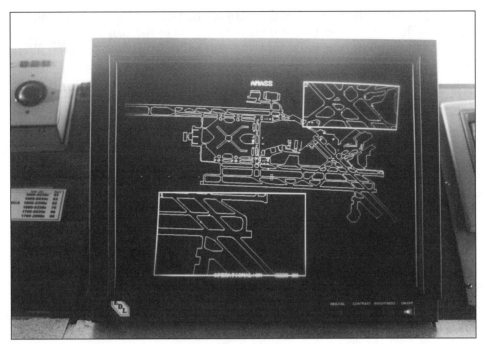

FIG. 1.10. Airport Movement Area Safety System (AMASS) alerts the local controller to potential conflicts on the runway.

because the controller has more tools at her disposal than does the pilot. More and more local controllers have radarscopes in the tower to confirm what they are looking at. Each also has the distinct advantage of having watched dozens of airplanes on any given day. As a result, she knows how the winds at altitude are affecting the speed of the inbound airplanes and she knows how the visibility may be distorting the visual cues for both pilot and controller. In short, the local controller almost always takes into account several different factors before making a final decision.

GIVE AND TAKE

Having said all that, I don't mean to imply that a pilot shouldn't at least mentally question the local controller's decisions. If, after carefully looking at the takeoff or landing clearance picture, a pilot believes that clearance would put him in a questionable or uncomfortable situation, he always has the right to refuse the clearance. The final responsibility for such a decision always lies with the pilot. But it is imperative to advise a controller as soon as possible that the clearance she just issued cannot be accepted.

It is also the pilot's responsibility to double-check any controller's instructions, and doing so with those of the local controller is particularly important. This is not because the local controller makes more mistakes than anyone else, but rather because events around any airport, especially when traffic is heavy, can develop with amazing speed. Any time a pilot is cleared for takeoff or landing, it is good insurance to take a few extra seconds to make absolutely sure there are no other airplanes in the way.

The more often that both pilot and controller watch out for each other, the more likely that early detection and quick resolution of most problems will occur. Here are a few of the more common mistakes that have happened unbeknownst to the local controller: pilots have taxied to the wrong runway; pilots have landed on the wrong runway; and pilots have landed on taxiways thinking them to be runways. In one of my all-time favorites (for which I was unfortunately present), a glider landed alongside of one of the primary landing runways at Pittsburgh Airport one afternoon and no one in the tower was aware of it until the pilot called on the phone to apologize.

There are a few practices for pilots and controllers that can make most of those errors a thing of the past. For starters, even when flying out of an airport with only one runway—which in actuality is two runways—always, always state the runway name in your transmission to the local controller when requesting takeoff clearance. Saying "Pittsburgh Tower, Mooney 445 Delta Tango ready for departure at runway 28 Left" can do wonders for ensuring both pilot and controller are on the same page. Whether landing or taking off, take a moment to carefully look at those numbers and letters painted on the approach end of the runway. Do they coincide with where you are supposed to be? As large as those numbers and letters are and as difficult as it seems it would be to miss them, they are often missed. Don't assume anything unless you have confirmed it.

Having dutifully considered all that has been said, it is time to get on to the business of flying. When the local controller gives a pilot takeoff clearance, the instructions he issues along with the clearance depend upon what type of airspace the pilot will be entering and what other traffic is around. If the airport is a smaller one unencumbered by the regulations of Class B or Class C airspace and a pilot wants only a standard departure from the traffic pattern, then the controller will simply say, "cleared for takeoff." If that same pilot requests a right turn when left traffic is standard, then most likely the controller will say, "right turn approved, cleared for takeoff."

On the other hand, if the departure airport is within the confines of Class B or Class C airspace, the local controller will either issue a specific heading for a pilot to fly or she will tell him to proceed on course. Proceed on course, though, does imply that the chosen heading will be somewhere in the general direction of his destination as stated to the clearance delivery controller. Heading off in the opposite direction of what is expected will, to say the least, cause some raised eyebrows in the tower. Regardless of what particular instructions are received from the local controller, it's good practice to repeat the instructions back to the controller along with acknowledgment of the takeoff clearance. It is just another confirmation of an important clearance.

Having made a mental note of that departure frequency the controller working clearance delivery gave him, it is time for the pilot to use it. For some inexperienced pilots, receiving the departure control frequency as part of the initial clearance leads to the misunderstanding that it is supposed to be the frequency on which to contact the tower controller. But that is not the case.

At some point after takeoff, the local controller will advise the pilot to contact departure, without restating the new frequency. The common thinking is, why should she take time to restate something that was previously issued and no doubt copied down? What happens if a pilot does forget to write the frequency down, or if he loses that little slip of paper somewhere in the shuffle? All is not lost; the universal problem solver is also the easiest and best solution to this oversight. All the pilot needs to do is ask the tower controller to give him the correct frequency one more time. It is better to ask for help than to fly off into the wild blue yonder, hoping the right answer will miraculously emerge from hiding within your grey matter.

Terminal Radar Approach Control (TRACON)

A *Terminal Radar Approach Control,* or *TRACON,* is simply the radar room where approach controllers work. So why are you talking to an approach controller when you are leaving the airport? Shouldn't it be the departure controller? To a certain degree, whether a pilot is talking to an approach controller or a departure controller is irrelevant. In truth, at many airports the same controller refers to herself as approach control when talking to arrivals and departure control when talking to departures. When all the controllers in a TRACON are referred to collectively, it is as approach controllers. This makes it easy to remember what to call them. When departing an airport and you are advised to contact the radar controller, call her *departure control,* when arriving at an airport make the call to *approach control.* The only time controllers really get upset about a pilot's identification of their occupation is when an approach controller is called a center controller (as in the en route center) and vice versa, and that stems from a mostly friendly rivalry with respect to who really does the most work. Having worked in a TRACON all of my controller life, I of course know the truth about the subject.

For the sake of argument and political correctness, when leaving an airport local control will advise a pilot to contact departure control. That controller is the first person a pilot works with who depends entirely upon radar to direct and separate traffic (see fig. 1.11). That fact alone significantly alters the pilot/controller relationship by shifting much greater responsibility to the pilot. From this point on, a pilot must take more care to ensure that the instructions he receives from the controller and the transmissions he makes in response to those instructions are appropriate and as accurate as possible.

Radar controllers work with the distinct disadvantage of not being able to look out the window and instantly see whether or not a pilot has correctly received and is properly executing the instructions just issued. Consequently, every communication between a pilot and a controller takes on a much greater significance.

Few, if any, radar systems used in air traffic control are capable of detecting every movement of an airplane, and none offer instantaneous information and presentation to the controller. Depending upon how often the radar updates

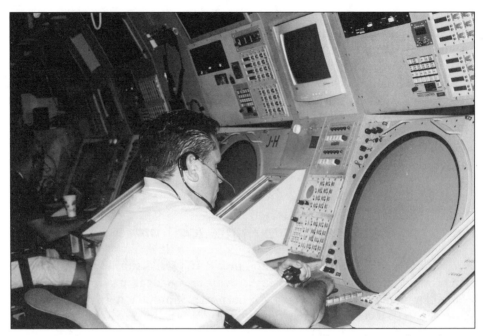

FIG. 1.11. The radar departure/approach controller is one of several controllers who work in the airport radar room.

the returned information (a function of how quickly the radar antenna rotates), depending upon what system is being used (primary or computer-generated), and depending upon where an aircraft is in relation to the updating radar sweep when an instruction is issued, a controller will receive feedback quickly or slowly on a previously issued instruction. Frequently there is a time lag of five to ten seconds before a controller sees an aircraft's change in position relative to any given instruction. While that might not seem like a lot of time, it can be just enough to get a pilot headed in the wrong direction at an occasionally very inopportune time. Add to that the fact that both pilots and controllers are no less prone to mistakes than anyone else and it becomes apparent that each needs to stay alert for the possibility of misunderstood communications.

I remember once, having taken a fearful flying friend for his first ride, when a controller mistook us for a flight taking a planeload of skydivers to their drop zone. When I reported level at our assigned altitude, the controller replied, "Roger, advise when your people have left the plane." I, in turn suggested that, since neither of us had a chute in our possession it might be best if we stayed in the airplane. Realizing his mistake he made some additional wisecrack and we both had a good laugh about it, but it took some time for my now panic-stricken passenger to return his eyeballs to their sockets.

LISTEN CAREFULLY

The first rule then is to listen carefully and decide if the instruction or transmission received from the departure controller makes sense. To do that, you must have some idea of what the departure controller's job is in relation to your flight and how she accomplishes her objectives. As mentioned earlier, the departure controller's office—the radar room—may be located in the same building as the control tower or it may be in an altogether different location many miles away from the airport. Where the radar room is physically located is of little or no concern to a pilot. Both his actions and the controller's responses are unaffected by where the controller happens to be sitting.

What should concern a pilot is what is that departure controller supposed to be doing for the pilot and how will she fulfill her obligations? The departure controller's job is to get each departing pilot away from the airport traffic and on course at his requested altitude as safely and efficiently as possible. To do that, the departure controller must first have the necessary flight information for each departure and she must establish radar contact with each aircraft after it is airborne.

Being another member of the team of controllers assigned to an airport, the departure controller will have already received a pilot's flight information before that pilot makes his first transmission to departure. Whether it is passed along on a flight strip that is sent down from the tower by an old fashioned, gravity-flow drop tube, or passed along electronically or verbally on an intercom, everything you told clearance delivery follows you on your journey. The departure controller knows, or should know, where you are going. Next she just needs to identify you on her radarscope.

TALKING TO DEPARTURE CONTROL

After turning on the aircraft's transponder, what should a pilot say on his initial call to departure control to help the controller do her job most effectively? Normally, initial contact with departure is a simple routine that can be kept relatively short. The controller needs to know five things: (1) your aircraft identification, (2) from where you departed (when other than the main airport associated with the TRACON), (3) your current altitude, (4) the assigned altitude, and, if one has been issued, (5) the assigned heading. While some controllers may argue that both the assigned altitude and heading are known quantities and need not be repeated, I know from experience that misunderstandings occur with respect to those assignments. Said correctly, neither takes much time and the additional safeguard makes it worth the effort.

An example of the result of your efforts would be: "Manchester Departure Mooney 801 Delta Whiskey departed runway 32 Nashua, out of seven hundred climbing to three thousand, heading two seven zero *assigned*."

To which the departure controller's response might be: "Mooney 801 Delta Whiskey, Manchester Departure Radar Contact." The first point a pilot needs to be aware of is to listen carefully for the words "radar contact." Those are the magic words that enable the departure controller to legally do the rest of her work. If a pilot doesn't hear them shortly after departure, it is worth a query to the controller to ask if radar contact has been established.

The second point to consider is that the absence of additional instructions from the departure controller does not mean a pilot is free to proceed on course. If and when additional instructions in the form of heading or altitude assignments can be issued or when traffic permits a pilot to continue under his own navigation, the controller will make that point abundantly clear. Until that time, be patient and fly the procedures as assigned.

One exception to passively complying with departure instructions is if something doesn't seem logical. As I mentioned earlier, although the departure controller should know where you are going, mistakes occasionally do happen. If a given heading or altitude assignment seems totally incongruous with your anticipated plan of action, ask for confirmation or clarification.

Once, on an instrument flight with a student, we unnecessarily flew an extra twenty miles out of our way because our previous controller failed to notify our current controller that he had assigned to us a heading for traffic that was since, long gone. I'm not sure how long it would have taken either the controller or my student to become alert to the problem, but I was reasonably sure we weren't going to get to Providence, Rhode Island, by way of Albany, New York. As the pilot, you need to know what should be happening and ask questions when an unexpected change seems to unilaterally alter your expectations.

At some point, the departure controller will advise a pilot to contact approach control on another frequency. The reason for the instruction is that, particularly within the airspace of a busy approach control, that airspace is divided into many different sectors with a different controller responsible for the traffic within each. Whenever a pilot is instructed to contact approach on a different frequency, it means that he is about to fly into another controller's airspace. For a pilot, no special problems are created with this transfer of communications, so no unique actions are required.

RADAR ROOMS

Along with airspace sectors, radar rooms vary so much in location and physical appearance that it would be impossible to describe examples of all of them (fig. 1.12). Depending upon the amount of traffic normally encountered within the airspace, there could be anywhere from two to twenty or more radar control positions within one approach control facility, with each position being staffed by a different controller responsible for a certain sector of airspace. In addition, there would likely be several other controllers working coordination positions in addition to clerical positions that have been developed to assist the radar controllers. The larger and busier the airport associated with a TRACON, the more likely it is that a pilot will have to make several frequency changes as he flies through the airspace.

When making those frequency changes to talk to the different controllers, remember not to treat each one as though she were an island unto herself. No matter how many different people you talk to along the way, each has already received information about your flight prior to that contact and each will be working to get you through her airspace as efficiently as possible. As a general practice, each call to a different controller needs only include your aircraft identification, altitude, and any instructions from the previous

Fig. 1.12. Monitoring panel in TRACON for radar and instrument navigation system.

controller with which you are still complying. If a controller needs more information than you have given her, she will ask. There have been many complaints about controllers, but being too shy has never been one of them.

By the time you work your way down the line to the last controller in the tower and approach control chain of command, the procedures should be familiar and routine. While there are often a lot of people responsible for a piece of airspace that is usually not that large, each has a similar job—to get you through their little corner of the world with the least amount of delay and confusion as is possible. Don't let the fact that there are a lot of different people with different job titles hinder or intimidate you. They have a job to do, but so do you.

Air Route Traffic Control Centers (En Route Control)

There is one other group of controllers that provides pilots with various services as they fly. They are the air traffic controllers who work in the *Air Route Traffic Control Centers*, or as they are more commonly referred to, the "centers" (fig. 1.13). Although, historically, the centers were the first air traffic control facilities developed to provide separation for pilots flying on instrument flight plans, it has only been within the last twenty years that the centers have afforded VFR pilots many of the same services the IFR pilots receive.

Fig. 1.13. Each en route controller is responsible for a different sector of airspace. (Photo provided courtesy of Lockheed Martin Air Traffic Management. © 1999 LOCKHEED MARTIN CORPORATION. All rights reserved.)

The en route centers are large, strategically located complexes that collectively are able to provide radar services for pilots flying almost anywhere in the United States. Rather than being associated with any one airport, the controllers in each center are responsible for separating the airplanes traveling en route from one airport to another.

Whereas approach control radar only covers the area within forty or fifty miles of the airport it serves, the long-range radar used by the center controllers can effectively cover an area that is several hundred miles long. Although the en route center radar is not terribly effective at lower altitudes due to the line-of-sight characteristics of all radar, pilots flying at altitudes of about three thousand feet or more can almost always avail themselves of the services offered by the center controllers.

Before a pilot can determine whether he should contact a center or an approach control facility for service, he must first know how the airspace is divided up. At the beginning of creation (probably somewhere around the tenth day), all of the airspace in the country was delegated to the various en route centers. Each center then redelegated portions of its airspace to the various approach control facilities that were within the lateral boundaries of their airspace, except that approach control airspace seldom goes higher than ten or twelve thousand feet MSL. Above those altitudes the airspace overlying an approach control is still the responsibility of the en route centers. Where there is no approach control facility taking care of traffic at the lower altitudes, the airspace remains under the jurisdiction of one of the en route centers, from the surface up to the higher flight levels.

For a VFR pilot, the problem then is how to know whether to contact an approach control or a center for service. The place to look for an answer is the *Airport/Facility Directory*. In the Tower En Route Control section, there are diagrams of all adjacent approach control facilities within its area of coverage. For the VFR pilot flying at the lower altitudes, if he is flying in one of those areas for which an approach control is listed, his first ATC facility of choice should be one of those approach controls. If, however, the A/FD shows no associated approach control facility for the area in which he will be flying, any ATC service he may receive will have to come from the center in whose airspace he will be operating.

The centers still primarily provide service to the IFR pilots, so when flying VFR, finding the correct frequency on which to contact a center controller can be a bit of a challenge. Although the IFR Low Altitude En Route charts do list center frequencies at various locations on the charts, the VFR sectional charts do not. If a VFR pilot needs to find a center frequency for a particular area, the easiest way is to contact Flight Service and ask a specialist there for the information.

Every center is similar to an approach control radar room with respect to its physical layout, except that a center is much larger and usually houses fifty or more radarscopes and at least twice as many controllers. But, as with the approach control sectorization, every center controller working radar is responsible for one particular piece of airspace (fig. 1.14).

FIG. 1.14. The en route center controller uses flight progress strips, posted to the right of the screens. (Photo provided courtesy of Lockheed Martin Air Traffic Management. © 1999 LOCKHEED MARTIN CORPORATION. All rights reserved.)

SERVICES AVAILABLE

Although each sector of airspace in a center is much larger than its counterpart in an approach control facility, the services a center controller can offer to a pilot are much the same as those offered by the departure or approach controller at an airport. Most often for the VFR pilot, a center controller limits her services to those of flight following and issuing traffic alerts and advisories. But for many pilots, having another set of eyes to help with looking for traffic that may be a problem and having someone on the ground keeping track of their whereabouts can be a comforting advantage.

As the ease with which both approach and center controllers can enter flight information into the National Airspace System computers increases, more and more VFR pilots are being provided with the same level of continuing service given to IFR pilots. In addition, if any pilot should need help in the form of navigational guidance, weather avoidance information, or any type of emergency assistance, to the extent they are able to provide it, center controllers are trained and equipped to do the job. Pilots should think of a center as an extension of the line of departure controllers he just left. The center controllers are doing the same job; they are just doing it from a different location.

RADAR HANDOFF

Whether working with consecutive approach or departure controllers or those in the center, as a pilot goes from one frequency to the next, it is important to understand if a *radar handoff* has been accomplished. A handoff is simply the process of one controller transferring control/information and radio communications to the next controller down the line. It may be executed through automation or manually with controllers communicating on voice intercom lines. The method used is of no real concern to a pilot, but whether or not a handoff has been made is important to know.

If a handoff is made, as is almost always the case when transiting an approach control's airspace, then when a pilot checks in on the next frequency he need only give the standard aircraft identification and altitude. If a handoff has not been made, then the pilot has to treat his initial call to the next controller as though he were starting from scratch. All the information regarding altitude, direction of flight, and services requested will have to be repeated to the new controller. This is not necessarily a problem as long as a pilot knows if or when he is required to begin the game anew.

It is fairly easy to figure out if a handoff has been made to the next controller. If a pilot is not advised that his radar service has been terminated, and if he is advised to contact the next controller on a specific frequency, then a handoff has been made.

However, if a pilot is advised that his radar service has been terminated, regardless of whether or not a new frequency is provided, a handoff has not been made. Occasionally, if a pilot's flight information has not been entered into the ATC system computer, a controller may not have time to forward that information and manually accomplish a handoff, but she may be willing to provide a frequency on which a pilot can request continued flight following. It is not quite as good as having been handed off to another controller, but it is the next best thing. If even that service isn't provided, a pilot may still request the next appropriate frequency and then negotiate with the new controller for whatever services she can provide. The best way to avoid any ambiguity and assure that a handoff will be made is to ask the current controller, at your earliest convenience, if she will hand you off to the next controller. Unless she happens to be more than a little busy, she will be happy to take care of that request.

Increasing Pilot Safety

Having talked to almost every controller in the tower, more than a few in the approach control, and still more in the center, you will have worked with every type of controller within the ATC system. You will no doubt also have figured out that the system is not as complicated as some would have you believe, and it is an excellent opportunity to increase safety and efficiency on almost every flight. When you know what to expect and what the normal sequence of events will be, the entire business of working with controllers becomes a lot easier. Eventually, with repeated practice, it will become second nature to you.

2

Radio Communications:
How Do You Hear Me?

SINCE THE RELEASE of the first edition of *The Air Traffic System* in 1987, much has changed in the world of light-plane flying, and many of those changes relate to how pilots and controllers communicate with one another. Aircraft radios, for example, have undergone tremendous improvements in the last ten or fifteen years. Gone are the old "coffee grinders" and the "com and a half" radios where you could communicate or navigate, but could do neither simultaneously. Now, even the most basic trainers have at least one communication radio in which one or more frequencies may be stored and brought to the active mode with the touch of a button.

Yet for all the technological advances that have come to the equipment we use to talk to each other, many of the human problems that existed over fifteen years ago are still with us. It is an interesting irony that one of the things we all do so much of the time—communicate—is the very thing that creates so many problems for pilots and controllers alike.

In 1987 I wrote about an old friend who, at the very beginning of his flying career, shared a real concern with me. It seemed that although his lessons were, for the most part, going well, he wondered if problems with his hearing were going to cut short his newfound hobby. He could never seem to get through a single lesson without missing at least half of the radio transmissions that were made to him.

A couple of months later my friend and I again ran into each other and returned to a discussion about our aviation interests in general and his hearing problem in particular. With a bit of a sheepish grin on his face he acknowledged that, rather than a problem with his hearing, most of the missed radio calls stemmed from the basic fact that his almost total inexperience with all that surrounds flying an airplane was really the culprit. As many of the elements of learning to fly began to fall into place, his hearing miraculously improved. Not so surprising when we think about it but, in and of itself, that revelation does little to help us overcome the resulting problems.

A common experience for almost every student pilot is that she develops tunnel vision or, in many cases, tunnel hearing. She concentrates so much on whatever task her instructor has put before her that everything else falls by the wayside. While we may see ourselves as being capable of multitasking, the truth is that most of us can only consciously concentrate on one thing at a time. For a new student pilot, that one thing is usually trying to keep the airplane's shiny side up and headed somewhere in the neighborhood of where it is supposed to be going. Listening to the radio isn't high on the list of priorities, but it needs to be.

While nothing but time, practice, and experience will remedy the situation, there are some things beginning pilots can do to significantly condense the learning curve and speed up the process of becoming effective communicators. The first and probably the most important step is to try to relax. For anyone still trying to master the basics of flying an airplane, that may sound like telling someone sitting in a dentist's chair looking at a pair of vice-grips about to be shoved in his mouth to just relax. But it isn't quite as difficult as it sounds.

Accept the fact that learning to fly isn't as easy as learning to drive a car, although having taught four children how to drive, I'd say it is certainly safer. In the beginning there will be missed radio calls and misunderstood or completely unintelligible communications from the controllers. That's just part of the learning process and one of the reasons why an instructor is along for the ride. If you are diligent about studying and learning as much as possible about your new endeavor, as time goes on, your ability to work with various controllers will improve. In the meantime, the best thing any student can do is to rely on her instructor's judgment and ability and believe in herself.

That does not mean that overnight a beginning pilot will become one of those easygoing airline pilots who never seems to miss a call. Unlike an inexperienced pilot, whenever a veteran pilot or controller misses a transmission, she simply does not think twice about asking to have it repeated. She knows it is a lot better and infinitely safer to ask for a repeat than it is to plod along doing something just because she thinks it is the right thing to do.

But experience alone isn't the whole answer. One of the worst aviation disasters of all time happened on the island of Tenerife when two Boeing 747s piloted by highly experienced pilots collided on the runway. The captain of the aircraft waiting to takeoff evidently misunderstood the tower controller's instructions and began his takeoff on a fog-shrouded runway as the second aircraft was back-taxiing on the same runway. By the time either pilot realized what was happening it was too late. The truth is that, at some point, flying the airplane becomes the easy part. Knowing how to effectively communicate with each other remains the ongoing struggle.

Headset Benefits

Where does a newcomer start to resolve some of the issues related to using the radio? For the light-plane pilot, one of the greatest difficulties she must overcome is the problem of cockpit noise. Besides being a significant contributor to pilot fatigue, the constant, albeit comforting, unabated drone of the engine can do more to disrupt communication than any other condition. Fortunately, it is one of the simplest problems to resolve.

Having spent thousands of hours listening and talking over the radio, I can say with absolute certainty that the single most effective reliever of radio confusion is the use of a headset. In addition to the most obvious benefit of being able to hear every transmission with remarkable clarity, a headset equipped with a microphone and a push-to-talk button for the control yoke can be handier than having a second pilot aboard. It lets a pilot transmit and receive without having to interrupt whatever else she may be doing. As a most welcome plus, a headset also reduces the drone of the engine to a pleasant hum.

Fortunately, the number of aircraft equipped for headset use and the number of pilots availing themselves of the benefits of a headset have dramatically increased in recent years. Airline pilots have long known the values of using a headset, particularly during the high-activity portion of their flights. General aviation pilots have finally started following suit. So instead of thinking of a headset as a luxury not worth the price, look at it as being some of the most economical and reliable help available.

Sterile Cockpit

Another principle that airline pilots long ago adopted and one that the rest of us would do well to copy is the idea of a *sterile cockpit*. Establishing a sterile cockpit simply means that during certain portions of every flight—for the airlines, most often when operating below ten thousand feet MSL—the only talking within the cockpit will be related to those considerations directly affecting the flight. What's for lunch or who is winning the Super Bowl are discussions to be saved for a less-demanding time.

Since most general aviation pilots spend little if any time flying above ten thousand feet, what constitutes sterile cockpit time can be adjusted as necessary. But minimizing distractions when attention to piloting duties is a full-time job is an excellent practice to maintain. A simple strategy might be that any time a flight is in the departure or arrival phase when concentration and activity are at their highest, extraneous conversations will cease. Let your passengers know that any discussions, short of serious safety concerns, should be saved until things slow down.

It's Just a Radio

Many of the other problems associated with talking on the radio revolve around the issue of being too self-conscious about its use. It is true that, in many ways, talking on a radio is similar to having a telephone conversation on a very large party line—a more updated version of which is a chat room with talking instead of writing—but in many ways it is just as different. Regardless of how she envisions a radio frequency, when she makes her first transmission, every pilot feels as though the whole world is listening to her and laughing at her technique or, more likely, lack of it. It may be completely natural to feel that way, but the reality is, that is not what's happening.

For starters, though it is true that there will be other pilots on the same frequency, they are usually too busy taking care of their own flying chores to pay much attention to a conversation that has nothing to do with them. Those who may be listening will no doubt either empathize with a contemporary's efforts to conquer the system or they will reminisce about having dealt with their own struggles some time in the past. What they won't do is spend any time laughing at someone else's efforts to become a better pilot. Pilots still take great pride in helping one another, not ridiculing beginners.

Accept the fact that for a little while, it is going to take a determined effort to overcome both the fear of sounding foolish and the oddities of using a radio. None of us started out sounding like a professional, but with a little time and a lot of practice, we became comfortable using the system. Through it all, we kept telling ourselves using the radio doesn't have to be something strange that should be avoided. It is there to allow us to communicate, that's all.

But knowing that a dozen different thoughts and feelings will be going through your head during those first few hours of practice, a good habit to develop is to always think before you transmit. Put what you want to say in simple and concise form, write it down if necessary, and then key the mike. If responding to a controller's request, think about what he really wants to know and then answer his question.

One of the classic examples of a pilot's best intentions gone awry was when a fellow controller with whom I was working asked a pilot the fairly common question, "What are your intentions?" The pilot innocently replied that he was on his way to his sister's house to celebrate his niece's first communion. Realizing too late that the controller wasn't moonlighting as a society writer for the local paper, he no doubt regretted his error for the remainder of his time on our frequency. It was embarrassing, maybe, but it is better to make a mistake and be embarrassed than to avoid talking and blunder into a potentially dangerous situation.

Other problems stem from the fact that, as much as pilots try to make radio communications and telephone conversations synonymous with one another, they are different. Certain things that are understandable and acceptable when used with a telephone just will not work with a radio. The sooner we understand these differences and adapt to them, the better our chances will be of using the radio to our best advantage.

The positive side of everyone on the frequency being able to listen to everything you say is that you get to listen to everything everyone else is saying. Experienced pilots know how valuable that opportunity can be. Wise pilots listen to many of the transmissions and, in the process, develop a mental picture of which other airplanes are close by, what kinds of weather conditions they are experiencing, what instructions they are receiving from the controller, and ultimately, how all that information affects the overall safety of their own flight.

Phraseology

Because everyone is using the same frequency to communicate and because each pilot has her own individual way of expressing herself, there are a couple of other points to consider when talking on the radio. Many standard words and phrases have been developed for use in most of the routine conversations between pilots and controllers. This *phraseology* provides a number of distinct advantages for anyone using it.

First, since frequency congestion has become a major issue at all but the most isolated airports around the country, using the standard phraseology whenever possible enables both pilots and controllers to keep their respective transmissions as brief as possible. When a pilot spends the minimum time possible on the frequency, she frees up that frequency for other pilots to use and also frees up more of her own time to use in some other way. Why bother to say "I have received your last transmission," when all you really have to say is "Roger." My own experience as a controller was that "Roger" had also evolved into the universal response for "I don't have a clue what the controller just said to me, but if I wait long enough the flying gods will send me a sign." But, when used correctly, good phraseology is one of the benchmarks of a true professional.

A second and more important function of standard phraseology is that its use eliminates, as much as possible, the chance of a misunderstanding between pilot and controller. Although the quality of aircraft radios has improved greatly in recent years, there are still times when talking to a pilot is like conversing with a friend who is using a cellular phone as he drives along the base of the Grand Canyon—it comes and goes. At those times, sticking with a limited number of standard phrases reduces the chances of being misunderstood.

Keep in mind, too, that even if you never fly outside of the United States, our country is so large that in everyday conversations, people from different regions often use the same words to refer to things that are sometimes quite different. Try ordering a cup of "regular," as opposed to decaf, coffee in New England and your java likely will come with cream and sugar. It is just one of the inevitable by-products of our many cultural and geographical differences. These colloquial differences can be cute and amusing most of the time, but when they occur within the context of a conversation between a pilot and a controller, the results could be anything but entertaining. Besides being more efficient, it is always safer to use standard phraseology whenever possible.

However, using standard phraseology isn't always possible. Although the existing system of conventions serves us well most of the time, when we combine the complexities of flying with those of just being human, the number of possible yet necessary conversations that could develop is practically endless. Whenever one of those unusual situations occurs, the best remedy to the problem is to use a combination of commonsense and plain English. Ask yourself, "If I weren't in an airplane and I wanted to respond to this query, or if I needed to get this point across, how would I do it?" Then, forget you are using a radio to communicate and just talk to the controller. It is the quickest way to make sure that he is going to understand what you want to say.

Having thought about the best way to compose what it is you want to say, it is worth taking some time to think about some of the potential pitfalls of using the radio to convey that message. Probably the biggest issue that confronts many inexperienced pilots is that they tend to do too much thinking after they have keyed the microphone. It is understandable that a newcomer to flying will be a little hesitant when talking into a keyed mike, but it can be very frustrating and sometimes even hazardous to take a couple of minutes to say what could have been said in less than thirty seconds. More often than not, every transmission can be broken down into two basic elements: who you are and what you want to do. Just take a moment to think about the briefest possible way to get those points across.

Listening and Hearing

It is equally important to spend a little time thinking about the other side of the communication process, the listening part. Many people believe that listening has become a lost art, and most controllers would probably agree. There is no special magic that makes some of us good listeners and others less able. But those who have mastered the art of listening would likely acknowledge that a big part of the process is slowing down long enough to hear all that is being said and also concentrating on nothing but that message until it has been received in its entirety. Pilots often seem to think they possess the innate ability to listen to a couple of different conversations at the same time, read a chart or two, and fly the airplane, all without missing anything of significance. Controllers, too, are frequently involved in several different tasks while simultaneously trying to listen to pilots. No matter who is doing the juggling act, when they do it, the act of listening and actually hearing suffers greatly.

Even when you listen, you may miss some of it. Many pilots seem to believe that air traffic controllers take great pride in talking as fast as they possibly can. Without question there are a few controllers who could moonlight as the speaker on those commercials where fifteen disclaimers are offered in a span of about eight seconds. They are the same ones who squeeze five different instructions and a joke into one transmission. Fortunately, those folks who can make any pilot's day difficult are in the minority.

Most controllers make a conscious effort to talk as slowly and as clearly as possible. If they know the person on the other end of the microphone is a student—because the student identified himself as such on initial contact—controllers will take even more care to reduce the possibility of creating confusion. In reality, even when a student doesn't identify himself to a controller, more often than not the controller knows anyway. Some things are just too hard to hide.

Regardless of the listener's status, controllers know that talking too fast just ends up being a waste of time. The fast-talking controller ends up having to spend so much of his time repeating all those things pilots didn't get the first time around that he uses up more valuable time than his rapid-fire delivery saves. Still, every pilot needs to understand that when a controller gets busy, he has to increase his speech rate just to get the job done. During those times it is not a matter of choice, but rather one of necessity.

One of the ways that a pilot can improve the likelihood of hearing specific transmissions directed to her is by developing her ability to selectively listen for her own aircraft call sign. Since, with only rare exceptions, controllers are required to begin every transmission with the identification of the aircraft for which the communication is intended, the first thing a pilot will always hear is those familiar numbers and/or letters that are painted on the side of her aircraft. If the aircraft you fly isn't always the same one, as is true for many of us who fly rental aircraft, look for the placard on the instrument panel that displays the call sign. If there isn't one displayed in the plane, write your identifier on a slip of paper and keep it somewhere in plain view. As a flight instructor who has on many occasions flown several aircraft in the course of a day, I always make sure I know my aircraft's name when starting out on a new flight.

Still another point to consider may be a bit more difficult to recognize but it is equally important to the listening process. One of the stumbling blocks, I believe, might best be explained in terms of pilots creating and thinking about misguided objectives when listening to a controller. Instead of listening to a controller's transmission to determine the intent of his instructions as they relate to a pilot's current situation, many pilots listen with a totally different goal in mind. Rather than pay attention to what was said and why, some pilots try to memorize the message so they can accurately read it back, verbatim, to the controller. Repeating any message back to a controller is extremely helpful, but if in so doing it prevents a pilot from thinking about what the controller said, little is gained from the exercise.

As an example, in a flight with an instrument student, we had been directed to a point where the next instruction should have been "Mooney 801 Delta Whiskey, turn left heading two seven zero...cleared VOR Alpha approach." Instead, due to the controller's error we were turned in almost the opposite direction and cleared for an approach to some other airport many miles away. My student, who was concentrating on the words rather than the meaning of the clearance, dutifully read the instructions back to the controller and started to comply with them as well.

A routine approach clearance is one of those events that almost always carries with it several different yet important instructions. In addition, the ability to read back that clearance correctly to the controller is, unfortunately, also one of the ways by which a student tends to gauge his progress on the way to becoming an instrument pilot. My student was so intent on reading back the approach clearance as a professional would that he gave little thought to determining whether or not it made sense. Understanding what the controller said and knowing if it made sense is substantially more important than memorizing words and giving little thought to their applicability. In other words, slamming into a mountain while having used impeccable phraseology does little to mitigate the consequences of a premature arrival.

How then do the uninitiated aviators learn the well-kept secret of how to hear and understand everything a controller says, regardless of the complexity of the message or the speed with which it is delivered? The secret is that experienced pilots almost always have a good idea of what a controller is going to say before the words ever leave his mouth. This does not mean that a pilot has to become a mystic to master the art of listening. What it does mean is that she has to acquire some of the knowledge that her elders of the air previously acquired somewhere along the line. One way to do that is to listen to the air traffic radio frequencies as often as possible. The more often a pilot listens to a radio frequency, the more her ears will become attuned to hearing how different words and phrases sound in the course of everyday practice. In addition, listening to a radio helps new pilots become more familiar with the normal sequence of events. During any flight, certain routine instructions are issued with clockwork regularity. If a pilot learns what the instructions are and under what circumstances they are given, the entire process of deciphering radio transmissions will be markedly easier.

For pilots who are just beginning to interact with controllers or for those who do not get the opportunity to fly very often, there is still a way to develop and exercise the ability to listen. It is as easy as finding a scanner or, even better, a handheld transceiver and taking a few minutes each day to listen to the interaction between pilots and controllers. Besides having the advantage of adding a valuable backup to your bag of tricks, using a handheld transceiver to listen to a frequency can soon make the standard instructions and even some of the unusual ones, when they later occur in flight, nothing more than routine chores to address.

Common Practices of Experienced Pilots

In addition to understanding some of the concepts of the communication process, it is helpful to be aware of a few common practices that seem to separate experienced pilots from novices. Here is a list of ten procedures that all pilots should be familiar with when using a radio to communicate. Some of the items will help you avoid dealing with or, even worse, becoming an occasional nuisance. Others could keep you from taking that first step down the path that might eventually lead to disaster.

1. If your aircraft is equipped with more than one communication radio and particularly if there is an audio switching panel associated with the installation, take the time to learn how to use it. Problems can result

from basic unfamiliarity, such as forgetting to switch a frequency from the stand-by position to the active one and switching frequencies on one radio but failing to adjust the corresponding audio panel button to the correct radio.

2. Whether using a microphone or a boom-mike on a headset, ensure that either is just touching your lips when transmitting. Each was designed to cancel out as much background noise as possible. If a microphone is too far away from the speaker's lips, it also cancels out his voice.

3. Make it a point to momentarily pause after keying the mike before beginning to talk and, likewise, pause briefly before unkeying the mike after finishing a transmission. Otherwise potentially important information may not get transmitted to the person on the other end of the conversation.

4. When finished transmitting, always be sure that the transmit button on the microphone is unkeyed. Otherwise you may be the culprit behind the *stuck mike* on the frequency. The major consequence of that condition is that the frequency on which a pilot is unknowingly transmitting is blocked to every other person tuned in. In one year alone, the FAA estimated that known frequency blockages across the country resulted in almost four hundred hours of unusable frequency time, which thereby created hundreds of unsafe situations for pilots. What is worse is that, not only does a stuck mike block the frequency for everyone within broadcast range of that pilot, it leaves the person responsible for creating the situation incapable of receiving any transmission that could warn her of the problem. So, if a frequency rife with conversation suddenly goes quiet, the place to start troubleshooting is in your own cockpit.

5. Whenever switching to a new frequency, be considerate enough to listen for a few seconds before you start talking. It is easy to begin talking impatiently in an effort to complete a necessary task. But if another pilot or a controller happens to be in the middle of a transmission, the result would render both speakers' communications unreadable. Listen to almost any UNICOM frequency on a busy day and witness firsthand the collection of garbled words and loud squeals that often cause the frequency to become almost totally useless.

6. Make a determined effort to answer every transmission made to you as soon as possible. Controllers understand that a pilot's first responsibility is to fly her airplane, but usually a verbal response is the only positive indication a controller receives that guarantees his transmission reached the intended pilot. One exception is that often, when a controller needs to supply the same information to every pilot on the frequency—such as a change in runway or weather conditions—he will transmit a message such as "Attention all aircraft, information Bravo is now current. Acknowledge receipt of this transmission by identing." Then, rather than five or ten pilots verbally responding to his transmission at the same time, each may do so by pushing the ident button on her transponder. In that instance, the controller receives visual verification of message receipt without creating havoc on the frequency.

7. Be aware that often one controller is using two or more different frequencies to communicate with pilots. If ever you hear the controller talking, but you fail to hear the pilot's response to his message, it means the controller is, in fact, talking to that pilot on a different frequency. When that happens, although there is no sure method of determining when that other pilot has finished answering the controller, try to leave a reasonable amount of time for the other pilot's response before you start talking.

8. After initial contact with a controller, know that there are legitimate ways to shorten any additional transmission you make. You may, for example, omit using the name of the tower, approach control, or center in any subsequent communications. Your aircraft call sign may be shortened to your type of aircraft and the last three digits of the call sign. The only exception would be if the controller advises you that, due to another aircraft with a call sign similar to yours being on the frequency, you should continue to use your full call sign until otherwise advised.

9. Always identify yourself with at least the shortened version of your call sign whenever responding to a controller's transmission. Although the brief "Roger" can be heard all too frequently when flying, it bypasses a valuable safeguard that helps ensure the correct pilot responded to the controller.

10. Don't let the previous nine suggestions confuse or intimidate you. Take the time to learn how to use the system to your advantage.

It may seem as though learning about and using the proper radio procedures can become an overwhelming and all-consuming preoccupation for the inexperienced pilot. But that is in part due to the fact that much of what experienced pilots have learned over the years has been condensed here into just a few pages. After having had the opportunity to think about the methods mentioned here and, after having exercised them in practice over time, you will most likely be able to mold and modify them to best suit your own skill and experience levels. With a little more time and practice, most everything should logically fall into place. Whenever something still seems strange, ask for clarification.

Effectively communicating with others has become as important to assuring a safe outcome for a flight as is correctly flying the airplane. It is vital that every pilot take the time to learn how to work with the system and how to use that knowledge to her best advantage. When each pilot becomes as comfortable using a radio as using a telephone, she not only sounds like a more professional pilot, she becomes one.

Here is a brief checklist of useful tips.

1. Use approved phraseology whenever possible, and otherwise use plain English. If anything is unclear, ask and ask again until it is clear.

2. Learn and practice the art of listening.

3. Learn how to accurately use the radio equipment on board each aircraft you fly.

4. Pause briefly after keying the mike before talking, and briefly pause when finished talking before unkeying. Always be sure the transmit button is unkeyed after every transmission.
5. Listen briefly before talking on a new frequency.
6. Make a determined effort to answer every transmission as soon as possible.
7. Be aware that controllers may be talking on two or more different frequencies simultaneously.
8. After initial contact, omit the name of the tower, approach control, or center facility. Use only the type aircraft and the last three digits of the aircraft call sign unless otherwise advised by the controller.
9. Always identify yourself with at least your abbreviated call sign whenever you answer a transmission.

3

Radar Systems:
Beauty or Beast?

RADAR! MORE THAN ANY OTHER single event, the addition of radar to our National Airspace System and its adoption as the primary means for separating aircraft within that system has permanently altered the way pilots and controllers do business. Whether it has been a helpful or a harmful addition depends almost entirely upon whose opinion is being expressed. Some advocates of freedom from government interference see radar as just another way for Big Brother to intrude on our freedom as pilots to go where we please when we please. Many other pilots understand that although radar unquestionably allows air traffic controllers to see where a pilot is and what he is doing almost 100 percent of the time, it is that very capability that has enabled pilots to increase the efficiency and utility they enjoy from their aircraft.

Regardless of which side you take, the reality is that radar is here to stay. It is an interesting irony that the system that has been dubbed by many as the ever-present eye that watches all we do, is the same system that has greatly expanded the flight options for every pilot. Few pilots fully understand the advantages and limitations of the radar systems that have become so much a part of our flying experiences.

The main reason radar technology was adapted for use in our airspace system is that, over the years as the country's air traffic steadily increased, it became apparent that a more effective and efficient method of safely separating aircraft had to be developed. Not only were the time-consuming and restrictive nonradar procedures of old wasting too much of the instrument pilot's time and too much of the nation's ever-decreasing airspace, but issues of safety were also becoming more prevalent. In addition, the skies around more and more of our airports were becoming too congested to handle safely the growing combination of public transport IFR aircraft and the general aviation VFR and IFR aircraft. Radar, it seemed, could be the solution to many of those growing concerns.

It is important for pilots to have a basic idea of how, by using radar for traffic separation, our shrinking airspace can be more effectively utilized. As a significant sidebar, it is worth noting that without some type of radar, be it ground-based, satellite-based or some other variation, the concept of *free flight*—pilots essentially developing their own individual routes—is much less likely to succeed. When all is said and done, the advantages of having a nationwide radar network for air traffic separation greatly outweigh any disadvantages.

Radar Basics

Before the existence of radar, all air traffic control was based upon separating aircraft by time, distance, and altitude. This was accomplished primarily through a combination of constant pilot reports to the controllers and, whenever possible, visual sighting by controllers. Using this method for keeping IFR airplanes apart meant that pilots and controllers alike had to constantly maintain a mental picture of the rapidly changing relationship among all the aircraft in a given area. Although keeping that mental picture was and, even with the addition of radar, still is a healthy by-product for both pilots and controllers, the process can occupy a significant portion of a pilot's time and require an intense level of concentration from the controllers.

Those pilots who have had occasion to fly in a nonradar environment know that the additional workload associated with it can quickly develop into a formidable task. Lengthy clearances via airways, VOR radials, DME fixes, and the like are the norm when flying nonradar, as are reports made by pilots to controllers advising of both their present location and estimates for their arrival at several of the subsequent fixes and compulsory reporting points along their route of flight. Then, as the approach portion of the flight is entered, most of the time, pilots must fly some type of procedure turn, DME arc, or other published route to transition from the en route phase to the beginning of the instrument approach. All of this uses a lot of valuable time and airspace.

Although these days, through the use of GPS, much of the computational work required of pilots to determine those estimates of ground speeds and times to the fixes has been all but eliminated, the separation standards by which controllers must operate have not kept pace with those advances. That combined with the reality that there are still many pilots who have not yet been able to acquire GPS units for their aircraft mean the nonradar separation standards of today still require an abundance of airspace to provide an adequate margin of safety for pilots. Generally speaking, to guarantee a pilot's safety when flying in a nonradar environment, the separation standards by which controllers keep airplanes apart must be three or four times greater than those used in a radar environment. It would be impossible to keep all of the airplanes that use the system each day flying efficiently if we used a nationwide system of nonradar control.

In addition to giving pilots the opportunity to move throughout the airspace more efficiently, one of the other significant benefits of radar that pilots enjoy is the tremendous amount of flexibility it affords them. Without radar, pilots who fly on IFR flight plans are restricted to routes that have been very carefully laid out and, most often, published. Since all nonradar separation is based upon knowing where the airplanes are at all times, without controllers having the benefit of actually being able to see them, pilots basically fly the exact same routes either one behind the other or using different altitudes. Either way, nonradar separation provides pilots with few opportunities to fly anywhere other than their planned route. Going direct to somewhere or deviating around weather becomes much more difficult to accomplish without having radar to help make it happen.

Radar is not just a tool used to make pilots' lives easier, however. To most controllers, radar is the difference between dreaming the impossible dream and sitting down in front of a radarscope to a reasonable job. Trying to use nonradar procedures to separate today's air traffic would be similar to a football announcer trying to describe and broadcast a long touchdown pass without seeing it firsthand. First he receives a series of position reports from all the various players and then, using some pretty fancy mental gymnastics, he combines them into a mental picture that makes sense of all the individual elements. It can be done, but it certainly isn't easy.

If you put that same announcer in a booth high above the playing field, where he can maintain an overview as the play develops, the entire job becomes decidedly easier. Basically that is the kind of help that radar provides for the controller. Instead of trying to maintain his own mental picture of where each airplane is and its relationship to the others around it, the controller can look at a radarscope and instantly see where all the traffic is. That, in turn, eliminates the need for pilots to continuously report their current whereabouts and how soon they will reach the next checkpoint. One result is that there are fewer and fewer compulsory reports that pilots, IFR or VFR, are required to make when flying under radar control. Another is that the inflexibility required in the nonradar world gives way to an environment filled with countless more options for both pilots and controllers.

Since each controller has a reliable and up-to-the-minute picture of where every airplane within her airspace is, she can use that overview to maneuver aircraft through all of the sky under her direction, not just those portions of it that are used for published airways. Particularly in more recent times, with airplanes of widely varying speed and performance characteristics being capable of operating at the same altitudes, trying to line up five high-speed jets behind a slower one would be difficult if not impossible to achieve. Radar allows the controller to essentially develop one or more passing lanes to move the jets to the head of the line.

Not only does radar increase efficiency, it also expands the controller's ability to function as a safety backup for pilots in a variety of different ways. Any time a pilot starts to head in the wrong direction, climbs above or descends below his assigned altitude, or just generally operates contrary to what is expected, the controller has the capability to catch the mistake before it develops into a serious problem. Unfortunately, that is the reason that some pilots most of the time and all pilots some of the time dislike controllers with radarscopes at their disposal. They feel the controllers are like police officers looking for speeders. The truth is that most controllers do not see themselves as the gendarmes of the sky. They despise the resultant paperwork as much as the pilots for whom it is destined.

Whatever the system, there are pilots who believe that air traffic controllers exist only to service their needs. Therefore, they believe controllers have no right to abuse their authority by looking over a pilot's shoulder and correcting him when he makes a mistake. But one of the underlying assumptions of the design of the air traffic system is that, since it is impossible to develop a predominantly human-dependent, error-free system, creating an error-tolerant system of interaction is far more advantageous. It then becomes the controller's job, not his option, to point out a pilot's mistakes. After all, the alternative of letting a mistake go unnoticed could easily end up damaging a lot more than just that pilot's pride.

Before passing that final verdict, keep in mind that radar also gives controllers the tool to routinely provide dozens of traffic advisories for all pilots flying through their delegated airspace. It gives each of us another set of powerful eyes that have the capability to see a long way off in every direction. Once, a long time ago, I issued traffic to a pilot as "six o'clock [directly behind his aircraft], five miles same direction." The pilot replied, "Roger, up periscope." His point was that his plane didn't have any windows in the back, so it would be helpful to keep him advised of the traffic.

But it is important to keep in mind that the availability of traffic advisories and the almost continuous reinforcement of the belief that controllers always issue pertinent warnings to pilots has become something of a double-edged sword. Without question it is a tremendous benefit to have a controller looking for and warning pilots about traffic that has the potential to become a collision hazard for them. But many pilots, when they hear the magic words *radar contact*, become too relaxed in their own scanning for traffic and too reliant on the controllers to take over all responsibility for collision avoidance. When that happens, the designed safeguards of the system disappear almost entirely.

So, if beauty is in the eye of the beholder, whether radar is the beauty or the beast depends on the lens through which the vision is seen.

Making and Fixing Mistakes

I remember a controller once relating to me an experience he had at his airport shortly after their new radar system was installed. Though the radarscopes had been operating in a seemingly normal manner for several days, the controllers could not use them for traffic separation until the system had been flight checked and certified by an FAA inspection aircraft. Until that time, although the controllers could watch the airplanes they were working with on the scopes, they had to continue to use their old nonradar practices to keep them apart. What he saw over the course of those next few days was pilots cutting corners, inaccurate position reports and estimates, and a few pilots so confused that they totally abandoned their own protected airspace in search of greener pastures. Yet he also saw many more pilots doing exactly what they had planned to do and doing it with consistent accuracy.

The point of all of this is to emphasize the simple fact that all of us— novice or experienced pilots, fresh or seasoned controllers—make mistakes. On more than one occasion I have seen firsthand that, even with all the advanced avionics and moving map displays, pilots get disoriented. The cockpit of an airplane is anything but a static environment. Things change and happen all the time and mistakes sometimes result. When the traffic is light, these mistakes are less likely to develop into serious problems. When the traffic is heavy, however, the tolerance for those mistakes is significantly less, and that is when detection should be on everyone's mind.

With the assistance that radar provides, controllers can more quickly notice when an error has occurred and work to reduce or eliminate the effects of that mistake, be they those of a pilot or another controller. Although it might seem otherwise depending upon how the message is delivered, controllers are not consciously looking for ways to make pilots feel incompetent. Rather they are trying to live up to their responsibilities inherent in the pilot/controller relationship.

After all, radar allows the reduction of separation standards, which in turn reduces tolerance for errors. It seems only right that radar should become the tool to mitigate the consequences of the resulting mistakes. Radar gives a pilot another set of eyes to look for mistakes and a much different perspective from which to recognize them. Besides, proficient pilots do not mind being watched by controllers; it just gives them another opportunity to show those folks watching from the ground just how good they really are.

How Radar Systems Work

It was not all that long ago that those in the know complained that the equipment behind our air traffic system was just plain archaic. The components that ran the system were so large and cumbersome they had to have their own dedicated suites just to house them. So much of the radar, navigation, and communication equipment was tube-type technology that, as the older technicians began retiring, there were real concerns that no one with any knowledge of the equipment would be around to replace them. Overall, the system had become just too ancient to be reliable, let alone safe.

Since that time, much has changed. The computers that now provide the brains behind the systems have increased tremendously the capacity and speed of gathering and processing information. Most if not all of the radar, navigation, and communication equipment is state-of-the-art technology and, as a result, is modern enough that just about any knowledgeable person can repair it when the need arises. Additionally, controllers now have thousands of pages of electronic information at their fingertips. At the touch of a button or a computer screen, they can recall anything from initial approach fixes for any approach in the country to what the special of the day is at Bud's pizza shop down the road. Although the former might be better suited to a pilot's needs, the latter can seem like a lifesaver to a late-arriving crew that is craving nourishment.

But despite the almost quantum leap forward that the FAA has finally taken into the twenty-first century, many of the advances are transparent to controllers and almost all of them are transparent to pilots. Everything is working at a much faster speed, with much greater reliability, resulting in significantly more system capacity. Still, the basics by which controllers direct pilots and how pilots, in turn, function within the system have changed very little. Whether that is due to some very insightful designers or an air traffic system that is slow to evolve, only time will tell. If the truth be known, it most likely is a little of both.

Whatever the reasons, the end result is that the equipment with which pilots and controllers work is composed of some basic elements that, if not the brains, are the heart of the radar systems being used. Our larger airports employ all the components of the most complex radar systems, while many of the country's smaller airports use portions of the same systems or simpler variations of the basic ideas. Each of the systems is capable of providing controllers with the information they need to separate airplanes safely. But the more-advanced equipment makes the job easier and, as a result, enables each controller to increase her individual capacity without diminishing safety.

PRIMARY RADAR SYSTEM

The most fundamental component used to be the only one that existed and it is still the one upon which all the rest are based. It is called the *primary radar system* and it is likely the type of system most of us imagine when we think of radar. Primary radar is a continuous series of energy bursts transmitted from a rotating antenna located somewhere near the main airport it serves. When these bursts of energy hit anything that has mass, be it a building, a storm cloud with significant precipitation, or an airplane, a portion of that energy is reflected off of the object and sent back to the antenna.

The reflected energy is received by the antenna and is then electronically translated into a video picture. The resultant video presentation, which is similar to a television picture, is what the controllers see on their radarscopes. The time it takes the energy to travel from the antenna to an object, reflect off of that object and return to the antenna can be calculated and then translated into the distance that object of reflection—or the target, as it is commonly known—is from the antenna.

With the aid of range marks, which are nothing more than concentric circles superimposed on a radarscope usually at five- or ten-mile intervals, a controller can easily determine an aircraft's distance from the antenna. In addition, through more electronic wizardry called a *video map*, controllers are able to display on their scopes things such as airports, towns, highways, and a host of other ground and navigational references. So, the information that is converted from the radar antenna reception provides the more complete presentation that controllers use to offer many different services to pilots.

Although going from nonradar to primary radar was like going from the Dark Ages to the Industrial Revolution, primary radar still has a number of inherent flaws that make it undesirable as the only source of information for controllers. The amount of energy returned to the antenna after it is reflected off of an object can vary greatly depending upon the composition and size of it. A small fabric-covered airplane does not reflect nearly as much energy as a large metal airliner will. A stealth bomber, with its advanced composition and development, takes many of its design cues expressly from the concept that, if enough radar energy is absorbed or reflected away from the antenna, the return will be invisible to a controller. Consequently, the aircraft presentation a controller sees on a radarscope can be anything from a relatively large, discernible solid line to an almost invisible pinpoint dot, even though the different airplanes reflecting the energy may be at relatively the same distance and altitude from the antenna.

Another major drawback that had to be addressed with primary radar was that, since it reflects off of anything that has mass, a method to eliminate unwanted returns also had to be developed. Controllers hardly ever want to see a primary return from anything that isn't in the air, but one of the most prevalent types of interference with primary radar is called *ground clutter*. Buildings, trees, nearby hills, ridges, and even large vehicles are all picked up on radar, yet they do nothing more than create annoying clutter on a controller's scope. That makes the job of seeing and separating air traffic more difficult. The solution was the creation of an electronic system called *moving target indicator (MTI)* that eliminated ground clutter.

Still another circuitry set can be activated if the radar system begins to display precipitation returns. VFR pilots need to remember that radar does not detect clouds with a low density of moisture in them, and if it doesn't detect them, controllers will not see them. As those clouds become more densely packed with moisture, that moisture will reflect energy back to the antenna. If the precipitation becomes widespread, the result can be such a large display of weather that a controller may have a difficult time seeing the airplane targets through the precipitation returns. When that happens the amount or the pattern of energy transmitted from the radar is reduced or altered, respectively, to eliminate the lighter areas of precipitation.

The problem with almost all of the solutions to reducing or eliminating unwanted clutter on a radarscope is that, because the level of the transmitted energy is reduced, a primary return from an aircraft—the skin paint, as it is known—is also reduced in intensity. That could mean that an airplane that was originally presented as a weak target because of size, location, or composition, could, with the implementation of any of the available circuitry, disappear altogether from the scope.

The last major disadvantage controllers must deal with when working with primary radar is that, other than some slight variations in intensity, all primary returns look exactly alike. What a controller sees on her scope is a lot of little lines and dots moving in different directions. To correlate each line or dot with the airplane it represents, the controller has to get an accurate position report from the pilot, or she has to issue a series of identifying turns to the pilot. As the turns are issued, the controller watches the target she thinks is the correct one to see if the resultant changes in its flight path direction correspond to her instructions.

Once the time-consuming process of identification is completed, the controller has to remember which line represents which airplane as it moves across the scope. Should it, at any time, merge with another target at a different altitude, she then has to reidentify the aircraft after the targets separate. For a controller using only primary radar with even a minimal amount of traffic, the level of concentration required is significant and the number of airplanes that can be handled safely is relatively low. All of these points are worth remembering for the time when a controller states that her secondary or automated radar is out of service.

SECONDARY RADAR

Fortunately, *secondary radar*, one of the other major components of today's radar systems, has helped to solve a host of problems that primary radar systems simply could not resolve. Secondary radar has done almost as much to modernize the air traffic system as primary radar initially did. Although its name is actually something of a misnomer, in addition to characteristics that are uniquely its own, secondary radar performs many of the functions of primary radar and it performs them much more effectively. Under certain circumstances, controllers are permitted to use only secondary radar to separate aircraft.

Secondary radar is a series of radio signals sent from an airplane to a ground-based station. The piece of equipment in an airplane that sends these signals is the transponder. The ground-based counterparts are the receiver located on top of the radar antenna and a component called an interrogator that determines what presentation a controller will see as a result of the interaction. When the process of sending, receiving, and converting the radio energy is complete, the result is that the controller sees a *beacon target* on her radarscope.

The beacon target that the controller sees on the radarscope can be anything from a single enhanced line overlaying the aircraft's associated primary target to two or three parallel lines in place of the single slash. A beacon target provides a number of advantages to the controller. The most significant advantages of the secondary target are that it is a larger and stronger return than a primary target, and it is unaffected by almost all of the shortcomings associated with primary radar. The size of the return is independent of the size of the aircraft sending the signal. In addition, all that circuitry that was developed to reduce clutter does not affect the strength of the secondary return. In fact, other than sharing the same antenna stand, primary and secondary radar systems are completely independent of each another. The result is a much more consistent and reliable presentation for the controllers.

While for the most part and with the exception of operations within Class A airspace, controllers need to have both systems up and running to completely do their jobs, secondary radar has become an invaluable backup. Since secondary radar requires aircraft to be transponder equipped to function, when using only secondary radar to provide ATC services to pilots, controllers are unable to provide any advisories or separation from non-transponder-equipped aircraft. Although there are still aircraft flying today without transponders, the reality is that their numbers are diminishing and the airspace in which they may fly legally is likewise shrinking.

When I was working as a controller in Pittsburgh, all of us who worked the morning rush into the airport one day spent the first forty-five minutes doing it without our primary radar. Since our airspace was what is now the equivalent of Class B airspace, we had become so accustomed to working only transponder-equipped aircraft that, instead of being the essential component of our system, primary radar had become little more than a backup.

Besides providing controllers with targets that are easier to see and immune to the shortcomings of primary radar, secondary radar has made the whole process of identifying individual aircraft easier and faster. Gone are the identifying turns and the oft-resulting confusion and misidentification and in their place is a procedure that is completed with the push of a button. When a pilot is assigned a transponder code and asked to *ident*, whether by virtue of an illuminated solid block appearing over his aircraft's target or the letters *ID* flashing in conjunction with his target, a controller can instantly identify an airplane by noting the change taking place. The exact presentation a controller sees on the radarscope as a result of the ident is really immaterial for a pilot; the workload reduction, on the other hand, is not.

AUTOMATED RADAR

Secondary radar's single most significant contribution to the modernization of the air traffic control system was to pave the way for the addition of computer technology to the radar systems. Many of the computer systems now being used to enhance the air traffic system are directly linked to the secondary radar components. Additional advances may eventually overshadow those currently being used in conjunction with beacon radar. For now the *automated radar* that is the result of secondary radar technology being mated to computer technology is the golden egg in the controller's basket.

Explaining all of the benefits and advantages the air traffic system has enjoyed as a result of that technological progress would easily fill an entire book. However, there are a few major changes that have been especially instrumental in making everyone's job easier and the entire system a lot safer.

Many pilots flying today have known nothing other than automated systems that have freed them and the controllers from the tedious tasks of old. But occasionally even the best systems fail, and an idea of what is lost when they crash can provide a valuable perspective on what the consequences will be as a result.

One of the most valuable benefits for controllers has been that instead of relying on a combination of information derived from flight progress strips and memory to keep track of each individual airplane, automation now records critical data and displays them alongside each associated radar target. The process begins when a controller issues to a pilot a *discrete transponder code*—a unique four-digit code—that has been assigned automatically by computer or is fed manually into the computer by the controller. This discrete code then becomes the identifying signal by which the computer recognizes a specific airplane.

As soon as the computer receives that code from the airplane's transponder, a presentation called a *data block* automatically appears on the radarscope next to the aircraft target. One of the most important bits of information contained within the data block is the individual aircraft's call sign. Instead of a controller having to rely on her memory to differentiate among five or ten identical targets to determine which is which, she now need only look at the associated data block, or tag, to see the identification. This information alone so greatly reduces the level of concentration required of controllers that many believe it to be the single most significant enhancement to the old radar systems.

The next most significant contribution to pilot safety and workload reduction for both pilots and controllers is that, for those aircraft equipped with altitude encoding transponders (Mode C capability), the *actual pressure altitude* is continuously displayed in its associated data block. The altitude is shown as a three-digit number on the radarscope and correspondingly changes any time the aircraft alters its altitude.

The benefit of being able to see an aircraft's altitude instantaneously and continuously cannot be overstated. Controllers are separating airplanes that are operating in a three-dimensional environment, but they are performing the job using two-dimensional radarscopes. The addition of altitude information to those scopes is essential to maintaining the correct mental picture. In addition, Mode C readouts significantly reduce the workload for pilots and controllers by eliminating the countless radio transmissions that used to be necessary to pass critical altitude information along to controllers. Thus, the good news is that controllers always know your altitude. The bad news, depending upon your level of proficiency, is that controllers always know your altitude.

The better news is that Mode C altitude information helps controllers reduce the number of traffic advisories given to any pilot and that means pilots don't have to scan for unrelated traffic. When separating aircraft, controllers are only permitted to use Mode C readouts that have been verified to be correct within plus or minus three hundred feet. But when issuing traffic to a pilot, they are allowed to pass along unverified altitude information as part of the advisory. Almost without exception, even the unverified altitude readouts are accurate, so a pilot looking for traffic can concentrate his attention on a less-generalized area. When the readout of the traffic is verified and it is in excess of about one thousand feet above or below the affected airplane, the controller most likely will not even issue an advisory. All of this saves time and reduces some of the apprehension created by flying toward a totally unknown target.

One of the last bits of information contained within an aircraft's data block is a computer-calculated and continuously updated groundspeed read-out. As more and more pilots equip their aircraft with more sophisticated avionics, each can have groundspeed information available in the cockpit. For the rest of the population who have yet to move up to the next-generation equipment, knowing that the information can be obtained from almost any controller at any time can be a distinct advantage when trying to determine actual winds aloft and time to their destination.

Accurate groundspeed data are also valuable information for controllers. This informaton helps them ensure that whenever minimum separation standards are being used, a following airplane will not reduce those standards by flying faster than the one ahead. That alone can be an invaluable aid for a controller when traffic or weather conditions dictate that she use all of her airspace as efficiently as possible.

Increased Reliability and Safety

With the advent of computers to the air traffic system, the reliability and safety of the system have been greatly increased. Many of the control decisions that a controller used to make based solely on the wisdom she gained from past experiences now can be supplemented or confirmed by computer-generated information. These readily accessible, objective data afford controllers the ability to make the correct decisions more often and more quickly, and that makes the system work more effectively for everyone.

What is both interesting and satisfying to note is that even with the significantly increased ability to gather information and make decisions based upon available data, the basic procedures developed as a result of adding radar to the air traffic system have remained virtually unchanged. What the distant future holds is anyone's guess. For the foreseeable future, pilots and controllers will continue to be the irreplaceable cogs in a unique and complex machine.

Radar may not be the answer to every pilot's prayers and there are those who would argue that it has outlived its usefulness. For the time being, radar still provides more efficient use of our nation's airspace and more safeguards for pilots than any other system currently available. The next time you tire of feeling as though half of the world is watching you as you methodically plod along through the sky, take a minute to think about the opportunities and benefits all those extra eyes can offer.

4

Airspace: The Alpha, the Omega, and Some In Between

SOMETIME LATE IN THE LAST CENTURY—if the 1800s immediately came to mind, this especially pertains to you—all of the airspace within the United States changed, or at least the names of the various categories of airspace changed. In keeping with the International Civil Aviation Organization (ICAO) and the rest of the world, our government decided it was time to designate airspace in a manner similar to the rest of the international aviation community (fig. 4.1).

For pilots who came to their calling after the reclassification was completed, the issue of airspace that used to be this, but is now that, isn't really an issue at all. But for many of us who grew up under the old ways, those habits truly do die hard. I suspect it is a lot like learning a second language. Instead of reading or speaking in the new language, beginners first mentally translate into their native tongues and then try to comprehend the new material. So it is with we older pilots. Let's see, Class B, that used to be a TCA, and so on.

Since it is time to move with the rest of the world into the next century, this book will make no more comparisons. Neither will it make an in-depth study of all the intricacies and nuances of the different types of airspace. That approach is better left to piloting texts and a good program of classroom instruction.

This chapter will illustrate some of the different types of airspace in the context of the pilot/controller relationship. What is each player expected to

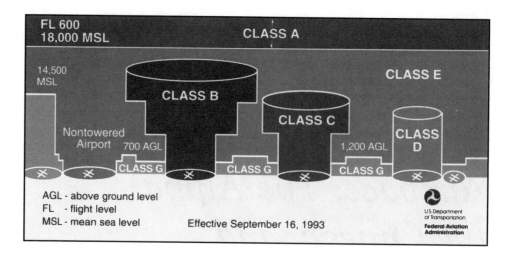

FIG. 4.1. U.S. airspace at a glance.

Airspace Classes	Former Airspace Equivalents	Changes
A	Positive Control Area (PCA)	None
B	Terminal Control Area (TCA)	VFR: clear of clouds
C	Airport Radar Service Area (ARSA)	None
D	Airport Traffic Area (ATA) and Control Zone (CZ)	Upper limits 2,500' AGL
E	General Controlled Airspace	None
G	Uncontrolled Airspace	None

do and how do those actions affect the other? With all the different types of airspace in which pilots must play and all the procedures seemingly unique to each of them, it still seems as though Parker Brothers must have been a consultant to the FAA. We frequently have to play all kinds of games to get from one place to another and, occasionally, you just can't get there from here. Circle the water tower three times, collect two hundred dollars, and then enter the traffic pattern over boardwalk. If you do not have a transponder, lose one turn, and on it goes.

Airspace architecture and design are an attempt to bring order out of chaos. Air carrier pilots want a system that will keep them in positive controlled airspace—in which every pilot must have an ATC clearance—from takeoff to landing. General aviation pilots, on the other hand, want to be able to fly into and out of airports without much hassle. Still others do not want to be subject to any kind of government assistance at all, be it voluntary or otherwise.

Unfortunately it is impossible to please every faction within the aviation community all of the time. The result has been that most of the air traffic system and the airspace that defines it is a series of compromises. They do at least provide all pilots with access to our public airports. With that access, however, comes regulations, procedures, and responsibilities each of us must follow in order to accommodate everyone.

Nowhere is the idea of *government assistance* more appropriate than in a discussion of airspace restrictions, procedures, and requirements. Thanks to some of the most confusing writing in existence, understanding exactly what a particular regulation means or exactly when it does or does not apply to a specific flight can seem all but impossible. Often it is not just pilots who feel as though they have been left in the dark. Controllers also occasionally feel as if they have been charged to direct traffic with rules that are obscure or incomplete. Regardless of which side of the issue we are on, the more each of us understands what the other is supposed to be doing, the easier and safer it will be to fit ourselves into the big plan.

Airspace Classifications

The place to begin is at the beginning and, ironically, at the end. The airspace classifications begin with A and end with G, with the one exception being that, in the United States, there is no equivalent to the internationally designated Class F airspace and so none exists here.

With respect to air traffic procedures, Class A is both the most restrictive and yet the easiest to understand. It begins at eighteen thousand feet MSL and continues to Flight Level 600. Any pilot who wants to operate in Class A airspace must do so on an instrument clearance, as a properly rated and current instrument pilot, in an aircraft equipped and certified for instrument flight. No more, no less. It is not common knowledge whether the Space Shuttle or other vehicles, upon departing Class A airspace for points higher, must maintain VFR conditions when leaving it. Then again, the answer to that question is beyond both the intent of this book and the scope of its author's knowledge.

The other end of the airspace spectrum is also the other side of the air traffic coin. If Class A airspace is the most restrictive, then Class G airspace is the least restrictive. But for the unsuspecting pilot, it is not without its own unique characteristics and hazards. From an air traffic perspective, it is critically important to note that controllers view Class G airspace as no-man's-land. That is, controllers neither have, nor want, responsibility for or authority over pilots flying in Class G airspace.

In fact, the only ways in which controllers get involved with flying activity within Class G airspace are by one of two methods. Either by virtue of the absence of approval or denial to operate within Class G airspace or by implicit or explicit issuance of a caveat relieving them of any responsibility for a pilot's welfare while flying within it, controllers are telling pilots that they are on their own. Which no doubt is fine with most pilots.

One difficulty that results is that pilots who generally rely upon controllers to alert them about, if not prevent them from, flying into a hazardous situation frequently don't get that added protection in Class G airspace. Compounding the problem is the all-too-frequent misunderstanding that the situation is otherwise.

For example, when a pilot on an instrument flight departs an airport that is in Class G airspace, the controller issuing his departure instructions will preface them with the phrase "when entering controlled airspace" followed by the appropriate control directions. In essence, that phrase informs the pilot that all the responsibility to avoid obstructions or other aircraft prior to her entering controlled airspace lies solely with the pilot. To expect that controllers will provide the protection normally afforded instrument flights in other circumstances is to court disaster.

Having offered that warning for the instrument pilots, I want now to mention a valuable side benefit that exists for pilots who join the world of IFR. With the exception of special-use airspace, such as Prohibited Areas, Restricted Areas, Temporary Flight Restrictions (TFRs), and the like, flight through any controlled airspace is decidedly easier for the instrument pilot. Once she has received an instrument clearance and the authorization to depart an airport under it, she is authorized to fly into or through any and all airspace she encounters along the way. That means if her flight will take her through Class B airspace, additional authorization to enter it is not required. The same is true for every other category of airspace, including the previously mentioned Class G areas. It is still true that no air traffic separation services will be provided in a Class G area, but if a pilot files to fly through it, controllers will not deny that request.

If only it could be as simple for VFR pilots, but alas it is not. Starting with Class D airspace, the plot begins to thicken. Class D airspace can best be described as an imaginary boundary that surrounds any airport that has an operating control tower (fig. 4.2). Its shape basically consists of a circle with a 4.4 nautical mile radius around the airport it serves. Within that radius, Class D airspace begins at the surface and extends up to 2,500 feet above the airport ground elevation. But for each airport, the actual size, shape, and height of the associated Class D airspace will likely have minor variations to accommodate requirements specific to the local area.

Fortunately, determining if Class D airspace exists around an airport and then, if it does, determining the actual dimensions of the affected area are not that difficult. When looking at a sectional chart, every airport that has an operating control tower will be shown in blue. If the selected airport is blue, then the next thing to look for is a circular blue dashed line surrounding the airport. That line represents the airspace that is included within the Class D

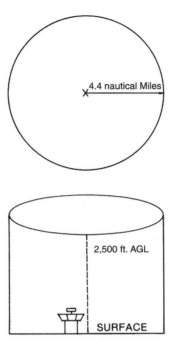

4.4 nautical Miles

2,500 ft. AGL

SURFACE

FIG. 4.2. Class D airspace is established only around airports with operating control towers.

airspace. Next, somewhere nearly adjacent to the airport symbol is a box enclosed with blue dashed lines and a set of numbers within it. Those numbers indicate the ceiling of the Class D airspace in hundreds of feet above *mean sea level (MSL)*.

For example, when selecting an airport if a pilot notes the symbol [27] alongside the blue airport symbol, it indicates that the top of the Class D airspace is 2,700 feet MSL. Since the indicated altitudes pilots read from their altimeters are also MSL altitudes, assuming the correct barometric pressure is set into the altimeter, no mental conversion is required to figure out whether or not a selected altitude for a flight will penetrate any Class D airspace along the way.

There is one little quirk with which pilots need to be familiar. If, in that blue dashed box, a minus precedes the numbers, the top of the Class D airspace goes up to it but *does not include* that altitude. So if, from the previous example the indication changed to [–27], the top of the Class D airspace would then be 2,699 feet MSL. Although somewhere there is no doubt a logical explanation for that one-foot distinction being necessary, but what that might be is beyond my feeble imagination to consider. Regardless of the top of the Class D airspace, the bottom always begins at the surface.

Just in case you are feeling a little too comfortable with having figured out where the airspace is and where it isn't, there is another point to consider. If the Class D airspace in question lies beneath either Class B or Class C airspace, and either airspace has a floor that is lower than the altitude designated within the Class D airspace, the more restrictive airspace takes precedence. For example, if the Class D airspace around an airport has a ceiling of 2,700 feet MSL denoted by the [27] symbol, but it lies beneath an area of Class C airspace that designates the floor as being 2,500 feet MSL, then the Class D airspace in that area stops at 2,499 feet MSL. The closer to the beginning of the alphabet the letter of the associated airspace is, the higher the trump card it has to play, so D always loses to C or B.

Having discussed where the airspace is and what it looks like, it seems only fair to mention why Class D airspace exists. As mentioned earlier, it creates an imaginary boundary around the airport it serves, and the primary reason for that boundary is to provide some order for the airplanes flying within it. Since every pilot who wants to operate within Class D airspace must establish two-way radio communication with the controller in the tower prior to entering it, it affords that controller a means to organize the flow of traffic around the airport.

Radio Communication for Class D Airspace

It might seem that what constitutes two-way radio communication would be obvious; that isn't necessarily so. The FAA has determined that if a controller answers a pilot's contact with the aircraft's call sign, that verbal bond has, in fact, been established. If, however, the controller replies with something like "aircraft calling, stand-by," instead of stating the actual call sign, it would be wise not to cross the line into the Class D airspace. In the eyes of the FAA, communication has not actually been established.

Yet inexperienced pilots, when faced with regulations and conditions that do little to clarify an obscure topic, sometimes have a way of interpreting the rules on their own. The tower chief at our local tower, after more than a few instances of students seemingly taking matters into their own hands, decided to vent some of his well-founded frustrations on the closest member of the college faculty he could find, me. The problem as he related it to me was that our students would rightly contact the tower prior to entering the Class D airspace, at which time they were told, "Cessna 674 Delta Whiskey, remain clear of the Class D airspace." At those particular times the area had become saturated with airplanes and the controller needed to restrict additional operations within the area until traffic thinned out a bit. Our students, however, deduced that since the controller had replied to them with their aircraft's call sign, the welcome mat had been laid before them. Such was not the case. In spite of the fact that two-way communications had been established, an air traffic instruction specifically directing a pilot to remain clear of the airspace preempts such a conversation.

There is one last issue regarding the communications relationship. What works when flying into Class D airspace does not necessarily apply when leaving it. Unless specifically requested to do so by the controller, a pilot is not required to advise the controller when she is leaving the airspace. Under normal circumstances, when a pilot initially informs ATC what her direction or destination is going to be, the controller working local formulates his own mental picture with respect to her flight path and approximately how long she will be in the Class D airspace. Unless a pilot changes her plan or some other unusual circumstance dictates otherwise, the controller, after a reasonable amount of time, will assume a particular plane has left his area. Making a transmission to state the obvious just wastes everyone's time and ties up the frequency in the process.

Control Tower Closed

What happens when, at those locations where the tower does not operate twenty-four hours a day, it closes down for the night? When the control tower is not in operation, the Class D airspace likewise ceases to exist. At those airports where the control tower does not operate continuously, on a sectional chart there is an asterisk just after the frequency listing for the tower. In addition, there is a notation that states, "See NOTAM/Directory for Class D/E (sfc) eff hrs.," to designate when the airspace reverts to a Class E surface area instead of Class G airspace. Pilots may then either consult the *Airport/Facility Directory* or the end sheet on a sectional chart to determine the hours of operation for the selected tower. When the tower is not in operation, usually the frequency designated as the control tower frequency becomes a *common traffic advisory frequency (CTAF)*, and is used in a manner similar to using a UNICOM frequency for traffic advisories and position reports.

Pilot/Controller Partnership

After making all the right calls and chatting with the controller, what does a pilot get in return for all her efforts? In many ways she gets her first real taste of being a partner in the pilot/controller relationship. With the exception of aircraft operating on the runways, what she does not get is separation from any other VFR traffic flying within the Class D airspace.

The controller's role in that partnership is to provide traffic advisories, sequencing, and a more structured flow of traffic into and out of the airport. Although more and more busy control towers have some type of radar display to assist the controllers with regulating the traffic, much of how a controller accomplishes his job is based upon a combination of pilot reports and what he sees through the tower windows. More often than not, when a pilot first contacts the tower to confirm that she may continue into the Class D airspace, the controller at the other end probably cannot visually locate the airplane.

If a pilot makes an incorrect position report, which unfortunately happens, the controller will often be unaware of the error until an airplane he was expecting to see arriving from the southwest ends up flying into the picture from the northeast. Maintaining accurate situational awareness then becomes a primary responsibility for pilots. When unsure of her position, at the very least, a pilot needs to inform the controller so he can spend a little more time working with that pilot to eliminate as much confusion as possible.

Sometimes controllers unintentionally add to the confusion by using local landmarks as reporting points for inbound pilots. While that system works well for pilots who are equally familiar with the immediate surroundings, newcomers to the same airport don't fare nearly as well. If the controller directs you to report Al's Funky Tavern on your way inbound and you don't have a clue where that is, make your dilemma known right away. Arriving early and unexpectedly at the airport isn't a matter of bad manners, it has the potential to become very unsafe.

Another of the controller's responsibilities is to point out traffic that either may be of concern to a pilot or traffic that the pilot is to follow. In return, the pilot's responsibility is to look for and find the traffic and advise the controller that the traffic is in sight. The wise pilot will be a bit cautious when looking for traffic, not assuming the first aircraft she sees is the correct one. And she will be equally skeptical after sighting the traffic and will confirm it is the correct traffic only when sure no other similar planes are in the same general area. Whenever a doubt exists, she will ask the controller for confirmation. Likewise, if traffic that was previously spotted somehow disappears amidst the ground or the clouds, the controller needs to know what has happened. Even the best pilot in the world cannot visually follow an airplane she can't see.

Remember that even though controllers directing traffic within Class D airspace, for the most part, are not providing separation for the aircraft involved, they will be issuing instructions that pilots are nevertheless legally bound to follow. The controller's job is to ensure a safe and organized flow of traffic into and out of the airport. Although much of his ability to do that effectively depends upon his individual experience and skill levels, without alert pilots paying attention and reacting correctly, the opportunities for a successful outcome shrink considerably.

Finally, for the pilot who intends to fly close to but not within Class D airspace, the best advice is to let common sense and good judgment be the controlling influence regarding whether or not to contact the controller. When flying just outside of or slightly above Class D airspace, it is a good idea to let the controller know you are there. In addition to making yourself known to him and other pilots flying in the same general area, should a slight miscalculation put you within the Class D airspace, you are covered. When you are well above or away from the airspace, it is probably more convenient to just stay alert and continue on your way, without the radio call.

Order in the Airspace

Class D airspace was created to establish some sort of order within the airspace around many of our moderately busy airports. Statistics and experience have proven that there is a much greater potential for midair collisions around the busier airports. But if we limit the number of aircraft flying in a given area and we require their pilots to obtain air traffic authorization prior to entering the airspace, we can and do effectively reduce the chances of a collision occurring. It is true that our flying becomes somewhat more restricted, but it is also true that safety improves considerably.

5

Radar Services for VFR Pilots: Is the Cure Worse Than the Disease?

NOT LONG AGO RADAR SERVICES for VFR pilots were the exception rather than the rule. Radar separation, traffic advisories, and sequencing of airplanes to or from an airport, or from one place to another were the domain of the instrument pilot. Radar, after all, was developed for use in air traffic control because the nonradar system could not handle the increasing number of pilots who were operating on instrument flight plans. VFR pilots were left to their own devices, to see and be seen, and little more seemed necessary.

Then someone, somewhere along the line got the idea that maybe VFR pilots ought to be able to take advantage of at least some of the services afforded IFR pilots when they were operating under radar control. More and more regularly, VFR pilots were mixing it up with air carrier flights as well as the instrument-rated general aviation pilots. Every once in a while, their mixing was a little too close for anyone's comfort.

In addition, the method of sequencing VFR aircraft into or out of an airport was becoming inadequate to handle the increasing number of pilots flying around the country. Even at airports serviced by a radar-approach control facility, the normal routine for VFR pilots was to bypass the approach controllers and contact the tower when they were inbound for landing. At that point, the tower controller usually would advise the pilot to proceed to a point somewhere close to the airport, report reaching the designated location, and then await further instructions. Instructions often included circling the area until the tower controller could coordinate with the approach controllers to negotiate for an opening among those aircraft (almost always IFR aircraft) that were being sequenced for the approach by the controllers in the radar room. When a slot was provided, the tower controller had to make sure that the VFR aircraft in that little holding pattern would fit into that slot.

Much of the time it worked, but sometimes it didn't. For any number of reasons, whether it was the speed of the VFR aircraft, its location relative to the slot, or a breakdown in the communications process, the fit was not right. The airplane that was under the direction of the tower controller got to the position to which it had been relegated too early or too late. Someone ended up going back out for another try and it was usually the VFR pilot who got delayed.

If more than one or two VFR aircraft were inbound for the same airport at the same time, the entire problem was compounded by the fact that several airplanes were circling fairly close to the airport and each had to provide its own separation from the other. It seemed that mixing apples and oranges that close to the runway, when a lot of relatively empty airspace went unused, was not the best solution to the problem.

The procedures that were established to accommodate VFR departures seemed equally inadequate. Essentially VFR aircraft remained under the direction of the tower controller and, as such, were ignored by controllers in the radar room who were directing IFR aircraft. IFR aircraft were provided separation from other IFR aircraft but not VFR. Thus, it was not uncommon to have a VFR aircraft that recently had departed the airport become a potential collision hazard for a pilot operating on an instrument flight plan.

Everything was legal and everyone involved was doing what he was supposed to do, but it was becoming evident that the procedures of the past just were inadequate for the days ahead. See and be seen is still one of the most basic tenets for all pilots flying in *visual meteorological conditions (VMC)*, but sometimes they just are not good enough. Two pilots may be doing their very best to see each other and still miss what seems to be the obvious until it is too late.

Finally, no doubt after many months of hand-wringing, negotiations, and laborious meetings, the idea was floated that perhaps VFR pilots, instead of being excluded from the world of radar, should be integrated into it. Consequently, over the years a number of ideas and iterations of programs designed to incorporate VFR pilots into the mainstream of the air traffic control system were developed, tried, adapted, and, in some instances, discarded as the ATC system slowly evolved into its present form.

Problems Pop Up

As with most changes that substantially alter the way in which people do business, bringing VFR pilots into the federal fold did not sit well with everyone. Many VFR pilots felt and on occasion still feel as though the cure has become worse than the disease. At one time or another, most controllers have heard pilots argue that they are quite capable of getting into and out of an airport without having a controller tell them every move, particularly when many of those moves seem inefficient from the pilot's perspective. As a pilot, I have often felt that angst as I was vectored to points C, D, E, and F when all I really wanted was to go from A to B. Given the greater number of pilots who use our airports today, whether I could have made my journey as safely as I did using the less-direct route provided by ATC is difficult to say. But, I do know that the procedures that were developed to include VFR pilots as players have made it much easier for controllers to separate all the airplanes more effectively.

Any partnership has issues that strain the relationship and the pilot/controller partnership is no different. A pilot's primary concern is and always should be the safety of his plane and his passengers. A controller's main objective is to ensure the safety of every person under her direction. Each has a unique perspective on any given situation, and occasionally the view from inside the cockpit is not as all encompassing as that from inside the radar room. When looked at collectively, the radar services and programs that are afforded VFR pilots today make the common goal of safety much easier to attain. As a valuable side benefit, the programs also provide a more efficient system for many more pilots.

Although some old codgers think that young people flying today rely too much on controllers to keep them out of trouble and get them to where they are going, they probably are the same ones who thought VOR navigation could not hold a candle to the old reliable low-frequency radio ranges. Yet, judging from the growing number of VFR pilots who use the services provided by controllers, someone must be doing something right.

Who Provides What

Before talking about the specifics of the various services that are available for VFR pilots, it is best to spend some time thinking about which controllers provide them. Although much of the discussion regarding radar services for VFR pilots will revolve around procedures developed for the terminal (approach control) environment, that doesn't mean that en route center controllers are not part of the program.

The emphasis on terminal facilities and their related programs stems from the premise that the greatest concentration of general aviation pilots for whom more structured programs needed to be developed were around our busier airports, mostly at altitudes that kept pilots below any center's airspace. Additionally, the practice of VFR pilots asking for, and receiving flight following and traffic advisories from center controllers is a relatively recent phenomenon. This is probably due to the fact that more and more general aviation airplanes are routinely flying at the higher altitudes of the en route center structure and because those same pilots have begun to recognize the advantages of having radar flight following.

No matter what the reasons—the ease with which VFR flight information can be entered into the automated systems is probably a factor—en route center controllers are as much a part of the game as their approach control counterparts. With the exception of sequencing air traffic for arrival at an airport, all of the services provided by terminal facilities are available when working with the centers.

Services and Contacts

How then does a pilot find out what services are available and whom to contact to receive them? If your preflight homework and planning don't reveal the answer, when all else fails, ask someone. Flight service specialists are often good sources for information you can't put your finger on.

An alternative is to check the *Airport/Facility Directory* (A/FD)or one of its privately published counterparts and the relevant sectional charts. In the A/FD, if radar service is available, the symbol ® precedes the approach or departure control service listed. When checking a sectional chart, if the area a pilot plans to fly through includes a *Terminal Radar Service Area (TRSA)*, Class B or Class C airspace, radar services for VFR pilots will be available. Yet, the absence of any of those types of airspace does not necessarily mean VFR pilots will be left to their own devices.

Once you determine that radar services are available, deciding what frequency to use for initial contact with ATC is the next step in the process. When departing an airport where procedures have been established for VFR pilots, the procedure is simple. Clearance delivery or possibly the ground controller will assign the appropriate frequency prior to your departure. The time to use it is when the tower controller advises you to contact departure.

When flying inbound to an airport that has radar capability or when just flying through an approach control's airspace en route to somewhere else, finding the correct frequency to use is not quite as easy but neither is it an insurmountable challenge. When planning to fly into a TRSA or Class C airspace, the appropriate frequencies are listed in a couple of different places: either on a sectional chart at the corresponding location over the ground where a pilot would make his initial contact or on the *Tower Frequency Tab* on the end page of the chart. Class B frequencies, although only printed at their corresponding locations on *Terminal Area Charts*, can also be found in the Tab List on each sectional chart.

Within each list, the frequencies are listed and the area for which each frequency applies is provided, as are the hours during which pilots may expect services to be available. For example, if after a particular frequency (270°–090°) appears, it means that, beginning from the 270 degree bearing from the airport and moving clockwise around to the 090 degree bearing from the airport, a pilot should use the frequency that preceded the parenthetical information.

Almost always, within each frequency section, two frequencies are listed and one of them, usually the second, is not available for use by most general aviation pilots. It is a frequency in the *ultra high frequency (UHF)* band and it is available for use by military or other government-sanctioned pilots. So skip trying to crank in 279.6 on the radio and, likewise avoid trying to plug it into the transponder. Neither action will achieve the desired results.

If you determine that your arrival into the airspace is going to be right on the line of the division between one communications area and another, do not waste too much time pondering the situation. You will not be banned from the skies if, after careful deliberation, you choose the wrong frequency. The controller with whom you first make contact will simply redirect you to the appropriate one.

So, after developing a good plan and establishing contact with a controller, what exactly do you get for your efforts? When the controller accomplishes the radar identification of your aircraft, the first thing you get is the magic phrase, *"radar contact."* Listen carefully for it, because without it, the rest of the game goes out the window.

Safety Alerts

The first item listed in the controller's bible under "Basic Radar Service to VFR Aircraft" is Safety Alerts. In the Pilot/Controller Glossary of the *Aeronautical Information Manual (AIM)*—a glossary that is also appended to the *Air Traffic Control Manual*—a Safety Alert is described as being "issued by ATC to aircraft under their control if ATC is aware the aircraft is at an altitude which, in the controller's judgment, places the aircraft in unsafe proximity to terrain, obstructions, or other aircraft." The definition itself is fairly self-explanatory, but there are exceptions. Placing too much reliance upon safety alerts as a means of collision avoidance would be a big mistake.

Every controller understands the importance of issuing safety alerts to pilots. By regulation and in everyday practice, controllers put the issuance of safety alerts at the top of their priority list. The reality is that it just does not always happen. One of the points to remember with respect to safety alerts is that, by the very nature of the situation under which they are issued, when a conflict with another plane exists, the controller involved is not working with the pilot of the other conflicting airplane. Were she in contact with both pilots, she would take positive action to prevent the collision. Since, to a certain extent, the other aircraft is then an unknown target to ATC, the controller issuing the safety alert may not see the impending situation in time to warn a pilot to react to it. There are any number of legitimate reasons why a controller might not be able to scan every square foot of her airspace every minute she is working the radar position. There could be a particularly complex situation developing at one end of the airspace while a potential collision hazard is developing in another completely different area. Or the unknown aircraft that appears with a much smaller data block than one being worked by a controller may be hidden among several other targets.

The issue is not why a controller might miss a potential danger, but rather to create an awareness that it happens. The fact is that controllers feel a strong moral commitment to keeping every pilot under their direction as safe as is humanly possible. While there can be no argument that a failure to provide that protection physically affects an airplane's occupants a lot more than the controller, to conclude that controllers care less than the pilots with whom they are working is blatantly wrong.

One afternoon as I was flying on an instrument training flight with a student who was busily doing his thing from under the vision-restricting hood that such students have come to loathe, I spotted an aircraft that was potentially a problem for us while it was still quite a distance away. As we closed the distance between us, it became clear to me that the other plane would pass five hundred feet or so beneath us. Still, I alerted my student to the fact that, if anything changed, I was going to take control of the plane to avoid any problems. Just as the other airplane was about to pass under ours, we received a rather frantic call from the controller alerting us to the problem. I realized later that I could have and should have let her know I had the traffic in sight long before it became a factor. But the tone of her voice clearly indicated to me that her concern for our safety was real.

In addition to issuing a safety alert, when appropriate and when time permits, the controller will also suggest an alternate plan of action for a pilot to take. For example, after issuing the alert a controller might add, "advise you climb to six thousand immediately." Notice that the instruction is prefaced with, "advise," which puts the execution of the controller's suggestion entirely within a pilot's prerogative to refuse or accept. If you are a VFR pilot and the alternate plan is going to put you in the clouds, the controller's suggestion does not carry with it any authorization to violate the FARs. Then again, depending upon your level of instrument proficiency, flying into a cloud would seem much less dangerous than risking a midair collision. It still would not be legal to venture into the clouds, but as pilot-in-command, you do have the authority to take whatever action is necessary for the safe continuance of your flight.

If, instead of another airplane, the ground or some type of obstruction is the culprit behind the issuance of a safety alert, the rest of the process remains the same. For sure, any pilot flying in VMC and most especially any VFR pilot is primarily responsible for ensuring his plane does not have an unexpected meeting with the ground or some errant tower, but within the realm of human capabilities, when unsafe situations occur, controllers will issue safety alerts.

The pilot's side of the equation is that he can help the controller immeasurably by appropriately reacting to the alert. Due to the serious nature of any safety alert, controllers are required to issue the alert repeatedly until a pilot advises that he has heard the warning and is taking some kind of steps to resolve the problem.

The options available to a pilot are relatively simple to understand. He may take the advice offered by the controller and climb, turn, descend, or whatever and that action should provide resolution for the conflict. Unfortunately, what many pilots do after initially receiving a safety alert is just continue on their original path with the hope that the situation will somehow resolve itself. Then, at the last available moment as traffic closes to an uncomfortable distance, they ask the controller for some directions to help them avoid the collision. The unfortunate part of this is that by the time the controller can formulate and issue an alternate plan, the time a pilot has to react may be too short to avoid whatever caused the alert. If an alert is issued along with an alternate plan of action, most pilots should accept the advice, act promptly, and inform the controller that he is complying with the controller's suggestion.

A second way in which a pilot can respond to a safety alert is to take his own steps to avoid the traffic or obstruction. If this occurs in Class B or C airspace and if ATC has assigned a heading or an altitude to maintain, pilots must inform the controller and, if time permits, receive authorization to deviate from the assignments prior to making any change. Obviously, if there is not time to notify the controller before making a change, the most important thing is to avoid a collision. But if that happens, the regulations require a pilot to inform ATC as soon as possible. The easiest way around all the problems is to tell the controller that you have the traffic in sight and ask for permission to maintain visual separation from it. Once received, that permission gives you the authority to deviate as necessary to maintain safe separation from traffic or obstructions.

A third action a pilot can take after receiving a safety alert is to do nothing and bet that the *Big Sky Theory* will save the day. That theory implies that with the sky being so huge and airplanes, relatively speaking, being so small, the odds that two of them will come together are just too low to worry about. I don't know many pilots who really believe that theory works, but, as a controller, I have witnessed many situations where pilots were willing to bet their lives on the theory's validity. The decision to do nothing is still a decision, but it is one that will be made by the pilot and not the controller.

I know from personal experience that, even on a clear day, other aircraft can be difficult to see. I also know from experience that receiving a timely safety alert from a controller can turn a potentially dangerous situation into a minor inconvenience. Whether or not a pilot accepts the service is his choice, but receiving a safety alert and advice to eliminate its accompanying hazard is one time when an unsolicited opinion should be welcomed.

Traffic Advisories

Traffic advisories are similar to safety alerts, but do not carry the same sense of urgency. Essentially, whenever a controller believes that another aircraft may get close enough to you to be of concern, she issues a traffic advisory. However, for all the reasons previously mentioned, controllers can't see every situation in which a traffic advisory should be issued. Additionally, because there are likely to be more airplanes that would qualify as traffic for a pilot, depending upon a controller's workload at any given time, she may see a situation and still not be able to issue the advisory. Issuing traffic advisories is a bit lower on that list than issuing safety alerts. See and be seen is still the rule of the day.

The methods by which controllers provide pilots with traffic advisories are not that difficult to understand. The most basic and often-used format is what I call the *clock method*. Controllers try to narrow down the area in which a pilot should look for traffic by referencing the position of the traffic to a position of a number on a clock face, with your aircraft being at the center of that clock. Traffic that is issued as "twelve o'clock" is straight ahead, traffic at "three o'clock" is off of the right wingtip, and so on.

Yet what seems simple in concept occasionally can get rather confusing in practice for both pilots and controllers. For example, I once issued traffic to an eastbound aircraft as being at twelve o'clock, five miles westbound. I then went on to some other traffic and momentarily quit observing the eastbound pilot and his traffic. When I did look back at the situation, my easterly headed pilot had made a turn to the north. When I queried him with respect to his unanticipated change in direction, somehow equating the top of a clock with the top of the world, he replied that he had turned north to see the traffic at twelve o'clock. That time the actions of the pilot did not create a particularly hazardous situation, but they did cause unnecessary confusion for both of us.

The second way in which controllers issue traffic is more straightforward in the methodology used but a little less precise in the results. Consequently it is used only in certain circumstances and less often than the first way. If the traffic is an aircraft that is maneuvering so rapidly or frequently that its direction of flight varies too greatly to be determined, rather than using the clock method, a controller will issue the traffic relative to cardinal compass points. An example would be, "traffic four miles northwest of your position maneuvering between three and four thousand." Assuming you know where northwest is in relation to your aircraft (a usually valid assumption for most of us most of the time), you know where to look for the airplane.

Once the traffic advisory has been issued, it is back to the pilot for his role in the exercise. When or if he sees the traffic, he should inform the controller so that additional advisories need not be provided. Otherwise, time permitting, the controller will continue to provide information regarding that traffic until it is no longer a factor. Clearly, if any action is required to avoid the traffic, a pilot should take it and likewise inform the controller of the changes in his flight path.

If, however, a pilot does not see the traffic but would like the controller to assist him in putting more distance between himself and the unknown aircraft, he must ask the controller for vectors. The controller most likely will not initiate the offer for vectors. Part of the reason is the additional work it creates for her, but I suspect a bigger part of the issue is the legal ramifications that could result if the controller suggests the idea to a pilot and something dire happens as a result of her suggestion.

It is important for pilots to remember that, if they want a controller's help in avoiding traffic they do not see, they need to make the request early enough for her to adequately offer the assistance. Even then, there are some times when vectors just cannot be provided. When I was a controller in Minneapolis, I ran across a pilot flying for one of the major airlines who had become somewhat of a legend within our facility. For whatever reasons, every time he departed the airport he would ask the departure controller for vectors around all unidentified targets.

One Saturday afternoon with much of our airspace saturated with VFR targets, this pilot checked in on my frequency and made his usual request. As he was approaching a rather large swarm of aircraft around one of the VORs, I advised him of the traffic and he reiterated that he wanted me to keep him away from all of them. After briefly considering whether or not I had that many vectors left in me I replied that I was not able to comply with his request. I just could not turn him often enough and fast enough to keep him away from all the targets on my scope. Fortunately, as I suspected, they were well below his altitude and he continued on without incident. Under normal circumstances his requests could be and were honored, but sometimes asking for vectors is asking for the impossible. It is important that pilots recognize the limitations that controllers face when trying to do their jobs.

The issuance of traffic advisories greatly contributes to enhancing a pilot's ability to see and avoid other aircraft that create a potential hazard. But it is important to remember that such advisories do not relieve pilots from being their own primary defense against collision. Controllers are not going to see every conceivable situation in which another aircraft might become a problem. The last sentence of the definition of traffic advisories in the Pilot/Controller Glossary makes the point best: "When a pilot requests or is receiving traffic advisories, he should not assume that all traffic will be issued." When in doubt, keep looking.

Limited Radar Vectoring

As it is written in the controller's handbook, the third of the four basic radar services is "limited radar vectoring *when requested by the pilot* [my emphasis]." That seemingly innocuous phrase adds an entirely new element to the pilot/controller relationship and one with which all VFR pilots need to become very familiar. Human nature in many pilots seems to be that, once a controller starts issuing vectors—vectors being nothing more than headings for a pilot to fly—much of the responsibility they held with respect to maintaining their own situational awareness somehow shifts exclusively to the controller. Such is hardly the case.

Several factors contribute to the false sense of security that pilots feel when being radar vectored. The first is that vectoring has become so much a part of the world in which pilots operate and it is accomplished with such a high degree of safety and reliability that almost all of us take it for granted.

If a controller starts vectoring me, then she will make it a point to keep me out of harm's way. True, with the exception that controllers are human too and every once in a while they need a pilot who is aware of his surroundings to provide the backup for those occasions.

Another is that, with only a couple of exceptions, any time a pilot is being vectored, the controller may only do so if the aircraft being vectored is at or above a minimum altitude that guarantees protection from the ground or obstructions. So, for many pilots, whenever a controller is vectoring them, being aware of their immediate surroundings seems to be less of a concern than when they are flying without assistance. One of those exceptions (along with when being issued a heading might not be the same as being vectored) will be covered in Chapter 6.

The other exception is one that should be of concern to every VFR pilot who ever accepts radar vectors to anywhere. Any time a VFR pilot contacts a controller and requests vectors, as long as the controller in question has not assigned him an altitude to maintain, the controller may vector the pilot *regardless of his altitude*. What can easily add to the dilemma is that whenever local procedures have been established to provide radar service for VFR pilots—as is the case with a TRSA—unless a pilot specifically informs the controller that he does not want radar service, the assumption is that he does. Either way, once the request for radar service is made, the burden of maintaining safe and legal clearance from obstructions and terrain features becomes one the pilot alone must bear.

For VFR pilots the idea that they alone are held responsible for keeping their airplanes away from solid objects that might hurt them, whether in the air or on the ground, is nothing new. It is or should be the rule by which we all fly when we are doing it VFR. The twist is just that common misconception that once a controller starts vectoring us, the responsibility for keeping us out of trouble shifts to the person on the ground. It doesn't.

That is not to say that any controller will intentionally vector a low-flying VFR aircraft into the side of a mountain or some high-flying radio tower. But not everything that can hurt a pilot is displayed on the controller's radarscope. Most controllers, even if it is on a subconscious level, tend to assume that VFR pilots, even those being vectored, will let them know if an assigned heading is going to put them in a dangerous situation. While it may not always be a valid assumption on the part of the controllers, it is important that pilots realize it is one that routinely is being made.

One final point to ponder with respect to VFR pilots receiving radar vectors: Depending upon the type of airspace in which the vectors are being provided, radar separation may or may not be part of the package. When flying within a TRSA, Class B or C airspace, some type of radar separation is being provided, the exact nature of which will be discussed shortly. In any other airspace, VFR pilots who are being vectored are not being radar separated from any other traffic. Again, that is not to say that controllers are playing Russian roulette with those VFR pilots under their direction. When conditions warrant, safety alerts and traffic advisories will be provided but with all the exceptions previously mentioned. It is just that the first and major line of defense against collisions is the person sitting in the cockpit. On too many occasions, when I was working as a controller and I said the magic words, "radar contact" to a pilot, I could almost hear their level of alertness go down several notches.

Radar services for VFR pilots have become an invaluable tool through which safety and efficiency have been greatly improved. While these services can be many things to many pilots, what they cannot be is a substitute for good judgment and constant awareness of what is going on around them. When it comes to asking for radar assistance from controllers, the rule should always be "let the buyer beware."

Sequencing

The last of the radar services available for VFR pilots is sequencing, at those locations around the country where procedures have been established for the purpose. Although there are no doubt some exceptions somewhere, generally speaking if an airport has an associated radar approach control and if those available services and the frequencies on which to receive them are published, it is a good bet that radar sequencing to the airport is also available.

Sequencing is nothing more than establishing an orderly flow of airplanes into an airport. The basic concept, simple as it is, carries with it some subtle responsibilities that pilots need to understand if they are to use the service safely. To begin with, as is the case with vectoring, sequencing aircraft inbound to an airport is not the same as separating them along the way. In many ways the process is similar to how a tower controller sets up a flow of traffic within a traffic pattern, except that in a radar environment the approach controllers do it and a sequence usually is established at a greater distance from the airport.

Most often an approach sequence is established using a combination of radar vectors and visual separation. That is, the controller will vector a pilot to a point where he can visually see the traffic he is to follow and at that point he will be instructed to follow it to the airport. A point to consider is that if, after having reported the traffic to follow is in sight, you are instructed to follow it, anything that interferes with your ability to do that needs to be reported to the controller.

If you lose sight of the traffic, let the controller know as soon as possible. The very fact that a controller points out traffic that is to be followed very likely means that the airplane ahead could become a problem for you if you do not see it. Otherwise, if, for example, the traffic ahead of you were so far ahead and so much faster that you couldn't catch it if you were a Lear Jet, the controller probably would not even bother to point it out. Instead she would just point out the airport and wait for you to let her know that you see it.

If, however, the traffic you are following to the airport is a heavy jet, a Boeing 757 or a large aircraft, controllers are required to provide wake turbulence separation from the traffic ahead. That means, in a radar environment, even when they are not technically providing separation for VFR aircraft, controllers must ensure that small aircraft are kept anywhere from five to six miles behind those types of aircraft—unless of course the controller points the traffic out, advises a pilot of the type aircraft, and then instructs him to maintain visual separation from it. At that point, how close or how far a pilot gets to the traffic ahead is his choice. Having once watched as a corporate jet landing behind a DC9 almost went up on a wingtip just at the landing flare, and having experienced wake turbulence on the final approach, I believe that too much distance is a lot better than too little.

One last point to mention with respect to being put into an approach sequence, and it is one that even more experienced pilots occasionally get confused about, is that an *approach sequence* is not the same as a *landing sequence*. The problem is not so much that pilots do not understand what each means, the names are self-explanatory. Rather, for most pilots, it is being aware that a distinction between the two even exists and under what circumstances one is different from the other. Getting the easiest part out of the way, the approach sequence is the order in which aircraft are aligned by the approach controllers for their respective arrivals to the airport. The landing sequence is determined by the tower controller and that is the order in which aircraft inbound on the approach will actually plant their wheels on the tarmac. The difference is that should the tower controller also have airplanes in the local traffic pattern or if, when appropriate, there are airplanes inbound that have declined the use of radar service, they will be mixed in with the approach sequence to create the landing sequence. Pilots who are unaware of the distinction between the approach and the landing sequence occasionally get caught off guard when the airplanes they have been following for the last ten miles are not the same ones they follow when landing.

Termination of Radar Service

Now that we have covered the basic radar services for VFR pilots and now that every pilot out there wants to take them on, how do we get rid of them when it is time to move on? With the exception of flying within Class B or C airspace, for a pilot it is easy. Just let the controller know that you would like to terminate radar service or flight following. The controller will most likely respond with "Radar service terminated, squawk VFR, frequency change approved." If you had been a good Do-Bee while traversing the controller's airspace you might even get a "good day" attached to the end of it.

There are a couple of reasons why a pilot might choose to terminate radar service even though the controller is willing to continue to offer it. The first is an area in which the interpretation of the rules is at best questionable. When a VFR pilot is flying in Class E airspace in which he is supposed to be unencumbered by all but the most basic restrictions, some controllers have the belief that, if they are providing radar service to that pilot, they have the right to both vector him and assign altitudes to maintain. This interpretation lends itself to debate, but it is a discussion for some other venue. Thus, whenever a pilot who is flying in Class E airspace begins to question the value of those or similar ATC instructions, he has only to request termination of radar service to eliminate the problem. Whether or not that is the best choice is a decision each pilot must make based upon his own judgment. Just know that it can be done, unilaterally.

Another reason to end radar control develops when a pilot starts to get caught between a rock and a hard place. For example, the airport that I have called home for the last fourteen years is located just outside of and beneath the Class C airspace of a larger airport just up the road. For many years pilots flying through the Class C airspace headed for my home airport, which is surrounded by Class D airspace, had a difficult time getting released by the approach controllers responsible for the Class C airspace in time to contact our tower controller before entering her airspace. As often as not, when their radar service was finally terminated, they had already crossed the line into the Class D airspace. They were welcomed by a very unhappy tower controller. Sometimes, however, the tower controller realized her frustration was caused by a fellow controller rather than an uncooperative pilot. Either way, it was the pilots who were hanging themselves out on a limb where a possible violation of an FAR easily could cut them down.

It may have been the radar controllers who were creating the situation, but ultimately it was still the pilots who were responsible for abiding by the regulations. Though there is no one correct way to deal with any such similar situation, one solution is to advise the controller in a forceful but diplomatic manner that a frequency change is not only requested but also required. The other is to advise the controller that, if you must remain on her frequency, she needs to coordinate the Class D airspace entry with the appropriate tower controller. Otherwise, maybe she could suggest a place to hold within her airspace until one of the two options can be approved.

Exactly when controllers will initiate the termination of radar services for VFR pilots is more nebulous. Most of the basic radar services provided for VFR pilots are subject to the capabilities of the radar involved and, more significantly, on the workload of the controllers at any given time. Although not an arbitrary decision, each individual controller is given the latitude to decide when and if she is able to add VFR pilots and the services they require into her traffic load. When traffic is relatively light, VFR pilots will be welcomed into the system. When traffic gets heavy, the weather gets difficult, or any other number of complex situations arises, pilots flying VFR will less likely be able to avail themselves of many of the normal services.

But having said that, on any given day almost anywhere across the country almost every controller will do her best to work with any pilot asking for her services. If anything, controllers tend to accept VFR pilots as part of their workload when they often do not have the time to give them all the attention they deserve. When there is constant chatter on a frequency and little being said to the VFR pilots in the area, a red flag should go up for those pilots that they could be more on their own than they might have thought. When the time comes that a controller recognizes she has reached or exceeded her limit to adequately service all the pilots on the frequency, she will most likely start to reduce her workload by terminating radar services for VFR pilots. Exactly when that will happen is impossible to predict for each individual controller, so for VFR pilots, expecting the unexpected is the best way to think.

More Airspace: The Good, the Bad, the Ugly

WHEN IT COMES TO AIRSPACE and the restrictions imposed within the various types, the eternal conflict between pilots and controllers is that typically most pilots want less of each whereas most controllers want more of each. Regardless of what each partner in the pilot/controller relationship wants, both have to work with what is there. Particularly for VFR pilots, developing a broad knowledge base and a sound understanding of the procedures, practices, limitations, and advantages of each type of airspace is essential to getting the most out of the ATC system. Having discussed the basic radar services that are available for VFR pilots in Chapter 5, the next step is to move on to more advanced procedures.

Terminal Radar Service Areas

A *Terminal Radar Service Area (TRSA)* is the one type of airspace that has no equivalent under international airspace classifications. Within the United States, TRSAs do exist and their development can be linked directly to a desire to afford VFR pilots the same services that IFR pilots have enjoyed since the inception of radar control. Specifically, in TRSAs as well as in Class B and C airspace, in addition to the basic radar services offered to VFR pilots, all VFR pilots who participate in a TRSA program receive radar separation from IFR and all other participating VFR pilots.

So, what is a participating VFR pilot and how does a person get to be one? As stated earlier, much of the airspace within our country is a compromise of one sort or another and TRSAs are no exception. The forerunner of Class C airspace, TRSAs were designed to fill the gap between limited or no radar service for VFR pilots and the all inclusive and more restrictive Class B airspace. Since many general aviation pilots had become both irritated and occasionally intimidated by the regulations and procedures associated with flying in Class B airspace, when the FAA began introducing the concept of more areas of more tightly controlled airspace, general aviation pilots reacted less than favorably to the idea.

The result was a major concession that allowed all VFR pilots the option of accepting or refusing radar service when flying within the confines of any TRSA. This concession continues to exist today and it continues to fuel the controversy of whether TRSAs are the best or the worst things that have happened to aviation in the United States. VFR pilots who choose to accept the radar services offered in a TRSA are said to be *participating* pilots. Those who refuse the radar service are *nonparticipating*. Either way, it is one of those rare instances in which pilots alone determine what, for them, is the best course of action.

Therein lies the controversy. Some pilots argue that there is no controversy at all. If they want the service they will ask for it, if they don't they will continue on their way without interference. Controllers, on the other hand argue that trying to provide adequate separation for participating VFR and IFR pilots in a TRSA while other VFR pilots are permitted to fly anywhere they want at any altitude without even having to talk to the controllers is, at best, extremely difficult. Each side has a valid argument but more often than not, normal practice for most pilots makes the argument moot. Over the years the majority of VFR pilots flying into or through TRSAs have come to recognize the value of participating in the program and the few who do not, seldom create real problems for other pilots or controllers.

To find out if your airport of intended use has an accompanying TRSA, look at a sectional chart. Each TRSA is depicted by a series of solid black circles and/or lines that define the exact dimensions of the airspace (fig. 6.1). The individual sectors within a TRSA are defined by solid black circles and/or lines that are just slightly narrower than those defining the outermost dimensions.

Within each sector is found either two sets of numbers or the letters SFC and a set of numbers. The numbers and letters define the floor and the ceiling in hundreds of feet above *mean sea level (MSL)*. For example, if 100/SFC appears within the innermost circle of a TRSA—which is almost always where SFC will be found—it indicates that within that associated area the TRSA begins at the surface and extends up to and including ten thousand feet MSL. Typically, the further away from the airport one looks, the higher the floor of a TRSA is above the ground. At the farthest reaches of a TRSA 100/50 could be found and that would indicate that the floor of the TRSA begins at five thousand feet MSL and the ceiling is at ten thousand feet MSL.

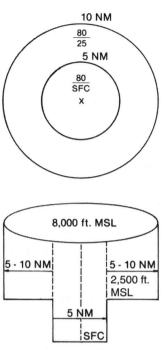

FIG. 6.1. The terminal radar service area (TRSA) is an integral component of radar service for the VFR pilot.

Not so incidentally, the fact that the charted altitudes for TRSAs as well as Class B and C airspace are MSL altitudes means that they correspond to the altitudes indicated on the airplane's altimeter, assuming a pilot has set her altimeter to the correct barometric pressure for the area.

The reasons for the gradual increase in the floor of a TRSA in those areas farther away from the airport it serves are several. One most likely reason is that its design mimics that of the Class B airspace structure that preceded the creation of TRSAs. Another is that, even though VFR pilots are not restricted from flying within the confines of a TRSA, the higher floor permits flight below it as pilots operate farther away from the primary airport. And if perception is reality, then presumably most pilots' reality is that the airspace below the floor of a TRSA is less restricted than within it. Those reasons aside, the main reason for the higher bases at the greater distances is that since radar is line-of-sight due to the curvature of the earth as well as obscuring terrain or obstructions, providing adequate radar service at lower altitudes in the outer areas is more difficult to accomplish.

However, there is one final glitch that complicates the ease with which pilots may fly into or through the airspace within the confines of a TRSA. Since only busier airports have TRSAs associated with them and since each of those airports has an operating control tower (at least some of the time), it follows that somewhere in that innermost region of a TRSA where it begins at the surface, there lurks some Class D airspace waiting to bite the unwary pilot. Approval from ATC is not necessary for flight within a TRSA, but flying into the Class D airspace that is coincidental with the center of the TRSA without establishing radio contact with the tower is still against the regulations.

Let's look at the Binghamton, New York, TRSA as an example. The innermost area of the TRSA begins at the surface and extends up to and includes 6,000 feet MSL. In almost exactly the same area, the Class D airspace also begins at the surface but extends up to and includes 4,100 feet MSL. Consequently, a pilot flying at 5,000 feel MSL legally could pass right over the top of the Binghamton airport without ever having to contact either the approach or the tower controllers. But, if that pilot were conducting the same flight at 3,500 feet MSL instead of 5,000 feet, although she would not need to contact ATC to fly through the associated TRSA, she would have to contact Binghamton Tower to receive permission to fly through the Class D airspace.

From the standpoint of practicality and ease, the simplest solution to the complexity and confusion is to take advantage of the radar services that are available. Then the issue of obtaining authorization to fly through the Class D airspace is not an issue at all. Once a pilot is radar identified, in the absence of any instructions from ATC to the contrary, she may proceed on course, even if on course takes her through the Class D airspace. One of the advantages of working with the radar controllers is that, if approval to pass through the tower's airspace is required, the radar controllers will coordinate that passage for a pilot. For those pilots who choose to make the journey without radar assistance, the choice is theirs to make, but they should at least be sure they are where they belong talking with whom they must.

Once a pilot determines that she will in fact be flying into or through a TRSA, finding out the correct frequency to use to talk to the right controller is relatively easy. Beneath the name of every TRSA on a sectional chart is a notation, "SEE TWR FREQ TAB." A pilot needs only to look at the end page of that sectional to find the proper frequency to use based upon her location from the airport. The same information regarding the frequencies can by found in the *Airport/Facility Directory* (A/FD).

After completing the necessary preparations, the pilot knows where the TRSA is and also knows the correct frequency to use to contact ATC. What's next? The next step is to contact the appropriate controller about five to ten miles outside of the lateral limits of the TRSA, keeping in mind that where a particular boundary lies depends upon your altitude. The higher your altitude, the farther out the TRSA exists. But keep in mind that, although a controller radar identifies you while you are outside of the TRSA, radar separation from other traffic will not begin until you are inside of it.

Exactly what to say to the controller on initial contact requires a bit of a digression. Unless your aircraft has been handed off to the controller responsible for the airspace within the TRSA that you will traverse, he has no prior knowledge of your impending arrival. Instead of already having a printed flight strip with your flight information, he must write one as you talk to him. That is where the dilemma lies.

Some controllers prefer that pilots establish initial contact giving nothing more than their aircraft type and call sign. Only after the controllers respond do they then expect to hear the rest of the information regarding altitude, route of flight, and additional requests. Another group of controllers want it all right up front and believe that anything less is a waste of valuable frequency time. Unfortunately, that means that for those of us who fly VFR, no matter what we do we can count on being wrong at least some of the time.

With respect to my own flying, what I say on initial contact depends largely upon how busy the frequency is at the time. If things are relatively slow and I know that getting a reply from the controller is not going to be a major issue, I keep the first call short, giving only my type aircraft and call sign. If, however, time on the frequency seems to be at a premium, as effectively and concisely as possible, I tell the controller everything I want him to know and expect he will ask for a repeat of anything he missed.

What that controller wants to know is as follows: type aircraft and call sign; my location; my altitude; the route of flight or destination airport; and, if required, that the current ATIS has been received. Usually everything can be said in a matter of seconds: for example, "Elmira Approach, Mooney 801 Delta Whiskey, fifteen miles southwest, at three thousand five hundred VFR, inbound for landing with information Bravo." Or, "Elmira Approach, Mooney 801 Delta Whiskey, twenty southwest, VFR, en route to Syracuse at five thousand five hundred, request clearance through the TRSA." After radar identification has been established the controller likely will respond with something like, "Mooney 801 Delta Whiskey, cleared through the Elmira TRSA on course, advise any change in altitude."

Why do you need a clearance to go through airspace that anyone can fly through any time and does that further imply that a controller can deny clearance through that airspace at some point? When a pilot contacts a controller and requests to enter a TRSA, essentially she is telling that controller that she knows the game and is willing to play by its rules in return for getting all the services, including radar separation. By issuing the clearance, the controller is responding with the implication that he too knows the rules and is willing and able to provide all the services the pilot expects to receive.

As a consequence of the responsibilities that fall upon a controller when he clears a pilot into a TRSA, that controller can deny clearance into the TRSA if he is too busy to fulfill all of his responsibilities to a pilot. However, there is a way out of the situation. Any time a pilot wants to decline the services offered within a TRSA, she has the right to do so. That holds true even after she has entered a TRSA. Once the services are refused, the controller is off the hook and the pilot is left to her own devices to navigate safely through the maze ahead. She can always listen to the various frequencies and get some idea of what is going on, but she will not be afforded separation from the other traffic around the area.

TRSA Services

If the controller provides services in a TRSA, what does that mean? A pilot gets separation from all other participating VFR and all IFR aircraft. The exact type of separation depends upon the situation. Visual separation is a frequent means by which controllers help pilots stay away from one another. It works well as long as pilots remember that when the controller states, "maintain visual separation from that traffic," the burden of preventing a near-miss or worse, shifts entirely to the pilot. The instruction does, however, imply that if a pilot needs to maneuver her aircraft by changing the heading or altitude to avoid the traffic from which she is maintaining visual separation, she is authorized to alter her flight path.

Vertical separation is also provided. VFR aircraft flying in a TRSA will be kept five hundred feet above or below all other participating aircraft within the airspace. Just keep in mind that, although five hundred feet is more than enough to ensure that two airplanes will not conflict with one another, for the uninitiated, watching another airplane pass 500 feet over the top of your aircraft can be a bit disconcerting. Especially if it is significantly larger than yours is. The one exception to the five hundred feet rule is that, if the other aircraft is a heavy jet or a Boeing 757, then the standard wake turbulence separation requirements supercede the VFR rules and one thousand feet vertical separation is used. That is still close enough to give the pilot of a smaller airplane an up-close and personal look at the underside of a Boeing 747, which even from a thousand feet can be somewhat daunting.

With the exception of wake turbulence requirements, the separation between small aircraft flying at the same altitude within a TRSA can also be somewhat surprising for the uninformed. Controllers may use what is known as *target resolution* to legally keep distance between the aircraft under their direction. In house, controllers occasionally refer to target separation as having "green in-between." That is, the white objects on the green radarscope must not touch. There must be green between them to have legal separation.

The actual distance is dependent upon variables such as the altitude of the airplanes involved and their distance from the radar antenna, and comes out to about one-fourth to one mile. In every instance, the distance represented by target resolution is just enough, with little extra to play with.

That combined with the understanding that there are always likely to be airplanes flying within a TRSA whose pilots are not participating in the program should underscore the point that those pilots who are receiving radar service are still responsible for looking for other traffic. Controllers do their best to provide all the necessary traffic advisories, but staying vigilant is always the responsibility of the pilot-in-command.

Once inside a TRSA, a pilot should also expect that both heading and altitude assignments on occasion will be issued to her. Although controllers will make every effort to allow pilots to do most, if not all, of the navigating on their own—if for no other reason than it results in less work for the controllers—occasionally some direction from the ground becomes necessary.

The VFR pilot has to keep a couple of points in mind when reacting to headings or vectors issued by a controller. Remember that as long as the controller did not assign an altitude prior to or in conjunction with the heading assignment, he can assign any heading regardless of the aircraft's altitude. If something is in the way, it is incumbent upon the pilot to both refuse the heading assignment and ask for an alternate instruction. Likewise, if a controller puts a VFR pilot on a vector that will cause her to fly into a cloud (since radar does not display the majority of clouds in a given area), she needs to speak up immediately.

Whenever a controller does assign a specific altitude to a VFR pilot, the burden shifts somewhat. A controller cannot assign an altitude that will put an aircraft below the safe and legal minimums for the area in which it is or will be flying. But he can assign an altitude that is not in compliance with the regulatory requirements of the hemispheric rules for VFR flight in controlled airspace. That is, ATC has the authority to assign an altitude of five thousand feet MSL to a VFR pilot flying within a TRSA even though five thousand feet is more commonly deemed to be an altitude reserved for instrument flight. When that assignment is no longer necessary, the controller should advise a pilot to "resume the appropriate VFR altitude." Any time a pilot is leaving a TRSA and a reassigned altitude is not issued, it is time to change anyway. Permission is not required to make that change. A pilot need only inform the controller that she will be climbing or descending to the correct VFR altitude for her direction of flight.

Leaving an Airport with TRSA

When a pilot wants to depart from an airport for which a TRSA has been created, the procedures to get going are not terribly complicated. As is the case when flying into a TRSA from outside of it, unless a pilot specifically tells the clearance delivery or ground controller that she does not want TRSA service on her way out, that controller will assume she is going to accept it. In that case the pilot is expected to inform the controller of her destination or route of flight and the altitude she is requesting. That information will be put on a flight strip and the pilot will be issued the appropriate departure control frequency and a transponder code. From that point on everything about a VFR departure from an airport within a TRSA is the same as one from any other airport except that the departure controller again may assign headings or altitudes as necessary to provide the required radar separation.

Pilots flying out of or through a TRSA will be afforded all the basic radar services for VFR pilots and radar separation from other traffic until they leave the airspace within it. At that point the controller will tell them that they are leaving the TRSA but he may not necessarily terminate radar service. If he is not too busy with other traffic, he may just tell pilots to remain on his frequency for traffic advisories. Although the radar separation part of the program ends with the TRSA, the basic radar services might easily continue for another ten or fifteen miles.

One final point about leaving a TRSA is that, if the controller had assigned a heading for a pilot to fly, as is true with altitude assignments, once out of the TRSA the pilot is free to fly whatever course she desires. In fact, had a pilot been flying an assigned heading, the controller should transmit an advisory to "resume own navigation" upon departure from the TRSA. Should he forget to make that transmission, the restriction is still cancelled. Though you may tell a controller who is still providing advisories any time you make a change, it is not a requirement.

Ever since TRSAs were incorporated into our National Airspace System, there has been a running argument with respect to their value. Opponents of the airspace say that when a pilot accepts the service she is letting herself in for a needless scenic tour of the countryside while being excessively separated from other planes in the area. Others believe TRSAs provide the most efficient method to get pilots into or out of airports, and they provide added insurance against collisions.

Radar service and separation have become for VFR pilots what an instrument clearance has always been for those folks who fly in the clouds. Not only does radar give controllers a tool that will ensure a greater margin of safety for pilots who participate in the programs designed for its use, but it also provides a more effective method of sighting those other pilots who are not using the service. Radar just does not miss nearly as many airplanes as we humans do.

Class C Airspace

The next step up in the hierarchy of airspace classification is *Class C (Charlie)* airspace. Originally, Class C airspace was created to address many of the issues associated with TRSAs and, in fact, many of the airports that are now encompassed by Class C airspace used to have TRSAs around them. The biggest problem that needed to be resolved with respect to improving upon TRSAs was that of how to eliminate nonparticipating aircraft flying in increasingly congested airspace without overly restricting VFR pilots in the process.

The solution to the problem was simple. Require that every pilot requesting flight into or through Class C airspace contact ATC for permission to do so prior to entering the airspace. Building a consensus among the various parties who would be affected by the new requirements contained in the proposal was not easy. Many pilots believed that TRSAs were filling the bill just fine. Additionally, they didn't care for the many similarities between Class C and Class B airspace. If it looked like a duck, quacked like a duck, and walked like a duck, regardless of what the FAA said, it was a duck—or in this case, a turkey.

Neither were controllers terribly pleased with the Class C airspace as originally proposed. Since participation in the Class C radar service program would be mandatory rather than optional, the way to keep pilots happy was to mandate that controllers would not be permitted to deny any pilot entrance into any Class C airspace at any time. With that addition, pilots became a little less hostile toward the newly proposed restrictions. Controllers reacted much less favorably.

All those folks who were working the front lines in radar rooms around the country realized that there were times when their ability to accept and provide separation for every pilot who wanted to fly into the airspace would be taxed beyond their limits. Their solution to that impossible problem seemed equally obvious. If they were not allowed to deny any pilot entrance into Class C airspace, then at some point, they would simply ignore many of the pilots until such time that the controllers could fit them into their workload. It was not what the designers of the airspace had in mind, but realistically it was an option that was bound to be used sooner or later.

Regardless of the evolutionary process that brought the airspace and its associated regulations and procedures to where they are today, Class C airspace has proven to be an acceptable compromise between the less restrictive TRSA and the more restrictive Class B airspace. That every pilot and controller associated with the daily operations within Class C airspace is satisfied with the end product is unlikely. All in all, what we ended up with has brought pilots and controllers about as close to that desired consensus as anyone will ever get.

Class C airspace is charted on both sectional and terminal area charts. If an airport has Class C airspace associated with it, most often a set of concentric magenta-colored circles will be displayed around the airport. Although there likely will be a few individual sectors within the outer circle and a few minor differences among them, the good news about Class C airspace is that its creation has been relatively uniform from one airport to the next.

Generally speaking, the charted inner circle of Class C airspace has a five-nautical-mile radius around the airport it serves and extends from the surface up to and including four thousand feet above the surface of the airport, charted in altitude above mean sea level (fig. 6.2). Similar to those altitudes found within TRSA airspace, the notation "43/SFC" indicates that the floor of the Class C airspace begins at the surface and goes up to and includes 4,300 feet MSL.

The outer circles, which are the ones that are more likely to contain several sectors in which altitudes and exact dimensions are not as uniform as the inner circles, are still more similar to each other than different. While a generic outer circle could be described as one having a ten-nautical-mile radius around the airport it serves beginning at 1,200 feet *above ground level (AGL)* and extending up to and including 4,000 feet above the airport elevation, the specifics of each are likewise depicted on the sectional and terminal area charts. The notation "43/12" indicates that in the outer circle, Class C airspace, begins at 1,200 feet MSL and extends up to and includes 4,300 feet MSL.

Finding the correct frequency on which to contact the controllers charged with providing services to pilots in Class C airspace is easy. Listed at the correspondingly appropriate locations on sectional charts are white boxes enclosed with magenta lines indicating either the correct frequency to use or advising an ATIS frequency to listen to for the required information. Those frequencies also can be found in the Frequency Tab List on the end page of the sectionals.

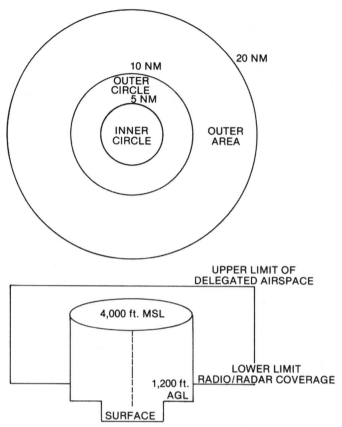

FIG. 6.2. The Class C Airspace is a compromise between the voluntary services of the Terminal Radar Service Area (TRSA) and the more restrictive Class B Airspace.

Obtaining authorization to fly into Class C airspace is very similar to the procedures used with Class D airspace. All VFR pilots are required to establish two-way radio communications with the appropriate controller prior to entering Class C airspace. But the same subtle nuances that have the potential for creating confusion and misunderstandings in Class D airspace likewise exist for pilots attempting to cross the line into Class C airspace. If a call to the controller is met with the response "aircraft calling, standby," two-way communications have *not* been established. If the controller responds to the same transmission with "Mooney 801 Delta Whiskey, standby," the requirement has been met. In the absence of any additional comments instructing a pilot to remain clear of the Class C airspace, the brief "standby" does not prohibit a pilot from entering it.

Additionally, although two-way radio communications and transponders are normally required before pilots will be authorized to fly within Class C airspace, in certain situations after having made prior arrangements, pilots may be permitted to enter the airspace. The intent of the exception is to keep the airspace from being unreasonably restrictive for pilots.

An interesting statement in the Class C Service section of the controller's manual further reinforces that notion. It states, "Class C services are designed to keep ATC informed of all aircraft within Class C airspace, not to exclude operations." Although controllers do have the authority to prevent pilots from entering the airspace when workload or other conditions warrant it, they are supposed to provide effective service for as many pilots as possible.

Once inside the airspace, everything that was true with respect to the requirements and responsibilities for both pilots and controllers in TRSA operations is also true in Class C airspace. ATC will provide all the basic radar services and separation from all traffic within the related area, and the separation standards that apply to aircraft flying within a TRSA are the same standards used in Class C airspace. The most notable difference between the two types of airspace is, with the exceptions noted earlier, that all aircraft flying within Class C airspace must be in contact with the controllers responsible for it.

Assuming that unknown traffic within Class C airspace is impossible, however, is not a wise assumption to make. My own experience when I was controlling traffic flying within Class B airspace was that, almost on a daily basis, there were pilots flying in the area who were either uncertain of their position relative to the airspace they had illegally penetrated or they were oblivious to its existence. Regardless of the reasons for their being where they were not supposed to be, believing those errant pilots would do everything else according to the rules was not a belief I cared to use as my safety net. That doubt and the fact that target resolution is the accepted procedure for separating aircraft at the same altitude within Class C airspace mean that pilots need to keep a sharp eye out for other aircraft.

One additional service that controllers are required to provide for pilots within Class C airspace is the mandatory issuing of traffic advisories and safety alerts between VFR aircraft. Not withstanding the value of either of those services, mandating something that is just about impossible to accomplish sets the controllers up for failure and gives the pilots false expectations. Controllers already are required to issue safety alerts whenever they notice a situation requiring them. Issuing traffic advisories is likewise optional only to the extent that higher priority duties first must be accomplished, so controllers are already charged with providing those services. Presenting an edict in the form of an additional mandatory requirement is not likely to be successful. However, I have no doubt that to the extent they are able, all controllers will attempt to comply with that requirement. That they always will be able to do so is something I would not bet my life on.

OUTER AREA

There is a segment of Class C airspace known as the *outer area* with which pilots should be familiar. The outer area though not charted on either the sectional or the terminal area chart normally consists of a third circle with a twenty-nautical-mile radius from the primary airport but its exact dimensions are in reality a bit more nebulous. The lower limits of the outer area are the lower limits of the associated approach control's radar and/or radio coverage. The upper limits extend up to and include the ceiling of the approach control's delegated airspace. Unfortunately, neither of those boundaries is likely to be known to the average pilot flying through the area.

Fortunately, with the exception of radar separation, which is provided only to pilots flying on instrument flight plans, the procedures associated with operations in the outer area are the same as those afforded pilots flying in a TRSA. ATC provides radar vectoring and sequencing for IFR and all participating VFR pilots. Controllers also provide traffic advisories, safety alerts, and one additional service called *conflict resolution*. Conflict resolution is what the name implies. If a potential conflict develops between two or more aircraft that are radar identified and in communication with the controller, he will provide such instructions as are necessary to ensure the targets do not touch.

If that sounds a lot like what happens when target resolution is used to keep airplanes apart, that's because it is. The distinction between that and conflict resolution seems to be that conflict resolution takes place in airspace for which ATC is not charged with ensuring separation between or among aircraft. The other difference is that, since the outer area is really nothing more than Class E airspace, pilots are not required to follow the controller's instructions. Although to do otherwise might not be the smartest thing to do, the option is there.

The fact that pilots have, at best, only a general idea of exactly where an outer area begins and ends is not really an issue. If they contact ATC when they are twenty miles away from the airport, the chances are good that they will get the most out of all the Class C services that are available. If they make their contact too soon, the controllers will likely advise them to wait a few more miles or they will assign a transponder code and have the pilots stand by for radar identification at a later time.

When flying out of an airport that is within Class C airspace, the termination point for radar service depends mostly upon who is doing the terminating. Pilots have the option of requesting the termination of service any time after they have left the confines of the outer circle of Class C airspace. Controllers are obligated to provide radar service for pilots until they depart the outer area for places beyond or in time for them to change to the appropriate frequency if they are landing at an airport adjacent to the Class C airspace. Either way, resolving the issue of when to call it quits is not a big problem for pilots.

Class B Airspace

Class B (Bravo) airspace is the most restrictive type of airspace in which VFR pilots are likely to fly. Unlike Class A airspace for which the regulations are relatively simple (because if you are not an IFR pilot on an IFR flight plan you cannot go there), Class B airspace has a myriad of rules, regulations, and procedures with which to comply. Although Class B airspace has existed for a long time, since many pilots learn to fly in less-congested areas of the country and since many of the regulations pertaining to Class B airspace do not exactly welcome student pilots with open arms, a lot of those same pilots have little actual experience flying in them. But with a little time and effort, most of what pilots need to know to operate in or near Class B airspace should become easier to understand.

Class B airspace is established around each of our major airports in the country (fig. 6.3). It is positive controlled airspace, which means that any pilot who wants to fly into the area must first receive an air traffic clearance prior to actually entering the airspace. For the IFR pilot, even though not specifically stated, that authorization is given when she initially receives her clearance to proceed via the instrument flight plan she filed. For the VFR pilot each request to enter Class B airspace must be met with a clearance in response. This is one time when pilots are not given a choice of whether or not they want to enlist the help of controllers. Besides being dangerous, entering Class B airspace without an ATC clearance is a violation of the Federal Aviation Regulations and doing so easily could lead to suspension of a pilot's flying privileges.

There are a couple of reasons why it can be extremely unsafe to fly within Class B airspace without a clearance. Though every pilot flying in VMC is always required to watch for other traffic, many pilots tend to become complacent with respect to that requirement when inside of any positive controlled airspace. It is human nature to believe that if every pilot operating in Class B airspace has been authorized to do so by ATC, and if controllers are providing separation for each of those pilots, there shouldn't be much to worry about.

The concern should be that some pilot is flying where she does not belong and that easily could end up being right in your face. Unfortunately,

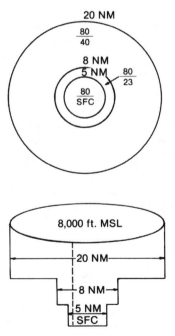

FIG. 6.3. Class B airspace is established around the busiest airports to provide all pilots with a greater margin of safety.

the *Global Positioning Systems (GPS)* with which more and more general aviation aircraft are equipped occasionally add to the problem. In spite of the manufacturers' best efforts to include appropriate airspace warnings as pilots approach Class B areas, too many pilots have a tendency to follow that straight line on the map, regardless of where it takes them. Occasionally it takes them where they do not belong.

Another less understood problem is that controllers subconsciously tend to filter out radar targets that, in their minds, do not belong in Class B airspace and, therefore, do not exist as traffic. An aircraft may appear on a controller's radarscope, but since that aircraft is only supposed to be in Class B airspace if its pilot first received a clearance to enter it, the controller may eliminate it from his mental picture. If, in a controller's mind the aircraft does not exist, the traffic information does not get forwarded to other pilots in the area. All the reasons behind the phenomenon may not be completely understood by human factors experts, but as a former controller I know the issue it creates is very real.

Class B airspace was established for the purpose of providing a definite and effective means of separating a lot of airplanes in a relatively small amount of airspace. Consequently, it only exists around those airports where there is a high frequency of heavy air traffic, most of which are large, high-performance airplanes carrying a lot of passengers. Because these planes consistently travel at high speeds and because they operate in all kinds of weather conditions, including those in which flight visibility may be greatly restricted, their pilots need a more reliable way than just see-and-be-seen to eliminate the potential of a collision with another airplane. Class B airspace then is one of the answers to the problem.

Any description of Class B airspace—including the FAA's own—usually includes a reference to an upside-down wedding cake. However, some pilots argue that some of the Class B airspace around the country more closely resembles the blueprint for a nuclear submarine than a wedding cake, upside down or not. Regardless of how the airspace is shaped, it has become a common element in our airspace system and as such, we should find a way to understand its elements and utilize the advantages it offers.

Finding out which airports are located within Class B airspace is no more difficult than was the case with Class C airspace. A glance at a sectional chart finds Class B airspace depicted by a series of solid blue lines and/or circles around an airport. In addition there will be a notation somewhere near the Class B airspace encouraging pilots to use the appropriate VFR Terminal Area Chart for flight within that airspace, and a white border on the sectional indicating the more detailed area that is included on that chart.

Before moving on to a discussion of the Terminal Area Chart, there is one additional item that, regardless of which chart is used, appears in connection with each area of Class B airspace around the country. Outside of the airspace at thirty nautical miles will be found a magenta circle with the notations "Mode C" and "30 NM." That circle indicates what is known as the *Mode C Veil*, which is an additional restriction that affects every pilot flying with 30 NM of the Class B airspace, regardless of whether they are actually within it.

To obtain all of the requirements relating to transponders and altitude reporting equipment and their use, consult FAR 91.215. In general, pilots flying within the boundary of a Mode C Veil need to ensure they have a 4096 code capability transponder with Mode C (altitude reporting) capability. The major exception is that older aircraft that were not originally certificated with an engine-driven electrical system or subsequently have not been certified with such a system, balloons and gliders, may operate within the thirty-nautical-mile radius of the airport if they are outside of Class B airspace and below the altitude of the ceiling of the airspace or ten thousand feet MSL, whichever is lower. For most of us, the simple interpretation is that if we will be flying within thirty nautical miles of the associated airports, our airplanes have to be equipped with transponders with Mode C capabilities.

The VFR Terminal Area Chart is very similar in both design and content to the sectional charts with which pilots are most familiar. The main difference between the two is that the scale of the Terminal Area Chart has been adjusted to allow for much greater geographical detail. Much of what is depicted on these charts has been included with the specific intent of enabling VFR pilots to navigate more easily around or within Class B airspace using only pilotage.

TERMINAL AREA CHART

There is a wealth of valuable information that may be gleaned from the individual VFR Terminal Area Charts and much of what is there can be deciphered after an hour or two of careful study. If, after that, there are still some items that seem confusing, getting some assistance from your favorite flight instructor or someone else who is more familiar with the charts and their use should easily resolve most of your questions.

There are several important pieces of information found on the Terminal Area Charts. In addition to the graphic information on the front of each chart, on the back is a condensed version of the information and regulations most pertinent to flight within the associated Class B airspace. This section is not all-inclusive with respect to the knowledge pilots must acquire to operate safely and legally within all Class B airspace, but it is an excellent starting point on the educational trail.

On the front, one of the more important pieces of information to notice is a more exact representation of the actual dimensions of the Class B airspace. Whenever possible, radius distances of the various circles and individual sector boundaries within the airspace will be denoted by distance measuring equipment, or DME (distance), and radials from an associated VOR. In addition to using pilotage, pilots who are flying aircraft with the capability to receive VOR (very high frequency omnidirectional range) signals (for all intents and purposes, everyone) can use this information to more accurately determine their location with respect to those boundaries.

Another very important piece of information that can be found on the chart is the correct frequency to use to contact ATC for a clearance into or through the airspace. The frequency for pilots to use to contact a controller is indicated within a white box located in the area appropriate for its use. It still is not the end of the world if a pilot makes her initial contact on the incorrect frequency. But because often there are a lot of controllers talking to a lot of pilots on a lot of different frequencies, getting the right frequency the first time can save everyone involved a lot of valuable time and energy.

When a pilot is instructed to contact another controller on a different frequency, it may sometimes seem like a big runaround when, after having made the change, she has to repeat to the new controller all that she said initially to the previous one, but there are valid reasons for doing it. If one controller's radar identifies an aircraft that is in another controller's airspace, several possibilities and potentialities exist.

First of all, it is unsafe as well as illegal for any controller to issue a pilot clearance to enter into airspace that is under the direction of another controller without first receiving approval from the affected controller. Sometimes, workload issues for either or both controllers preclude the necessary coordination from occurring. But to do otherwise could mean that the controller who wrongly authorizes a pilot into the airspace may be doing so without knowing where all the related traffic might be, and that, in turn, represents a real danger for other pilots in the area.

Second, when one controller takes it upon himself to authorize a pilot to unknowingly enter another controller's airspace, the second controller will suddenly see a radar-identified aircraft for which he is supposed to be responsible but about which he knows nothing. When that happens, particularly if he has other traffic close by, it can make him wonder if it's time to trade his ATC headset for one at the local fast-food drive-up window. Something as simple as finding and using the correct frequency for a given area can be one of the things that separates the amateur from the professional.

Most if not all of the rest of the information shown on the VFR Terminal Area Chart should be old hat by now. The combinations of letters and numbers depicting the floor and the ceiling of the Class B airspace use the same format as that used for TRSAs and Class C airspace. The symbol 80/SFC indicates that Class B airspace begins at the surface and continues up to and includes eight thousand feet MSL. Similarly, when compared to Class C airspace, normally the only segment of airspace that begins at the surface is that within the circle closest to the primary airport.

Farther away from the airport (in keeping with the upside-down wedding cake analogy), although the ceiling of Class B airspace remains the same, the floor becomes progressively higher. In keeping with the many airspace compromises mentioned earlier, different floors for the same Class B airspace in different areas afford different opportunities for various pilots. Those pilots flying into or out of the primary airport are able to conduct their flights without ever having to leave positive controlled airspace, thereby reducing the risk of collision. At the same time, other pilots who want to use the smaller, outlying airports have the choice of (1) obtaining a clearance to fly through Class B airspace or (2) flying below the higher floors and eliminating any requirement to contact ATC for authorization to conduct their activities. In the latter, the choice is up to each individual pilot to make. If the controller is not too busy, getting a clearance to fly within Class B airspace for as long as possible is usually the safer way to go.

REQUIREMENTS FOR CLASS B OPERATIONS

Although there are many similarities between Class B and Class C airspace, Class B is more restrictive and carries with it certain additional requirements that pilots need to know. Again, pilots planning to fly into any airspace in which air traffic control procedures are inherently intertwined with the flight operations conducted there need to take some basic preliminary steps prior to entering the airspace. Pilots need to research the related FARs, and when making an initial trip into Class B or C airspace, they should spend some time with an instructor to make sure they have all the necessary knowledge. Most of the procedures applicable to Class B airspace are not that unique, but because of the likelihood of heavy traffic in the associated areas, many of the ATC instructions attached to the procedures tend to come at a fairly rapid pace. An unprepared pilot could get caught up in the flurry of activity that exists routinely.

Pilots also need to be aware that even though there is no distinction among the various areas designated as Class B airspace within the United States, there are certain airports within select Class B airspace that have been designated as *High Density Airports*. The complete list of these airports are in FAR 93.123, and they require compliance with additional restrictions before pilots legally may fly into or out of them. All of those requirements are found in FAR 93.129. Because each of the airports listed meets or exceeds their acceptance rates during most of the day, pilots planning to fly into or out of those airports must obtain a reservation prior to conducting any flight operations there. Getting a reservation is not all that difficult, but for pilots not used to having to meet a schedule, arriving at the right place at the right time does add another dimension to their flying.

Aside from making airport reservations, what does a pilot have to do or be in terms of her own certification to be legally allowed to penetrate Class B airspace? If she holds at least a private pilot certificate, the answer is simple. As long as she meets all the currency requirements regarding a particular flight (such as those required before passengers may be carried), there are no additional requirements or exceptions. Flying in Class B airspace for anyone who holds a private pilot certificate or higher is just the same as flying anywhere else, and that includes flying into or out of the primary airport.

For the recreational or student pilot, however, it is not as simple. Because of the very nature of traffic conditions within most Class B airspace most of the time, some additional restrictions are necessary to ensure these pilots don't unknowingly disrupt the rest of the traffic. Although the restrictions seem to be organized in the usual hodgepodge manner of many of the FARs, the most significant restriction is one of the easier to understand.

Neither a student nor a recreational pilot, regardless of any training she might have received, is permitted to conduct solo flights to or from any airport listed in Appendix D, Section 4 under Part 91 of the FARs. Because of the consistently heavy traffic, the complexity of the airspace and airport operations, or a combination of both, the pilot-in-command must hold at least a private pilot certificate to take off or land at the following airports: Atlanta Hartsfield, Boston Logan, Chicago O'Hare International, Dallas/Fort Worth Regional, Los Angeles International, Miami International, Newark International, John F. Kennedy International, LaGuardia, San Francisco International, Reagan National, and Andrews Air Force Base. Training flights to or from those airports are not excluded, but when they occur, the flight instructor is the pilot-in-command for purposes of this restriction. Only solo flights by student or recreational pilots fall under the regulation.

For any other operations conducted in Class B airspace by student or recreational pilots (for these purposes recreational pilots are also student pilots), the restrictions are not quite as tight. Still, they do not permit flight-at-will into the airspace. Before a student pilot may fly solo within the confines of Class B airspace, she must first receive ground and flight instruction from an authorized instructor. The ground instruction must specifically relate to the particular airspace in which the flight will take place and, likewise, the flight training also must occur in the specific area in which any future flight will take place. In addition to the training, there must be an endorsement in a student's logbook made within ninety days of the proposed flight stating that the training was given and the student was found to be proficient to conduct the solo flight.

The same requirements and procedures hold true with respect to flying into or out of other airports within Class B airspace. Before any student may conduct solo operations at an airport in Class B airspace, first she must have received specific ground and flight training for that airport and her logbook must bear a similar endorsement to that required for flight into the airspace. Essentially, a student who is accompanied by an authorized flight instructor must fly a dress rehearsal to the same airport she would later like to return to on a solo flight.

For any pilot flying within Class B airspace, the expectations for understanding and complying with the regulations and procedures conducted there are quite high. Likewise, the pilot's responsibilities for conducting her flights in a safety conscious manner are equally stringent. There are, after all, a lot of airplanes flying in close proximity to one another. Regardless of a pilot's certification, be it student, recreational, or private, if she has never ventured into the world of the big time (even when the regulations do not require additional training), plunging into the fray without having all the necessary knowledge and tools to safely accomplish the journey is foolhardy.

THE AIRPLANE

The airplane also must be equipped with the accoutrements necessary to meet the letter of the law for Class B airspace. As recently as ten or fifteen years ago, many pilots argued that equipping their airplanes with all the stuff required in the regulations was expensive and unnecessary. Today, much has changed to alter that thinking. In addition to reduced costs and more options in the marketplace, what was once optional equipment is now the norm.

Consequently, the equipment required to fly in Class B does not seem at all unreasonable.

One of the most important pieces of equipment that must be installed in an aircraft is an operable two-way radio capable of communications with controllers *on the appropriate frequencies* for the associated Class B airspace. That is, if the frequency notation states that pilots need to contact approach control on 124.725 for clearance into the airspace, that capability must be available on the radio to satisfy the regulations.

A couple of considerations tend to mitigate the seemingly restrictive nature of that regulation. One is that, whenever possible, the frequencies with which VFR pilots are expected to contact ATC for authorization into Class B airspace have been selected specifically for the likelihood of their availability for most general aviation pilots. So, more often than not frequencies such as 124.75 or 125.9 will be the rule rather than the exception. Second, since many old radios have been declared officially defunct with respect to being legal for communicating with ATC, most aircraft flying today are adequately equipped to provide communications on the appropriate frequencies.

If, after conducting her preflight planning, a pilot determines that her older, but legal, radio does not have the capability to enable her to communicate on the posted frequency, all hope is not necessarily lost. A phone call to the approach control responsible for the airspace in question may provide the answer. Occasionally, pilots in similar situations have been able to negotiate with the FAA (really they have) for approval to make their contact on a frequency that is mutually available. The key is to not wait until you are about to cross the magic line to begin your negotiations. In this case, timing is everything.

The only other required piece of equipment for a VFR flight into Class B airspace is an operable transponder. All of the options for transponder types are spelled out in FAR 91.215. Generally speaking, for most light planes, a transponder with 4096 code capability and Mode C capability that provides automatic altitude reporting is adequate. Oh, and they must make sure the equipment is turned on. Lest they forget the obvious, there is an FAR to cover that eventuality.

There are exceptions that allow pilots to request and receive authorization to fly within Class B airspace when all is not quite right with their transponders. If the transponder is working but the Mode C altitude reporting capability is not, controllers may authorize flight into the Class B airspace any time conditions permit. If the entire transponder fails en route, a pilot may be authorized to continue to her destination or to a repair shop, even if that flight will penetrate Class B airspace. But if the plane does not have a transponder, according to the regulations a request to enter the airspace must be made at least one hour before the proposed flight.

Keep in mind that although, with respect to at least the first two instances, the regulations state that the request may be made at the last minute, it does not state that such a request will necessarily be approved. Rarely will a pilot be denied access to Class B airspace because of a partially or completely inoperative transponder, especially if the failure occurred en route. But pilots need to understand that the one piece of equipment that both enhances safety for pilots and significantly contributes to workload reductions for controllers is the transponder.

When traffic is light or moderate, obtaining approval to enter Class B airspace without an operable transponder usually is not a problem. But because of the added concentration required of a controller and because of the added verbal coordination that results, on certain occasions an aircraft without an operable transponder may be denied access to the airspace.

The best way to ensure that the lack of a working transponder does not prevent you from gaining access to Class B airspace is to make your situation known to the controllers as soon as possible. If, for example, you know prior to a flight that your transponder is not working and you will need to penetrate Class B airspace to get to your destination, the best advice is to contact the approach control facility responsible for the airspace and try to make suitable arrangements before you ever leave the ground. If a failure occurs en route either ask the controllers with whom you are presently working or contact the nearest flight service facility and ask a specialist to relay your problem to the approach controllers ahead. Often you can get approval to waive the transponder requirement long before you reach the point where turning around may be the only other option.

The exceptions should be used only in unusual or unforeseen circumstances and should not be overused. One morning when I was working approach control at Pittsburgh, one of the routine commuter flights reported to the previous controller that his transponder had just failed and he was requesting a waiver to continue into the Class B airspace. The traffic situation was such that I determined working the airplane without a transponder was not going to be an unusual burden or a hazard to safety. A few hours later another controller got the same story and being unfamiliar with the earlier situation, again granted approval for the aircraft to enter the airspace. Upon learning that the problem had occurred earlier, the controller advised the pilot to get the transponder fixed before the next run into our airspace. Still later, another pilot gave the same story for the third time. That time the answer was no, not just because the truth seemed to be fading fast, but because traffic was getting too heavy. Controllers may not always be the most astute group of individuals but, given enough time, even we eventually catch on.

One final equipment requirement that must be met prior to flying in Class B airspace only applies to pilots conducting IFR operations. In addition to the equipment required for VFR aircraft, each aircraft on an instrument flight plan also must be equipped with an operable VOR or TACAN (a military equivalent) receiver. In these days of dual navigation receivers, IFR approved GPS, and countless other goodies, it is doubtful that any pilot would or could even consider conducting an instrument flight without a VOR or TACAN receiver. The regulation, in this case, rather than creating unusual demands for pilots really does little more than state the obvious. Nevertheless, it is a regulation with which pilots must comply.

Whether we talk about pilots needing to ensure they have proper training and certification or we talk about aircraft being correctly equipped and certified, all the rules and regulations regarding each as they relate to flying within Class B airspace exist to enhance safety. Occasionally exceptions to some of the rules can be approved while others are nearly cast in stone. It is critical to our safety that each of us understands which is which. For the rules that are unalterable, we need to do it right the first time. For those with some latitude regarding enforcement, try to do it right the first time and if an unusual situation unexpectedly occurs, we need to work for the best solution possible. Whatever the final outcome, it is always better to prepare for the possibility of having to chose an alternate airport rather than betting everything on getting exactly what we want.

Flying in Class B Airspace

Figuring out if you are legally qualified and if your aircraft is properly equipped to fly within Class B airspace is actually a lot more difficult than actually doing the flying. In many respects it is the same as flying in Class C airspace. The differences are not all that difficult to understand. In spite of the horror stories you may have heard, Class B airspace has little in common with the Bermuda Triangle. Seldom does a pilot cross into the unknown never to be heard from again.

ATC CLEARANCE

The first and one of the most important points to remember is that every pilot, VFR and IFR, must obtain an ATC clearance prior to entering Class B airspace. Instrument pilots get that authorization as part of the instrument clearance they receive at the beginning of their flights. If the route by which they are cleared passes into or through Class B airspace, inherent in that clearance is authorization to enter it.

VFR pilots obtain their clearance by a different method. They must contact the appropriate controller at the right time. The right time is not moments before you are about to cross that imaginary line into Class B airspace, but rather when you are still at least five or ten miles from the boundary . Remember that a lot of talking will be going on with a lot of pilots and the controller may not be in a position to drop everything just to talk to you. Give yourself enough time to have a fighting chance.

This is also a good opportunity to develop a couple of important practices with respect to getting into Class B airspace. The first is to make sure that you specifically request "clearance into Bravo Airspace." That statement or a similar one makes it clear to the controller that what you want is to play in his backyard. Equally important is to make sure the controller responds "cleared into Bravo Airspace." It is not just a matter of establishing two-way communications, nor is it good enough if the controller says something something else like, "proceed on course." The controller may know what he means and he may mean to imply a clearance has been issued, but do not bet your pilot's certificate on that.

In the past there has been a lot of misunderstanding because pilots thought they had received clearances to enter the airspace when the controllers, sort of, almost, but not really, failed to clear them into the airspace. If a controller does not say the word "cleared," ask him to verify that you are, in fact, cleared into Bravo Airspace and do not cross the line until you hear it.

Because controllers are responsible for providing separation to all aircraft flying in Class B airspace, they have the authority to keep additional traffic out of their airspace when traffic, weather, or any other unusual conditions require it. When VFR pilots are held outside of Class B airspace, they should receive what is known as an *Expect Further Clearance (EFC)* time. In the world of instrument flight, an EFC time is basically a lost communications procedure. For VFR pilots, it is used more to inform a pilot of how long the delay will be before she will be authorized to enter the airspace. If, for example, a controller advises a pilot to expect further clearance in fifteen minutes and after fifteen minutes the pilot hears nothing more, the correct response is to contact the controller again instead of just driving into the airspace.

Once a pilot receives her clearance into Bravo Airspace, one of the most important things to keep in mind is to stay alert, pay attention to all that is going on, and answer every transmission as soon as possible. Although the sky will not be black with airplanes, traffic likely will be heavier than in other types of airspace and the controller's instructions probably will be coming at a fast pace.

Controllers are much more likely to issue heading and altitude assignments to provide the necessary separation for pilots in the area. Keep in mind that, for VFR pilots, regardless of what instructions controllers issue, it is the pilot's responsibility to ensure that complying with that instruction will not cause her to violate any regulations. In the Class B Service section of the controller's manual, there is a note that specifically states, "Assignment of radar headings, routes, or altitudes is based on the provision that a pilot operating in accordance with VFR is *expected to advise ATC if compliance will cause violation of any part of the CFR*" [my emphasis]. If what a pilot receives is not going to work, she needs to advise the controller immediately and ask for an alternate instruction.

On the other hand, when traffic is light, a controller may just as likely say something to the effect of "proceed on course, advise any change in altitude." At this point flying through Class B airspace is no different than any other airspace. A suggestion is, even if the controller does not specifically state "advise any change in your altitude," and even though one was not assigned, he needs to know prior to your making any changes. The same holds true with flying a different heading. A five- or ten-degree change in heading is not a big deal, but if a pilot suddenly decides to make a ninety-degree turn to the right, the controller needs to hear about the change before it happens.

CLOUD CLEARANCE AND SEPARATION STANDARDS

Cloud clearances that apply to VFR pilots flying in controlled airspace do not hold true when operating in Class B airspace. The only cloud clearance requirement VFR pilots must comply with is to remain clear of clouds. The assumption is that, since everyone in the airspace is supposed to be there only after having been authorized to do so by ATC and since everyone is being provided separation from everyone else, the cloud clearance requirements were relaxed quite a bit. That does not mean pilots should relax though. What is supposed to be true about those other pilots is not always so. Most of the time, the methods of separation by which aircraft are kept apart and the separation standards controllers use to accomplish the task are the same as those used in Class C airspace. Except where heavy jets and Boeing 757s are concerned, controllers can use five hundred feet vertical separation between VFR aircraft or between a VFR and an IFR aircraft and they can use target resolution between aircraft at the same altitude. The one other exception to that rule is that if one of the aircraft weighs more than nineteen thousand pounds or is a turbojet, then the lateral or longitudinal separation increases to 1.5 miles. Fortunately for pilots, it is up to the controller to determine the weight of the aircraft involved and if there is any question, the controller will ask.

Everything else that goes on in Class B airspace with respect to controllers' actions and pilots' responsibilities is the same as in Class C airspace. Traffic advisories, safety alerts, sequencing to the airport, altitude assignments, visual separation requirements, and notification of leaving the airspace are all the same. The most unique aspect of Class B airspace is that everyone who is authorized to be there is getting radar service and separation.

Staying Safe in a Crowd

Though clearance into Class Bravo airspace is not an instrument clearance, it is the single most effective way for VFR pilots to all but eliminate the risk of a collision with another plane. The positive control that exists within Class B airspace has been established for the protection of everyone who flies there and that is usually a lot of everyones. Though flying within it may require a little more knowledge and a good bit more attention on the part of the pilot, the result is that being there is almost always safer than flying in a busy traffic pattern at your favorite uncontrolled airstrip.

Nowhere is a complete understanding of the pilot/controller relationship more important than when flying in an area of high-density traffic, most of which is moving at a very fast clip. Both pilots and controllers have the responsibility to operate by the prescribed rules and the rules of common sense. If ever a situation arises when you do not know what action is the correct one to take, ask someone for help. I guarantee that when it is the controller who does not know the answer, asking is the first thing on his mind. A thoughtful, sensible pilot or controller is worth more than a thousand government regulations.

7

Landing at Major Airports: Flying with the Pros

I SUSPECT THAT MOST general aviation pilots who have never flown into a major airport have thought about what it would be like to do it. They imagine themselves flying where the pros go, lining up on final, looking out the windshield at a ten-thousand-foot runway, and seeing airplanes in the air and on the ground going about the professional business of aviating.

Often, a certain level of apprehension and uncertainty accompanies those thoughts, however. Getting through the Class B airspace is just the beginning. It is actually getting into that airport with the big-time players that has our chins sitting on top of the instrument panel and our noses pressed to the window in an effort to avoid missing anything. It may not be necessary to feel that way, but neither is it unnatural.

On many occasions, student and private pilots have asked me to accompany them to a major airport just so they could go through the experience with a safety pilot along for added protection. I even had a friend who was a senior captain and check airman for a major airline call one day and ask for advice about flying into the airport that had been his home base for quite a number of years.

His concern was not so much what to do when he arrived at the airport, but rather what he should do prior to that point. He had just purchased a new Mooney and having lived the instrument pilot life that is synonymous with air carrier operations, he did not know exactly what procedures he should use as a VFR pilot. Whom should he contact and when should he do it? What would be expected of him once he got into the Class B airspace? When he was flying a jet, the answers were easy, but take away the structure of airline flying and he was not quite as sure.

With his background it did not take long to answer most of his questions, but the situation pointed out that even the most experienced pilots lack some of the knowledge they need some of the time. The smart ones don't hesitate to take the steps necessary to educate themselves and, without question, my opinion of my friend went up several notches when I recognized he was more than willing to admit that he needed some assistance.

Although the best way to get comfortable with flying into a major airport is just to do it repeatedly, one place to start is to dispel some of the rumors that have been floating around probably since the time of Orville and Wilbur. At one time or another, we have all had the local expert on aviation (self-proclaimed expert that is) take us aside and fill us with horror stories about the terrible effects of wake turbulence, fast-talking controllers, and just plain chaos in general. To be sure, many of the issues behind the rumors should be legitimate concerns for pilots, but none are reasons to avoid flying anywhere we want or need to go.

Another point to consider is whether a major airport is the most suitable choice for a destination. Although our air transportation system has been witness to a number of airport closings around the country, many of the ones that are left have seen significant improvements in recent years. One of the side benefits of the increased congestion at major airports is that there is a developing network of excellent reliever airports that can be found outside of many of our larger cities.

These airports, some of which were once better suited to soapbox derby racing than airplane flying, have become safe, modern, and convenient stopping points for general aviation pilots. They are also less expensive than a major airport where landing and parking fees easily can exceed one hundred dollars. Besides being able to enjoy the friendliness and camaraderie that is common among general aviation gathering places, the ATC procedures developed for these airports are more suited to light-plane pilots.

On the other side of the coin, because most of the air traffic flying into the major airports is large, high-performance jets, the procedures designed to accommodate them are likewise tailored more to their advantage. While that is not to say that general aviation aircraft have been ignored, the reality is that if there is one category of aircraft that is predominant at a particular airport, most of the air traffic procedures were developed with it in mind. Most of the time it is just more convenient, efficient, and economically wise for general aviation pilots to use reliever airports instead of the major ones.

If, after serious consideration, a pilot decides that the only airport that will fit the bill is the same as that used by the air carrier pilots, then that is the one to use. Major airports are public-use airports and, at least as of this moment, general aviation pilots are part of the public. As long as a pilot and his aircraft meet the regulatory requirements that have been established for the airport of choice, he has the right to use it whenever the need arises.

Make the First Flight a Success

The secret of how to make that first flight into a major airport a successful and relatively uneventful occasion is really no secret at all. Success is possible with preparation. If a pilot knows what to expect ahead of time and if he knows which responsibilities for what belong to whom in the pilot/controller partnership, he should encounter few, if any, problems on that first flight.

One of the best ways to start the preparation is to learn as much as possible about the airport at which you will be landing. Publications put out by pilot organizations, private companies, and the government are filled with information on just about every airport in the country. Those, along with sectional and VFR terminal area charts should give you just about everything you need to eliminate any surprises along the way.

Except in very unusual situations, any pilot planning to fly into a major airport can make certain assumptions. The first is that the airport will either be in Class B or, at the very least, Class C airspace. As such, radar service, sequencing, and separation on the way to the airport will be provided. If for some reason the normally available radar services are not available, the place for VFR pilots to be is anywhere other than in that airspace. The pilots who have to be there and the controllers responsible for their separation will already have all that they can handle.

Finding the Right Frequency

Since there will also be more than one or two controllers directing all the traffic, there will be more than one or two frequencies used by almost every pilot along the way. It is a good idea to find as many of the appropriate frequencies as possible and write them down in the order in which they most likely will be used. For example, write down the frequencies for the arrival ATIS; approach control for the area in which you will be arriving; the tower controller or controllers, if more than one; likewise for ground control; and, assuming you will eventually be leaving, clearance delivery. For certain, there is always the possibility that a controller could issue a frequency that is not on your list, but if you have something written down, at least there is a source for some reliable information if things start to get mixed up.

Mixed up they can get, sometimes when we least expect it. As an example, on what must have been one of the first trips for this pilot into the airport, one pilot managed to make several wrong decisions in the face of adversity and pressure. It seemed that somewhere between talking to the approach controller and switching to the tower controller, he managed to get the wrong tower frequency. Evidently he had not written down any of the frequencies he had or was about to use and neither did he have a second radio in which to put the new frequency. Three trips around the pattern later, each without having communicated with anyone, he finally reached the tower controller and landed, much to the delight of the pilots and controllers who had been getting older by the minute. Had that pilot written down any frequencies, he could have contacted an approach controller or even a ground controller and received the help he needed.

Even though many of today's GPS/com radios have a database that includes everything about every airport, save maybe the price of a cup of coffee, having a hard copy of the most important frequencies is still a good idea. When a pilot gets close to the airport, where a lot is happening and airplanes are flying relatively close to one another, that is not the time to be looking inside the cockpit, flipping through the electronic pages of the radio to find a frequency.

The Lay of the Land

The next thing to become familiar with is the airport layout. Again, although there are many available sources on the market, one that provides excellent diagrams of the larger airports is the *Airport/Facility Directory*. In the back of each issue are detailed diagrams that include runway identifiers and their respective lengths, taxiway locations and identifiers, and, quite often, the locations of general aviation parking areas. Since getting on the ground and moving around once down are often more difficult than getting to the airport in the first place, some familiarization with what is there can be a distinct advantage.

Among other things, it is very helpful to know how many runways there are, how they are situated in relation to each other, and how long they are. For instance, if there are parallel runways, which is almost always a certainty at major airports, knowing how close they are to each other can help prevent a landing on the wrong one. Not only have pilots landed on the incorrect runway, but more than one or two have landed on taxiways thinking that anything that wide must be a runway. I once overheard a controller who was having trouble getting a pilot lined up with the correct runway say to the pilot, "Look for the wide white runway and let me know when you see it." Because the pavement on the assigned runway was decidedly lighter than the other two in question, his idea did the trick.

Although in the vast majority of cases runway length should not be an issue for most pilots who fly light aircraft, some of the larger airports have one or two short runways tucked away somewhere for the sole purpose of keeping general aviation airplanes out of the primary mix of traffic. A few airports even have taxiways that, under certain conditions, become authorized landing areas. Most of the time these runways are very much in keeping with what light-plane pilots are used to, but knowing ahead of time that there is a possibility that the runway of the controller's choice may be only 2,500 feet long can eliminate any last-minute surprises.

Land and Hold Short

In addition, many airports now employ *Land and Hold Short Operations (LAHSO)* to increase the capacity of their existing runways. LAHSO means that the tower controller can instruct a pilot to land on a runway and hold short of an intersection of a crossing runway so that simultaneous operations can be conducted on that other runway. In the past, controllers had to stagger operations on two crossing runways so that there was no possibility that two aircraft would reach the intersection at the same time. While a meeting of two airplanes at an intersection is not too high on anyone's list, in many instances the affected intersection is as much as five or ten thousand feet from the approach end of at least one of the runways.

In addition, there are a host of additional conditions that must exist before LAHSO legally can be conducted. Among them are the runway must be dry, no night operations are permitted except where specific lighting requirements have been met, weather conditions must be VFR, and wind shear must not be present. If these and a few others conditions are met, then any pilot landing at an airport where published LAHSO procedures exist should anticipate the possibility that he may be requested to comply with them.

In the *Airport/Facility Directory* there is a section pertaining to LAHSO that specifies at what airports they may be conducted, on what runways, what the hold-short point is, and finally, the distance to that point. With just a little bit of preflight preparation, pilots easily should be able to determine whether or not LAHSO procedures exist for their destination airport. But even if the instruction to land and hold short comes as a complete surprise to an inbound pilot (in practice it should not), he can always ask the controller for the available landing distance before he makes his decision to accept the restriction.

That brings up the single most important point to remember concerning LAHSO procedures: Every pilot always has the option to refuse to accept a restriction to hold short upon landing, with no exceptions. But with that in mind, it is also essential to remember that, if a pilot does plan to refuse the hold-short restriction, he needs to inform the controller immediately. This is not the time to play the Little Engine That Could, saying "I think I can, I think I can...oops I thought I could." If ever any doubt exists regarding whether stopping within the required distance is doable, pilots need to refuse the restriction.

Many airline pilots evidently have decided that under no circumstances will they accept a land-and-hold-short restriction. For whatever reasons, they have seemingly come to the decision that to do otherwise is to compromise the safety of their aircraft beyond what they are willing to accept. While I do not profess to know or understand the reasoning behind those decisions, I wholeheartedly agree with their right of refusal. Knowing that the professionals refuse LAHSO procedures should make it easier for a general aviation pilot to do the same, should the need arise. I would add, however, that stopping a Cessna Skyhawk is usually easier than bringing to a halt two hundred thousand pounds of jetliner.

On the other hand, it is also important for pilots of light aircraft to understand that the allowable distances under which controllers can conduct LAHSO are considerably less when it comes to most general aviation aircraft. For the basic single-engine aircraft that many of us fly, a runway length of as little as 2,500 feet is enough for a controller to instruct that Sky-hawk to hold short. For the higher performance singles and many light twin-engine aircraft, somewhere between 3,500 and 4,000 feet is the acceptable distance. Just because there is five or ten thousand feet of runway lying in front of you does not mean necessarily that it will all be there for the taking.

In addition to knowing the usable distance for a LAHSO restriction, run-ways on which they are used are required to have hold-short markings clearly painted on them. Although distance information alone should be enough for a pilot to decide whether or not he can comply with a restriction, looking for the hold-short lines while still in the air, can be a good way to confirm the point at which, at least for this time, his runway comes to an end.

Land and Hold Short Operations have become an effective, efficient, and safe way to increase the capacity at some airports where the creation of additional runways is not an option. But there is no question that using them decreases the margin of safety for everyone involved. Whether it decreases that margin below an acceptable point is directly related to how completely pilots and controllers understand their mutual obligations and responsibili-ties when dealing with LAHSO. As long as everyone knows what to do and performs his job in the appropriate manner, safety is not compromised. If anyone goes along for the ride without understanding fully his role in the plan, fixing the resulting situation becomes everyone's problem.

Now that a thorough perusal of the airport diagram and other associ-ated information has cleared up much of the unknown, keeping it available to be used as an in-flight reference might not be a bad idea. Besides being a valuable means by which to begin to develop a mental picture of what that airport is going to look like from the air, it can be a valuable tool for figur-ing out which runway is which. Many pilots, including yours truly, when faced with a mass of concrete spread out five or ten miles before them, have an ailment that prevents them from discerning which runway is the one they are supposed to be using. Directional gyros and a lot of other gadgets on the market are supposed to do the trick, and for some pilots they do. Others of us have found that taking a pictorial representation of the airport and turn-ing it to coincide with the direction from which we are approaching can be an invaluable aid for finding the right place to plant our wheels.

The Right Time

One last bit of preflight planning that effectively might ease the burden of a pilot's first experience with the big time would be to plan his arrival at a time when traffic around the airport is likely to be light. Especially with those major airports that are considered hubs for one or two major airlines, the time in between an arrival rush and a departure rush can be an ideal time to plan an arrival. For a twenty- or thirty-minute time period, the airspace around most hub airports can be all but deserted.

Since every major airport in the country has what is known as a *Traffic Management Unit* whose job it is to predict each hour's traffic flow into or out of the airport, finding out when traffic is going to be light is relatively easy to do. A quick phone call to the approach control responsible for the airport explaining that, as a general aviation pilot, you would like to know the best time to plan an arrival there would, I am sure, be met with a good response. Not only does good timing make it easier for the pilot, but having one more airplane change its arrival from a busy time to a slower one also does wonders for the controllers involved.

Proper preparation before every flight is not only good practice, it is a requirement. It is also one of the most effective ways for a pilot to shift what easily could become a very high workload during his arrival to a major airport to a time when life is a lot less hectic. Eliminating as much of the unknown as possible is one of the best ways to reduce the apprehension that goes with taking on a new challenge.

Time to Go

Probably the most effective and easiest way to cover the normal, routine events that typically take place at a major airport is to discuss them in the sequence in which logically they would occur. The first item on a pilot's agenda should be to listen to the airport's ATIS broadcast, and it is a good idea to do that when still fifty or sixty miles from the airport. Since that distance is usually well within the broadcast range of most stations yet far enough away from the point at which communications should be established with the controllers, it gives pilots an opportunity to listen to the ATIS at their leisure. If it takes more than one run-through to get all of the necessary information, there is time for that too and it can be accomplished without having to simultaneously listen to a second frequency for ATC instructions.

By checking the ATIS, pilots can start to develop a good idea of what the rest of the trip will entail. For example, expected weather conditions can be confirmed or unexpected conditions can provide an early warning that plans may have to change. By knowing what runways are in use, pilots can get a good idea which direction they will have to fly to fit into the approach sequence. If any unusual happenings are occurring at the airport, that will probably be on the ATIS broadcast.

Just remember that a new recording is made about five minutes before every hour, so if you check the ATIS just prior to that time, it may become necessary to listen again just after the hour to find out if any changes were added to the new information. Getting all of the information that is broadcast on an ATIS is easy; having all of it is essential.

First Contact

The next item to consider is where to plan to make that first contact with ATC and with that there are a couple of considerations pilots should keep in mind. The first is that as soon as possible, it is a good idea to begin listening to the frequency that you will be using. A lot of information can be obtained just by listening to the controller and the other pilots. It can give you a good idea regarding how busy the controller is and where most of the traffic is in relation to your location. You will also get to practice listening to the person with whom you will soon have to communicate. If it sounds as though the controller is rather busy, that should also alert you to the fact that contacting her earlier rather than later might not be a bad idea. It gives her more time to radar identify you and provide the required clearance without your having to circle somewhere outside the airspace.

A second point to consider is how your altitude affects where that first contact should be made. Although individual controller preferences are not always exactly the same, most controllers I know and have known prefer pilots to make their initial contact while still outside the farthest boundary, regardless of their altitude. If the Class B airspace, at its farthest, extends to twenty miles from the airport, then contact should be made prior to that point, even though pilots at lower and higher altitudes will not actually be in the airspace at that point. Generally speaking, by the time a pilot is inside the thirty-mile Mode C Veil, the controller responsible for the airspace would like to have notice that that pilot is inbound to the airport. For the pilot who runs across the few controllers whose preferences are otherwise, the worst they will do is advise the pilot to continue inbound and call again in another five or ten miles.

VFR Check Points

Having decided upon a distance at which to contact the controller, a VFR pilot has a few aids that will help him identify his location in such a way that will be clear to controllers. One good aid is the *VFR Check Points*. VFR check points are landmarks strategically located around both Class B and C airspace, which pilots are encouraged to use to reference their position when talking to a controller. These check points also are prominently displayed on each controller's radarscope, thereby giving the controller a quick and easy way to pinpoint the pilot's location.

VFR check points are identified on either a sectional or a VFR terminal area chart by a magenta flag adjacent to a landmark. For pilots using GPS, *VFR Waypoints* for navigation have been created using either identifiers that exist in the databases or latlon coordinates. In most instances the waypoints are collocated with the VFR check points, and the GPS identifiers can be found in parentheses just after the name of the check point. For the stand-alone waypoints, a listing of identifiers and their latlon coordinates can be found in the *Airport/Facility Directory*. In either case, being able to use GPS to identify and navigate to these check points is a tremendous advantage for VFR pilots.

Many of the VFR check points are satellite airports, but other landmarks that are frequently used include towns or small cities that are isolated enough to prevent misidentification, racetracks and even distinct towers or antennae. VFR pilots inbound to a major airport need only find the most convenient check point and reference their position to it when contacting the controller. It is not necessary to be directly over the check point when checking in on a frequency. A couple of miles away from one in any direction is more than adequate to give a controller the information he needs.

If there are no VFR check points convenient to where a pilot plans to contact ATC, the next best choice is a nearby navaid, the preference of choice being a VOR. The best way for a pilot to relay his position to a controller is with respect to a radial, an approximate distance, or, if equipped with DME, an exact distance from the navaid. Just remember when using VORs, pilots almost instinctively tune the receiver to a TO indication, which means they are actually on the reciprocal radial. TO the 270 degree radial means a pilot is inbound on the 090 degree radial and is, therefore, east of the station. As is true with VFR check points, almost all of the navaids in a controller's area of jurisdiction will be displayed on her radarscope and locating a pilot referencing any one of them is a relatively easy task. A controller faced with an easy task is usually a happy controller. Score one for the pilot.

What to Say

The time finally has come to make the initial call to the controller. The best approach to this and any subsequent transmissions is to take a few moments to think about what you need to say before keying the microphone. Remember, the controller does not need a lot of information and the exact format in which you present it is not nearly as important as getting your message across. All you really need to tell the controller is your name (aircraft identification and type), where you are (location over the ground AND altitude), what you want to do (destination), and that you have the current ATIS information. An example might be "Boston Approach, Mooney 801 Delta Whiskey, two northeast of Minute Man airport at five thousand five hundred, inbound for landing with Alpha."

Notice that all the little words and phrases that are usually so common and important in everyday conversation are omitted. Words and phrases like miles, feet, this is, I am, and I have received, are both unnecessary and undesirable in the world of aviation communications. The bad news is that it takes a little bit of practice to undo what your English teachers taught you. The good news is that fewer words spoken means fewer chances of getting tongue-tied in the process.

One other suggestion, either during the initial call to ATC or some time shortly thereafter, let the controller know that you are a first-time visitor to the airport and that you are also unfamiliar with the local area. Don't hesitate to tell ATC that a little extra help and some extra attention would be appreciated. Even high-time professional pilots end up at the wrong airport on occasion, so asking for some assistance does not brand you a fool.

Whether you are a student pilot or a low-time, inexperienced pilot, you can benefit from admitting your status to controllers. When a controller knows he is working with a pilot who is at the beginning of the learning curve, he takes the extra time to make the experience easier. He will consciously slow down his speech rate, he will try to keep his instructions basic and uncomplicated, and he will pay closer attention to all that the pilot is doing. Everyone has to have a first time for everything and the odds are fairly good that your controller was himself a student pilot at one time. Taking advantage of help that is available may be the sign of a beginner, but it is also the sign of a smart pilot.

Situational Awareness

Once a pilot has been radar identified and cleared into the airspace, he needs to understand some basic assumptions that will be made regarding his trip to the airport. The first is that, unless otherwise stated, the pilot is capable of navigating to the airport by his own means. Being unable to get to the airport without ATC assistance should be a very unusual circumstance. Although at some point the controllers will provide radar vectors to follow traffic or to establish a sequence, a pilot should never take that as a reason not to plan to fly the entire flight by his own means. As soon as a pilot expects ATC to take over his navigational duties, that is the time that traffic will be light enough for a controller to say, "proceed direct to the airport, report it in sight." Being unable to comply with that instruction could prove to be, at the very least, embarrassing.

The next assumption is that any time a pilot receives an instruction that either does not make sense to him or is beyond his abilities or the capabilities of his aircraft, it is his job to let the controller know immediately. For an inexperienced pilot working with a veteran controller, this may fall into the category of easier said than done, but to be unsure of anything is to be unsafe as well. Unfortunately a few controllers sometimes do their best to thwart a pilot's responsibility to question their actions by giving seemingly short-tempered responses to those legitimate questions. But when they shut down a pilot's inquiries, they undermine that pilot's safety and abuse their authority. Such instances are rare, but even one occurrence is one too many.

When a controller does start to vector a pilot, some of the responsibilities for keeping him out of trouble shift or are shared in a way that can be discomforting for the novice. It is not unusual for any pilot to lose his situational awareness after being taken off course and given five or six different headings. To a certain degree, once a controller starts vectoring a pilot, the controller becomes responsible for continuing the vectors until the pilot sees the airport or, upon completion of his vectoring routine, informing the pilot of his location so that he may resume his own navigation.

Unless the controller has assigned an altitude to maintain as well as a heading to fly, it is still the pilot's responsibility to ensure the resulting flight path will not put him into a hazardous situation. Likewise with the assigned altitude, if staying at the assigned altitude will put a VFR pilot into the clouds, he needs to speak up loud and early.

The easiest way for a pilot to maintain situational awareness in the face of multiple radar vectors is to use a GPS receiver with moving map capability. But even without GPS, pilots can create their own mental picture of where they are once the vectoring is under way. With the aid of a sectional or a VFR terminal area chart, as the headings are issued, the pilot can plot the approximate course changes on the chart and then confirm that what is outside the window matches up with the lines on the chart. If anything seems amiss at any time, the pilot should ask the controller for confirmation of his position over the ground. In one accident prior to which a student and instructor on an instrument flight had been receiving radar vectors, a series of events led ATC to forget the aircraft. The airplane subsequently flew into mountainous terrain and, in spite of the fact that the pilots had been receiving vectors, the National Transportation Safety Board (NTSB) produced findings that stated the pilots were contributing factors because they did not maintain their situational awareness. Radar vectoring is an essential element of air traffic control, but when it comes to accepting them, the rule is always, "let the pilot beware."

When the approach controller has just about finished her job of getting a pilot to a point to where he can see either the airport or the traffic he is to follow to the airport, the previously mentioned *clock method* (see Chapter 5) comes into play. If a pilot is to look for traffic to follow, advising where to look for that traffic is accomplished most efficiently by referencing it to a clock position. The same is true if there is no traffic or the controller has ensured that it will be no factor, in which case she will point out the airport in a like manner. For example, if the controller states that the airport is 10 o'clock and five miles, that is a signal for the pilot to start looking somewhere between the front of the plane's left wing and the nose of the airplane.

One word of caution: When a busy controller starts pointing out the airport to a pilot and the pilot does not see the airport, the correct response is not always the most pleasing to ATC. Some pilots, with little more than a mirage in front of them, have responded "airport in sight" just to appease a harried controller. Those pilots may have good intentions, but hoping to see something that just is not visible is the first step down a very slippery slope. By reporting a phantom airport in sight, a pilot may reduce the workload for one controller, but will likely make other controllers down the line pay the price for easing that burden.

Somewhere along the line to the airport, pilots should anticipate at least one and perhaps several frequency changes. At every large airport there are a lot of controllers handling air traffic within a relatively small section of airspace. It is extremely common that, as pilots work their way toward the airport, they will pass through several different airspace sectors. For each different sector there will be a different frequency to use. While it is still helpful for pilots to have made a list of the anticipated frequencies, the current controller will always tell a pilot what the next frequency will be.

These days, with the majority of general aviation airplanes being equipped with two communications radios and with each radio being capable of storing an active and a stand-by frequency, there are several methods for using that to your advantage. One method seems to be most effective when a pilot enters the arrival phase of flight. When they contact the approach control facility responsible for the destination airport, many pilots set one radio up with the tower frequency in the active position and the ground control position in stand-by. The other radio then is used for all other communications. Each time a new frequency is issued to a pilot, he switches the frequency he is about to leave to the stand-by position and tunes the newly assigned frequency into the active position. That way if for some reason the new frequency turns out to be incorrect, the previously proven one can be moved from stand-by to active to try the process all over again. There is an added advantage of having the tower and ground control frequencies at the ready on the other radio, and that benefit will be discussed shortly.

With each frequency change and with each new controller it might seem as though that goal of getting to the airport will never be reached, but each of those controllers is weaving pilots through the maze of airplanes flying into, out of, and through the airspace. Along the way, the novice will find that most of what is happening is not that much different from any other flight.

The Approach Sequence

Most of the flight consists of flying assigned headings and altitudes, looking for traffic, and responding to the controllers' directions and queries as promptly as possible. The controllers, in turn, direct the flight as necessary, issue traffic advisories, apply wake turbulence procedures and advisories when appropriate, and initiate radar handoffs to the next person in line. Then, finally, the pilot will be told to contact that one controller who will establish the approach sequence to the airport.

From that point on, the atmosphere tends to change a bit, especially if traffic is heavy. Although anyone who has ever flown into a VFR airport on a busy Saturday or Sunday most likely will have experienced heavy traffic, at a major airport it is still different. Most of the traffic, both inbound and outbound, will be large, high-performance air transport aircraft flying at speeds well above those of most general aviation aircraft. The approach controller's job is to create a space for the general aviation pilot among all those other planes and that is when some unfamiliar techniques could come into play.

With light planes, a controller's objective is to get them as close to the airport as possible without actually being in the arrival traffic flow. Once they are relatively close to the airport, the controller will create an opening in the approach sequence and fit them into the flow at what might seem like the last minute. Yet in actuality that controller was planning that move for quite a while. The reasoning is sound enough if we consider that most of the traffic inbound to a major airport is easily capable of flying the approach at anywhere from 170 to 200-plus knots. For those aircraft, being vectored to a twenty-mile final, though not terribly high on a pilot's wish list, it is not all that excessive or time-consuming. To attempt to put a general aviation airplane flying at around 120 knots in the same situation is not nearly as convenient for anyone. That twenty-mile final that was an inconvenience for a jet becomes a short cross-country for a light-plane pilot and all during the trip any following traffic has to be slowed to a crawl and vectored on their own endless journey. To serve every pilot as efficiently as possible, controllers juggle the traffic in a couple of different ways.

One way to handle the situation is to have general aviation pilots fly their aircraft parallel to, but outside of, the final approach course. It is similar to sitting in the travel lane of a highway while others in the passing lane overtake you. Then when your aircraft is four or five miles from the airport, an opening in the final will be created and becomes yours for the taking. Just as is expected when moving to the passing lane on a highway, matching your speed with the rest of the traffic in that lane is expected.

Obviously controllers do not expect a Cessna 172 to fly as fast as a jet, but they will ask many pilots to keep their speed as high as possible for as long as possible. In doing so, what they are hoping for is that a pilot will maintain a normal cruise speed until he is a mile or so on final, at which point a reduction to his approach speed is expected. How each individual pilot responds to that request must be based upon his own level of experience and expertise, but it is safe to say that if keeping his speed up on final is a first-time attempt at the maneuver, it might not be the best idea. To what degree a pilot complies with a request to keep his speed up is strictly voluntary. Controllers will always ask for and hope for the best, but they are trained to accept whatever a pilot can provide.

Considering that almost every approach to a runway at a major airport ends with a landing on a runway that is at least 5,000 feet long, flying a higher speed until a one-mile final should present no great problems for most pilots. But whether or not a pilot can comply with the controller's request is a decision he has the responsibility and the authority to make. If his flying skills are a little rusty or the runway is wet or anything else creates an unsatisfactory level of discomfort, a pilot's response to ATC should be a polite "unable."

The controller may not be pleased with that reply and the possibility of an additional delay for the pilot does exist, but neither of those consequences should be reason to try something that does not feel right. Keep in mind, though, that to a controller the only thing worse than a pilot advising her that he cannot keep his speed up on the final approach course is a pilot who says that he will and then doesn't. Occasionally controllers can be very trusting individuals and one of those times is when they desperately want or need help from a pilot. So when a pilot says that it is not a problem to get 180 knots out of his Piper Warrior, in the face of all logic and reason, that controller will react accordingly. When the pilot's best intentions and the controller's greatest hope both fall short, life is not nearly as much fun. The best advice for pilots is to say what you can do and then make certain you do what you said.

A second commonly used method of mixing slower inbound traffic with the faster jets is to have the pilot of the light aircraft fly to a point close to where a normal base leg entry would be made and then have him circle the area until a slot on the final opens up. When the opening becomes available it is then just a matter of leaving the holding pattern on a base leg and continuing inbound for landing. The best advice for a pilot faced with this option is to set up a circling pattern that is comfortable to fly and yet does not encroach upon the airspace over the runway. Again, the objective is to keep the airplane relatively close to the airport, not to make its pilot fly steep turns around a point.

Whatever the exact method a controller uses to fit you into the approach sequence, at some point the traffic to be followed will be pointed out to you. When you report the traffic in sight and the controller responds with "follow that traffic," as is the case with maintaining visual separation, how closely you follow the airplane is up to you. The burden of keeping a safe distance between your plane and the one you are following completely shifts from the controller to you. The same is true for wake turbulence avoidance and while nothing can guarantee you will not encounter its effects, learning the proper techniques for reducing the risks are critically important for every pilot.

When the controller neither points out traffic to follow nor makes any mention of preceding traffic, that means there either is none or she is providing the required separation from it. That does not mean that you should continue your approach blindly accepting her instructions as gospel. It does mean, however, that as long as everyone does his job correctly, there will be no conflicting traffic between you and the airport.

Talking to the Tower

By the time a pilot gets to his last hurdle—contacting the tower controller—most of the strange and unexpected events will be behind him. Either he will be cleared to land on the assigned runway or his presence on the frequency will be acknowledged with the landing clearance coming at a later moment. Whenever the clearance to land is given, if the controller does not state the landing runway in the clearance, which most often she will, pilots should always respond to the instruction by stating the runway that they will land on. When on short final, a quick look at the approach end of the runway to confirm that the pilot's expectation and the controller's clearance match the numbers painted on it can provide valuable insurance that what is supposed to be happening coincides with what is happening.

One of the last unexpected situations that a general aviation pilot might encounter when landing at a major airport is that, after having been asked by the approach controller to keep his speed up for as long as possible, the tower controller may advise that same pilot to plan to use one of the first taxiways to exit the runway. As incongruous as it might seem, that is because the approach controller and the tower controller do not always share the same objectives. The approach controller cares that a pilot stays far enough ahead of the traffic that is following him to the airport. The tower controller's concerns relate to the fact that before the second jet can land, the first must be clear of the runway.

Caught in the middle is the poor light-plane pilot who can either keep his speed up while on final approach or slow down and exit the runway with a minimum of delay, but he cannot do both. The best advice is to forward the approach controller's request to the controller in the tower and put the decision back in her lap by saying, "Tower, approach asked me to keep my speed up, I can either do that or slow down and clear the runway early, which would you like?" Being rather territorial and somewhat self-serving, the tower controller will probably ask you to slow down and plan the first available taxiway. If she restates the request to keep your speed up, that's okay too. Either way the decision has been moved to the controller and that gets you off the hook.

The only other unfamiliar methods that might be used at a major airport and the unknown expectations that accompany those procedures relate to getting off of the runway. It is true that, absent any contradictory instructions from ATC, when a pilot lands, the runway he uses belongs to him in its entirety. It is also true that even the rawest recruit in the FAA knows that the pilot of a single-engine light airplane does not, except under extraordinary circumstances, need ten thousand feet of runway to get his craft under control. Expectations being what they are, to commit such an act without first clearing the way with ATC may be legal, but it is not thoughtful or professional. When a pilot takes an unnecessarily long time clearing a runway, the odds are good that the pilot following him will have to execute a go-around and go to the back of the line.

The next situation is not as black and white. Clearing a runway and continuing to the ramp may seem as though it should be a subject open for little discussion, but it is a situation in which the written word and the expected practice do not align perfectly. Generally speaking, the procedures as written state that a pilot should clear the runway, get beyond the hold-short lines, and contact ground control for clearance before proceeding on any taxiway other than the one used to exit the runway. The origins of the problem stem from the fact that most of the taxiways that pilots use to exit a runway are nothing more than short connectors to a parallel taxiway.

The rules state that once beyond the hold lines, pilots should stop short of the next taxiway and contact ground control for clearance to proceed. The expectations at large airports are that, in the absence of instructions from the tower controller to hold short of a taxiway, pilots should continue moving off of the connector and contact ground control as quickly as possible. The one exception is that in no instance should a taxiing pilot cross a runway without specific authorization.

There are any number of variables that further complicate the problem. One is that some of the instructions the tower controller might issue to a pilot exiting the runway may leave room for interpretation. "Turn right next taxiway, contact ground point niner" is one. Should the pilot stop and then contact ground control, should he keep moving and call ground, and what is "point niner"?

The last question is the easiest to answer. Most ground control frequencies at airports throughout the country are shared by most of those airports. Since all communication is supposed to be taking place on the ground, interference from another pilot a distance away using the same frequency should not apply (a good reason not to use ground control frequencies when in the air). The shared frequencies are 121.7 and 121.9. Since the 121 portion of the frequency does not change from one airport to another, controllers are permitted to instruct pilots to contact ground using only the digit after the decimal point, in this case point niner.

The first two questions are not as easily resolved. If the tower controller does not specifically instruct a pilot to hold short of the next taxiway, she is expecting that pilot to clear the connector and contact ground control right away. When pilots stop unexpectedly and take their time switching to ground control, the result is that an airplane on the runway cannot clear it and an airplane approaching that same runway cannot land, and more than a few people are left unhappy.

The best solution to the problem is to use sound judgment and have the ground control frequency readily available. As long as the next chunk of pavement is not a runway and as long as the tower controller has not instructed you to hold short of it, look to see if there are any aircraft moving toward you from either direction. If there are, stop and contact ground control. If not, keep moving and call ground. If, as was suggested earlier, the correct ground control frequency has already been entered into the stand-by position on one of your radios, ground control can be contacted at the push of a button and most of the questionable issues should dissolve. Everything after that should be a matter of following progressive taxi instructions if they are needed or just taxiing to the ramp.

Be Prepared

With the right preparation, a good mental picture, and an alert attitude, flying into a major airport need not be any more difficult than going to a smaller one. Much of the structure required to get a lot of airplanes into the same airport can actually reduce the possibilities for confusion or misunderstanding. Most of the time the same rules of common sense and safety and the same air traffic procedures that are used at outlying airports all apply to flying in the big time.

The last thing to remember is that no pilot or controller knows everything there is to know about every airport in the country. Whenever something unfamiliar arises, the experienced professionals always ask a question. Besides being an extremely valuable learning experience, flying with the pros can actually be a lot of fun.

8

Special VFR:
I'll Take One Too

WHEN A PERSON SPENDS enough time working as an air traffic controller he is the recipient of more than a few amusing transmission and strange requests, but one that topped my list for years was a request I received from a VFR pilot one afternoon. The weather at the airport was below basic VFR minimums—ceiling of one thousand feet or greater and visibility three miles or better—and a couple of VFR pilots were trying to get out of the airspace and commence their various journeys. One pilot asked for and received a *Special VFR Clearance* out of the area. A second, upon hearing of the success of one of his compatriots, contacted me and said, "Ah ground, I'll take one of those things you just gave that other fellow." I did not know whether to laugh or cry, but his transmission reinforced what many controllers and pilots already knew, a lot of people do not really understand what Special VFR is all about.

Many student pilots, as they go through their private pilot training, never receive any formal training in the use of Special VFR procedures. Only after they receive their licenses and go out to conquer the world on their own does their exposure to Special VFR begin, and even then it is usually on a hit-or-miss basis. Add to that some confusing and seemingly contradictory information in FAA publications relating to Special VFR and pilots and controllers alike misunderstand and occasionally misuse Special VFR.

Special VFR procedures were developed to provide a safe and legal method for pilots operating under visual flight rules to do so only within certain designated areas of airspace. Below ten thousand feet MSL, within the lateral boundaries of those portions of Class B, C, D, or E airspace that have been developed in conjunction with an airport and that begin at the surface, special VFR operations may be authorized and conducted. For example, if a pilot wants to depart an airport that is within Class B or C airspace on a Special VFR clearance, the authorization only applies as long as she is flying below ten thousand feet MSL and is within that portion of the airspace that begins at the surface. Once she departs that inner circle and flies into a section of the airspace that begins at any altitude higher than the surface, she is bound by the requirements of that airspace and Special VFR procedures no longer apply.

Special VFR is used to provide separation for all aircraft that are authorized to be in certain types of airspace only when that airspace is below basic VFR minima. It is not intended to be used as a means to reduce flight visibility and cloud clearance requirements within controlled airspace in general.

One way to locate areas in which Special VFR operations for fixed-wing aircraft are permitted is to mention those places for which they are not authorized. In Section 3 of Appendix D to Part 91 of the FARs, there is a list of thirty-three airports around the country at which Special VFR operations for other than helicopters are not permitted. At each of the listed airports, regardless of the type of airspace that surrounds them, Special VFR flight is not an option for any but helicopter flights.

Incidentally, there are a number of ways in which the regulations that pertain to helicopter operations are eased or altered as compared to those for fixed-wing aircraft. For pilots caught up in the joys of rotorcraft machines, some time spent perusing the regulations can clarify the differences. For purposes of this book, all additional references to Special VFR operations will refer to the regulations only as they apply to pilots of fixed-wing aircraft.

Back to the list, in addition to Appendix D, on sectional charts and VFR terminal area charts, if Special VFR operations are not permitted at an airport depicted on the charts, it will be noted as such. For those airports "No SVFR" is printed on both types of charts just above the name of the affected airport. If that is the case at the airport in question, a pilot wanting a Special VFR clearance need not apply.

When to Use Special VFR

Now that we know where Special VFR flights may be conducted, the next question is when would a pilot use them? Special VFR operations are directly linked to the weather conditions reported, officially or otherwise when no official report exists, at the airport of intended use. For example, if the official weather report for Podunk International Airport indicates the ceiling is less than one thousand feet and/or the visibility is less than three statute miles, a pilot may request a Special VFR clearance to operate into, out of, or within the airspace associated with that airport. If weather conditions are better than those just mentioned, for all practical purposes, Special VFR does not exist and all flight operations within any particular type of airspace must be conducted according to its associated regulations.

On the other side of the visibility coin, Special VFR operations within a particular area may only be conducted when the flight visibility is at least one statute mile. In addition if a pilot wants to take off or land at an airport under a Special VFR clearance, the ground visibility must be at least one statute mile as well. If weather reporting is available, the visibility stated in the report is the governing factor. If no weather reporting exists, then flight visibility becomes the determining factor and, in a rather unique twist, flight visibility includes the visibility from the cockpit of an aircraft in takeoff position, in which case it must also be at least one statute mile.

In a bit of an unusual twist, the requirements regarding what visibility—flight or officially reported ground visibility—becomes the determining factor to a certain extent depends upon the intentions of the pilot. If a pilot intends to land at or depart from an airport for which there is official weather reporting and the report indicates the weather is below VFR minimums, she will be required to obtain a Special VFR clearance prior to entering the associated airspace.

However, if her intention is just to fly through the airspace or if weather conditions at the airport of intended landing or departure are not reported, then her flight visibility takes precedence over the officially reported visibility relating to the airspace. One example that might help clarify the regulation begins with the situation wherein the official weather at Rangoon International is a clear sky with two miles visibility in haze. A pilot wanting to pass through the airspace is above the haze layer and flying with unlimited visibility. Since she is operating in VFR conditions, she is not required to request a Special VFR clearance to continue her flight. If, however, she is required to obtain a clearance or establish two-way radio communications with ATC to comply with those regulations, irrespective of the weather, that does not change. She would also have to advise the controller that she is currently flying in good VFR conditions and will be able to continue to do so for the remainder of her time in the airspace.

Conversely, suppose a VFR pilot would like to land at one airport that happens to be within the Class D airspace of another airport that has both a control tower and official weather reporting. The controlled airport has weather that is above VFR minimums, but the pilot is looking at two miles visibility through her windows. She may request and receive a Special VFR clearance to enter the airspace on her way to the other airport. The same would hold true if she only wanted to pass through the airspace as opposed to landing within it.

One final restriction that impacts whether a pilot legally may request a Special VFR clearance relates to when she requests the clearance. Any time between sunset and sunrise (or in Alaska, when the sun is six degrees or more below the horizon), for a pilot's request for a Special VFR clearance to conform to the regulations, several additional conditions must exist. During those time periods, any pilot wanting to fly under the rules governing Special

VFR flight must possess an instrument rating, be current to fly as pilot-in-command in instrument conditions, and be flying a plane that is properly certified and equipped for IFR flight.

It is vital that every pilot understand these restrictions because, if a pilot makes a request for Special VFR after the sun goes down, rather than ask her if she is properly equipped and qualified, the controller will assume that she knows and is able to comply with all the pertinent regulations. The added requirements for nighttime Special VFR stem from the knowledge that what may be doable during daylight hours, that is, using outside visual references to maintain control of the airplane in marginal weather conditions, can be next to impossible at night. It is, therefore, essential that each pilot carefully review the legal requirements as well as her individual competency and proficiency.

What Special VFR Is About

With the where and when of Special VFR noted, what is it really all about? It is about allowing VFR pilots to operate as close to the world of instrument flight as they possibly can get and still remain in VFR conditions? With that in mind, it is critically important that any pilot venturing into that world understand all the implications and responsibilities associated with the procedures.

Any time a pilot is flying in an area where a Special VFR clearance is required, she is also flying in an area of very marginal weather conditions. For anyone who has flown when the flight visibility is only one mile, or the ceiling is less than one thousand feet, or both the ceiling and visibility are low, it should have been evident that the margin for error with which VFR pilots are normally accustomed to operating was significantly reduced. That is not to say that every or even any flight conducted under the rules and procedures of Special VFR is inherently dangerous, but it does suggest that each pilot who ventures into that arena needs to have a solid foundation of understanding and knowledge.

Add to that the fact that because Special VFR operations are conducted in instrument weather conditions and because most of the flying occurs in the vicinity of an airport where the rest of the pilots are operating under instrument flight rules, the expectations increase all around. Each pilot works under the assumption that every other pilot in the area knows what to do, so it becomes imperative that VFR pilots also understand and follow all the established procedures and regulations. Since almost all of the traffic separation responsibilities are borne by the controllers, they also expect that everyone involved knows the rules and will abide by them.

With that understanding, when a pilot determines that she is ready, willing, and able to safely conduct a flight while operating on a Special VFR clearance, nowhere is starting with a complete understanding of her responsibilities more significant. Before a controller can authorize a pilot to operate on a Special VFR clearance, that pilot must *initiate the request* for the clearance. Under no circumstances are controllers permitted to suggest to a pilot that what she needs to reach her objectives is that handy dandy clearance.

For a variety of reasons, that is one regulatory requirement that controllers hold on to tenaciously. The most important reason is that the restriction is based upon the fact that flying Special VFR changes the nature of the VFR pilot's world in a unique way. Because of the marginal weather conditions in which operations are conducted, the available options are reduced, the risk factors are increased, and the pilot's responsibilities are much more onerous. Controllers assume that if a pilot knows enough to request a Special VFR clearance, she likewise knows what lies in store for her when the controller authorizes it. If she does not know she is required to request the clearance, then she probably should not be flying in the area anyway.

Although less of a concern for the pilot, the other reason controllers will not attempt to sidestep the regulation and offer the clearance to a befuddled pilot is that to do so illegally puts their careers at risk. About as close as a controller will get to advising a pilot that, if she wants to continue her flight as anticipated and the weather conditions are less than VFR, is to tell her, "The Class D (or whatever) airspace is IFR. State your intentions." If, as all too many do, the pilot responds with, "Approach, I'd just like to come in and land," that may be close to what is required but it is not close enough. She needs to say the magic words: "I request a Special VFR clearance into the airport." Traffic permitting, ATC will grant the request.

What a pilot gets for all of her efforts surrounding obtaining the authorization to conduct her flight on a Special VFR clearance is approved separation from all IFR and other Special VFR aircraft operating in the area. Since the only pilots flying around in controlled airspace when the weather is less than that required for VFR flight must be flying on either an instrument or a Special VFR clearance, it follows that every authorized aircraft is being separated from every other one. Therein lies the benefit of Special VFR.

The exact methods by which controllers provide separation for Special VFR aircraft sometimes will differ from those applied to IFR aircraft. To begin with, Special VFR does not authorize a pilot to fly in the clouds. Whenever a controller assigns an altitude that a pilot must maintain, rather than issuing a specific altitude to maintain, the controller will advise him to fly *at or below* a certain altitude. This accomplishes two things. First, although the approved vertical separation may be reduced to as little as five hundred feet, it provides a positive means by which to keep any instrument traffic safely above the VFR pilot. Second, it gives the VFR pilot the flexibility to descend to a lower altitude should it become necessary.

An important point that pilots using Special VFR need to consider is that while it does allow pilots to reduce the VFR cloud clearances to just remaining clear of the clouds, Special VFR does not reduce or eliminate the minimum safe altitude regulations as stated in FAR 91.119. Controllers are not permitted to assign altitudes that have, as the upper limit, an altitude that is below the minimum safe altitudes. Controllers religiously adhere to that restriction. Pilots, on the other hand, often tend to let it fall by the wayside.

Along those same lines, the authorization to remain clear of the clouds that pilots receive with a Special VFR clearance applies only as long as they are flying within the airspace for which the clearance is authorized. Once they leave the associated Class B, C, D, or E airspace and head to points beyond, if those points are in controlled airspace, the requirements of FAR 91.155 still apply. Controllers are not likely to play policeman of the air and file a violation against a pilot because it seems unlikely she can comply with all the regulations in the face of flying beneath an eight-hundred-foot ceiling, but that does little to alter the reality of the situation. Just as important, a controller also will not deny a request for Special VFR if the official visibility requirements are within the prescribed limits. It may be their job to determine what is legal inside the designated airspace, but it is the pilot's job to determine what is going to be safe for the duration of her flight.

The rest of the time controllers will use radar, nonradar, visual separation, or a combination of all of the methods to separate Special VFR aircraft from the rest of the traffic. Regardless of how they keep the airplanes apart, an additional requirement to which controllers must adhere is that Special VFR flights may be approved only if they do not delay arriving or departing IFR aircraft. They do have a certain degree of latitude in applying that rule, but when it is a toss-up, those pilots looking for a Special VFR clearance are the ones who will be put on hold. In those instances, VFR pilots should be advised of the approximate length of the delay so they can decide whether to wait it out or go on to Plan B.

There are two other instances when a pilot may elect to request a Special VFR clearance. The first is referred to as *Local Special VFR Operations* and is really nothing more than requesting to remain in the local traffic pattern for takeoffs and landings. The most limiting factor that usually determines whether the request will be granted is how the request will affect any other traffic in the area. Since ATC is still responsible for providing separation between aircraft and visual separation may not be feasible, any regular flow of other traffic may negate the possibility of granting such a clearance. At other times, when no one else is flying, it can be a good opportunity to take advantage of an otherwise empty runway.

The other possibility for which Special VFR can be an effective means for VFR pilots to get up and going is when the only weather restriction to flight is visibility. If, for example, a haze layer that is only a few thousand feet thick blankets an airport, pilots may request a Special VFR climb to VFR conditions. The limiting factor that needs to be considered is that the clearance is almost always accompanied by a distance restriction. That is, a pilot must be able to reach the higher VFR conditions within a designated distance from the airport. Once there, she reports reaching VFR and goes on her merry way.

Exactly which controller a pilot contacts to obtain a Special VFR clearance depends upon where she is when the request is made. The easiest situation with which to begin the discussion is when a pilot is on the ground at a controlled airport. In that case she can make her request with either clearance delivery or ground control if there is no separate controller assigned to issue clearances. In addition to all the usual information regarding her aircraft identity and type, a pilot only has to make the specific request for Special VFR and state her direction of flight or destination.

If the airport is an uncontrolled airport but located within the Class D airspace associated with a different controlled airport, then a phone call or, if possible, a radio call to the tower requesting Special VFR should do the trick. If the departure airport is within a Class E surface area, the choice becomes a little less clear. If a pilot knows what ATC facility is the controlling facility for that airport, the place to begin would be with that facility. If she does not know, a phone call to flight service should resolve the issue. In any case, unlike when VFR conditions prevail, if the weather is IFR, a pilot cannot take off and pick up a Special VFR clearance once in the air. Besides being unsafe, it is against the regulations.

Because of the nature of the weather conditions that accompany flight under Special VFR conditions, what if things start to go awry before or even after a pilot receives a clearance? What does a VFR pilot do when either the visibility drops below the requisite one mile or she cannot continue at a safe altitude and remain clear of the clouds? Neither of those situations is one that a VFR pilot would willingly or knowingly place herself in, but each could occur without much forewarning.

The first answer is that if weather conditions deteriorate to the point where continued flight according to the regulations governing Special VFR is not possible, a pilot cannot expect to look to controllers for a quick and easy solution. When the visibility drops below one mile, the controllers' hands are tied, they cannot authorize Special VFR operations. The second answer, though not an easy one to consider or implement, is that if developing weather conditions prohibit a pilot from legally complying with the rules, she may have to exercise her emergency authority as outlined in FAR 91.3. In the latter case, a pilot faced with such a situation will need to use her best judgment and take whatever actions are necessary to ensure a safe outcome.

Having dutifully covered all the bases with respect to preparation, experience, and knowledge, when weather conditions are such that a pilot decides she needs a Special VFR clearance to conduct or continue a flight, usually she can expect to be able to obtain one without a whole lot of trouble. As far as controllers are concerned, as long as traffic conditions permit, the visibility is at least one mile, and the pilot requests the clearance, she can expect to have her request honored.

Flying Special VFR Safely

The ease with which a pilot may obtain a Special VFR clearance and the fact that no special training or pilot certificate is required to fly it—with the exception of nighttime operations—does not necessarily mean that there is nothing terribly difficult about doing it. The flying itself may not be very different, but the judgment and decision making required to make the flight a safe one move to a decidedly higher level. Any time a VFR pilot flies in marginal weather conditions, she must understand the complexities of that weather and the trends and conditions it foreshadows. Any instrument pilot would be the first to say that weather that is marginal but safe one minute can, almost without warning, turn hopelessly bad the next. If a pilot goes into such a situation without having given some thought to an escape plan if things turn sour, she may be heading down a dead-end path.

Every one of us has to realize that no one will be able to guarantee when it is safe to fly Special VFR and when it is not. Certain weather conditions can make a Special VFR clearance a safe and efficient tool. Other conditions, even though they may be better than the legal minimums, could present any number of hazards for an inexperienced pilot. Each of us has to evaluate both current and anticipated conditions optimistically and pessimistically for every flight with respect to our own particular experience, skills, and ability. When it is used with careful forethought and continuous reevaluation, Special VFR can be a safe and efficient way to counter less-than-ideal weather conditions.

9

The Pilot's Ultimate Responsibility: The Final Say

MANY YEARS AGO I was speaking at a safety seminar and during the question-and-answer session that followed my presentation, a pilot who had run into a difficult situation asked me what I, the controller, thought he should have done to better handle the events that had occurred. In this particular instance there were no specific regulations to cover his problem, yet he knew that if he did not do something, the situation would only deteriorate more. After he relayed how the events had unfolded, I discovered that what the pilot really wanted to know was what to do if a controller gave him an instruction that he believed would put him and his aircraft in an unsafe situation. Though there is no clear-cut answer to what is usually a complex situation, revisiting who is responsible for what in the pilot/controller partnership can shed some light on how best to react when some aspect of a flight seems to be getting out of hand.

The most important and the simplest point to remember is that the pilot and his passengers are the ones who will most directly suffer the consequences of a good situation turned bad. As a result, the pilot is also the person who is ultimately responsible for taking whatever action is necessary to ensure that the safety of his flight is never compromised. FAR 91.3, Section (a) is one of the few regulations that leaves little doubt with respect to its intent: "The pilot in command of an aircraft is directly responsible for, and is the final authority as to, the operation of that aircraft." Air traffic controllers neither possess nor want the authority to take that responsibility from a pilot regardless of the situation.

Although the responsibilities delegated to the air traffic controllers are not as neatly or concisely summarized, their manual states, "The primary purpose of the ATC system is to prevent a collision between aircraft operating in the system and to organize and expedite the flow of traffic." While not specifically mentioned, that also would include doing everything within their capabilities to keep pilots safe, or at the very least, not doing anything to put pilots under their direction into unsafe situations. The goals of the controllers are not that different from those of pilots.

That being true, how do a pilot and a controller end up on what appears to be opposite sides of the safety issue? More important, when it happens what can a pilot do to make the best of a less-than-ideal situation? The best place to start is by learning how to recognize when, either by self-induced means or outside influences, a pilot's authority to completely discharge his responsibilities is being eroded.

How to Stay Pilot-in-Command

This brings us to the issue of what our responsibilities are. In that regard, FAR 91.3 leaves something to be desired. But I believe it was written in an all-inclusive and nonspecific manner because to do otherwise would hinder pilots' abilities to correctly deal with whatever situations might arise. The almost infinite number of possible events that could cause a pilot to have to invoke the authority granted under this regulation mandates that he be permitted to use his best judgment in dealing with them.

Thus, as pilots, we are responsible for everything relating to our airplanes and the flights we conduct in them. That notion may do little to help us delineate our responsibilities in a manner that makes recognizing them easier, but it clearly points out the breadth of the subject we must consider. If our job is to remain as safe as possible in every situation, then some of what we need to consider is what the things are that will reduce our safety to an unacceptable level with respect to fulfilling our role in the pilot/controller partnership.

First of all, pilots should never encourage or allow anyone to make a decision on their behalf that could compromise their absolute and final authority for the safety of their aircraft. There is a distinct difference between requesting information from which an enlightened decision can be made and requesting that someone else take that same information and make the decision in our place.

In a year's time, every controller probably receives thousands of requests from pilots for information ranging from weather conditions along their routes and delays at the destination airports to names of the best restaurants in town. Time permitting, most controllers are happy to supply whatever information they have on the subject.

There is nothing wrong with asking a controller for whatever assistance she can provide, which often can be substantial. The problems begin when, in addition to the information itself, a pilot also wants that controller to evaluate the data and then make a decision that could affect the safe outcome of his flight. No controller is in a position to be able to understand how a given set of conditions will affect an individual pilot's ability to cope with the resulting circumstances. Questions such as how current and proficient am I, how comfortable am I with the situation, have I experienced similar conditions before, are questions that can only be answered in the cockpit. When a pilot asks a controller, "how does it look to you?" he is asking for omniscience that no controller possesses.

There is a fine line between asking for information that will enable a pilot to make a valid decision for himself and asking a controller her opinion with respect to the best decision to make, but it is a line no pilot can afford to cross. Any time a pilot gets into a situation where the outcome of continuing on his present path is, in his mind, questionable and he asks a controller to provide confirmation for his actions, the die may well be cast. Rather than relinquish his fate to someone less capable of evaluating the quality of his decision, the best course of action would be to remove himself from the problem and find the time and a place to reassess his plans.

A good example that just about every pilot or controller has encountered relates to what happens when weather activity along a route intensifies. During the spring and summer months, when thunderstorms frequently move through many areas of the country, there can be almost endless chatter on the frequencies as pilots and controllers exchange information regarding flight conditions (fig. 9.1). Pilots continually ask controllers questions about how rapidly the storms are developing and moving, how intense they appear, and whether there are any breaks in the weather line. Controllers counter with requests for visual confirmation of radar-depicted weather activity, pilot reports of flight conditions, and how airborne radar or stormscopes depict the same weather. On days such as those, the exchange of weather information between pilots and controllers is second only to separating airplanes with respect to its importance (fig. 9.2).

Both pilots and controllers have learned that these exchanges are one of the best ways to take full advantage of the resources each is able to bring to the situation. Experienced pilots know that what they can see through the cockpit window often gives them a more accurate assessment of the weather than what a controller is seeing on her radarscope. On the other hand, when a pilot's view of the conditions ahead is severely restricted or eliminated altogether, his airborne weather avoidance equipment combined with the controller's radar can be a safe and effective means by which to navigate the storms.

Using every resource available is definitely a pilot's responsibility and controllers can be valuable resources for a lot of useful information. Using a controller's knowledge and expertise to make up for, or supplement, the lack of it in the pilot is how well-intentioned pilots undermine their own ability to act as pilot-in-command. If you find yourself asking for information based upon facts or even expert interpretation, that is just fine. But if you ask for

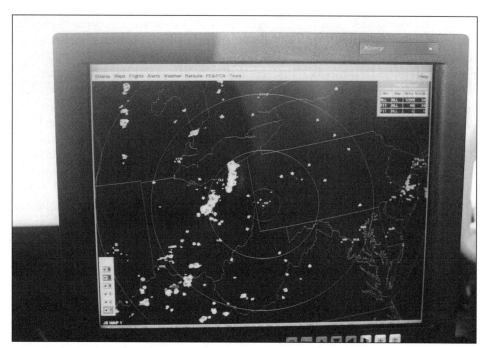

FIG. 9.1. Doppler Radar Display enables controllers to provide "real-time" weather information to pilots.

FIG. 9.2. The meteorologist's office is located steps away from the en route center controllers, giving them quick access to reports on the changing weather.

an opinion regarding what to do with it or how to act upon those data, you have gone too far. You have effectively eliminated, at least for a time, one-half of the pilot/controller partnership by asking the controller to make a decision in your place.

There is one small paragraph in the *Aeronautical Information Manual* (AIM) relating to the roles and responsibilities of pilots and controllers that says a lot in terms of how pilots fit into the ATC system. "The responsibilities of the pilot and the controller intentionally overlap in many areas providing a degree of redundancy. Should one or the other fail in any manner, this overlapping responsibility is expected to compensate, in many cases, for failures that may affect safety."

The air traffic system was created to be error tolerant, rather than error free, at least to a certain degree. No matter how hard pilots and controllers try, each is subject to mistakes. What the AIM is saying is that when a pilot makes a mistake, the controller should be there to correct it, and most pilots will bear witness to the fact that controllers are not the least bit shy with respect to fulfilling their obligations in that regard. But the AIM is also saying that the same holds true for pilots. When the controller makes a mistake, a pilot's role is to bring it to her attention.

Most controllers will admit that on occasion, an alert pilot prevented them from making a mistake that could have led to a more serious error later on. To do that, though, pilots must continuously work to maintain a high degree of situational awareness. Each pilot has to know where his airplane is in the air, and where he is in relation to the others around him. He needs to have a good idea of what should be happening next and he needs to have an understanding of how the controller's instructions play into it all. In short, a pilot is responsible for developing and maintaining as much of the controller's worldview as he can. When he does that, he becomes a more effective partner, and he gives himself firmer ground to stand on when the time comes to exercise his authority.

The Controller's Job

One of the next steps with respect to when a pilot should exercise his authority is to understand some of the situations that create the need for him to do it. If we accept that controllers make mistakes and need to be corrected, and if we accept that no controller intentionally tries to put a pilot into a hazardous situation, then we need to explore what other circumstances can put a pilot at risk. More important, we need to know what a pilot can do to prevent getting into an untenable position in the first place.

There are two major causes that often mandate what action controllers take with respect to how and why they maneuver the aircraft in their airspace. The first is how each pilot's objectives and requests relate to everyone else in the area, and the second is the legal or regulatory constraints by which each controller is bound to operate. If pilots can understand how and when each of these factors may affect their plans on any given day, they also can figure out how to avoid being placed in an uncomfortable situation to begin with.

More than anything else, the amount and complexity of traffic in a controller's airspace dictates how she is going to direct the various pilots through it. If traffic is light and conditions are relatively benign, each pilot who has a special need or request likely will find the controller to be willing to accommodate him as much as possible. But when there are more airplanes in the area and weather or some other conditions place additional or unexpected demands on a controller's capabilities, many of the otherwise available options begin to diminish.

One of the conditions outside of a pilot's control that may affect his plans is traffic. With the increase in air traffic in recent years, much of the airspace around many of our airports becomes saturated at various times throughout the day. When that happens the amount of reserve airspace—airspace as yet unused by a controller—is reduced or eliminated. Today, there are more and more times when a controller runs out of airspace to use.

When poor weather conditions develop, the problem of airspace usage is further compounded by the fact that every pilot in the vicinity wants to be in the same small parcel of unaffected air at the same time. It is understandable that what is beneficial for one pilot will most likely be beneficial for everyone else, but the problematic consequence is that, however much a controller would like to honor each pilot's request, it is not always possible to do it. In such instances, the easiest way for a pilot to avoid what could become an untenable position is to either avoid it altogether or have an alternate plan ready.

With just a little bit of preflight preparation, a pilot should be able to consider factors such as weather and anticipated traffic and then determine how they will likely affect his planned flight. If he can mitigate any of them by altering his plans, the outcome is apt to be much more favorable.

For instance, if weather conditions are reducing the acceptance capacity at a major airport, traffic that otherwise would flow through the airspace with little or no delay instead likely will be congested as a result of the bottleneck, and flyable airspace no doubt will be at a premium. Most of the scheduled carriers destined to that one airport have few alternative options and will use those that they have only as a last resort. General aviation pilots, however, are almost always in the enviable position of having literally dozens of other airports available for their use. When the conditions at a major airport seem to be inviting congestion and delays, the best way to avoid the difficulties that await inbound pilots is to opt for an outlying airport that is less affected by the conditions. It will make life easier for light-plane pilots, and it will mean fewer delays for other pilots who have no choice but to continue to their original destination.

Regulatory constraints, the other factor that directly affects any controller's ability to honor a pilot's request, are not entirely independent of the first. Often it is weather or traffic or both that influence how easily a controller can maneuver around or through the maze of legal requirements that bind her actions. Basically, controllers are faced with three absolutes that direct most of what they can and cannot do, except in emergency situations.

The first regulation, which controllers are not authorized to alter and which is most easily understood, is the required separation between or among aircraft. If the manual by which they operate states that, for a given situation, two aircraft must be separated by three miles laterally or one thousand feet vertically, that is the beginning and the end of the story. To decrease the required separation for any reason doesn't just reduce the allowable safety margin, it is not legal.

The second restriction relates to the minimum altitudes that controllers legally may assign to pilots. For instrument pilots there are a few possibilities, but for VFR pilots who are being radar vectored, the lowest altitude that a controller may assign is referred to as the *Minimum Vectoring Altitude (MVA)*. The MVA basically provides pilots with one thousand feet of terrain and/or obstruction clearance. MVAs can vary significantly depending upon the lay of the land and they are seldom readily accessible to pilots (a situation which does little to promote pilots' positions as safety back-ups). However, they are one of the foundations by which controllers do their jobs. While IFR pilots are seldom afforded the opportunity to descend below the MVA, VFR pilots are not so restricted. The controllers may not be able to assign an altitude lower than the MVA, but a VFR pilot can always initiate a request to descend to a lower altitude, as long as in doing so he does not violate any of the other regulations pertaining to maintaining a safe and legal altitude. That may not always be a viable option but it is one to keep in mind. Otherwise, the MVA is the bottom line for both pilots and controllers.

The final constraint that affects how a controller may move her traffic through the airspace is less easily understood by pilots but it is one with which compliance is mandatory. A controller may never allow an airplane she is directing to penetrate the airspace of another controller unless she first has received authorization from the second controller. One of the issues for pilots is that they have no way of knowing how the airspace in which they are flying is divvied up or when they are about to leave one sector for another, nor do they often care. Unfortunately, the result can be one of the more frustrating and least understood reasons for having a request denied, and it becomes decidedly more so when the controller does not seem to be terribly busy.

As an example, a VFR pilot asks for a different heading to avoid clouds ahead of him. After a reply of "stand-by" and what seems to be an interminable amount of time, the less-than-swamped controller advises she is unable to authorize the course change. Typically pilots wonder what gives? The guy on the ground is talking to all of three airplanes. The problem stems from the fact that controller number two, whose airspace you are not yet into but would like to be, is too busy to accept one more airplane. Controller number one has no choice but to deny your request. It may seem like another exercise in the bureaucratic shell game, but flying unannounced into any controller's airspace is an invitation to disaster.

Knowing some of the regulations that tie a controller's hands may not make an uncomfortable situation any better, but keeping them in mind could help you avoid the situation in the first place. Knowledge and preparation are two crucial elements in staying ahead of the game, but even the best-prepared pilots occasionally run across the unexpected.

When that happens, the next best way to avoid going from bad to worse is to give ATC as much notice as possible regarding any pending changes. The more time a controller has to accommodate a pilot's request and the less drastic the request is, the better the chances are that change will, in fact, be possible. Asking a controller for a heading change of twenty degrees to avoid clouds that are ten miles ahead is much preferred to asking for a ninety-degree change in course that must be accomplished within the next mile or two in order to avoid violating any regulations. Even if the earlier request cannot be approved, it buys both pilot and controller time to negotiate an alternative way out of the problem. Waiting until the last minute only increases the likelihood of ending up in a no-win situation.

If preparation is not the only answer and if making an early request for a deviation likewise does not provide a pilot with a suitable solution to his problem, what should he do when faced with either doing what he thinks is in the best interest of safety or following the instructions from a controller? The time to ask yourself that question is not when the right answer is likely to be clouded with a lot of emotional baggage. The time to think about it is long before your plane ever leaves the ground.

Saying No to a Controller

Begin by accepting the fact that telling a controller you are unable to accept her instructions is difficult. Over the years I have heard countless variations on the theme that to refuse to accept an ATC instruction means an almost endless interrogation at best, or losing your certificate, at worst. The truth is seldom so dire, but the fear of self-destruction seems to stay firmly implanted in the minds of many pilots.

The first step in overcoming any reluctance to make the correct decision is to think rationally about the truth. Experienced pilots calmly but insistently negotiate with controllers dozens of times on a daily basis. A controller issues an instruction, a pilot recognizes it is not within either his ability or the capability of his aircraft, and he tells the controller so. Most of the time, either the controller asks the pilot what he can do and then acts accordingly or she issues an alternative instruction and life goes on. No one gets called on the carpet for violating a regulation because none has been violated.

The next step is to think about what the consequences would be of invoking or not invoking the pilot-in-command authority in a given situation. If telling a controller you cannot accept her instruction is not a big deal but the alternative might create a hazardous situation for you and your passengers, the answer seems obvious. While it is when comfortably sitting on the ground, the same is not always true when faced with an authoritatively cranky controller on the other end of the mike. But the correct answer doesn't change with when it is asked.

I have always been amused and amazed by the survey that found that more people place the fear of speaking in public higher on their lists of fears than they do the fear of dying. I have always assumed that's because while we can envision standing up in front of a crowd and speaking to them, we cannot effectively imagine what it is like to die. I suspect that for too many pilots, refusing to accept an ATC instruction versus flying into a potentially deathly situation is very similar. Be that as it may, even knowing some of the worst the FAA has to offer in terms of compassion, the correct answer for me does not involve pain and agony. Stealing from a beer commercial, "know when to say no."

Fortunately, once a pilot has come to grips with the idea that, at one time or another, refusing to accept an ATC instruction goes with the territory of being a pilot, the process of acting upon his decision is much simpler than going through the mental exercises it took to arrive at that point. When the time comes (and it will), all a pilot has to advise a controller is that, for reasons of safety, he cannot comply with whatever instructions he just received. The more specific a pilot can be with his response, the easier it will be for the controller to come up with an alternate plan. Rather than just a general comment, saying, for example, the assigned altitude will put him in the clouds gives the controller an idea of how to resolve the problem. But regardless, when the time comes that a pilot has to take action to ensure his plane remains safe, the only way to do it is in a timely, firm, and, if necessary, insistent manner.

How the Controller Responds

There are several possible ways a controller may answer when a pilot refuses the controller's instructions. The first and most common response basically has been covered. The controller, after making some inquiry with respect to what the pilot can do, will issue an alternative instruction and the problem should be resolved quickly.

A second possible situation, although highly unlikely, is that the controller may take a somewhat confrontational position wanting to know in more detail why the pilot cannot comply with her instructions. If such a situation does arise, the most important point to keep in mind is to do as little as possible to aggravate or escalate the intensity of the moment. A firm but diplomatic response to the effect that you will be happy to provide a more lengthy explanation on the telephone after landing should be more than enough to cut the discussion short. Should the controller continue to press for some other explanation, mentioning that to do so would be to compromise other more pertinent duties definitely should end the conversation. The point is not to worry about whether the controller understands, or what she thinks about your abilities as a pilot, the concern is to keep a less-than-ideal situation from getting out of hand.

The last possibility is that the controller, for reasons of her own constraints as previously discussed, has no legal options other than the instructions she just issued. Because of traffic, airspace, or terrain, the controller and, unfortunately, the pilot are both caught between a rock and a hard place. Although not an option that any pilot wants to consider, the possibility of declaring an emergency always exists. Such a declaration serves two purposes. First, it provides authorization for a pilot to do whatever is necessary to ensure the safety of his plane is not compromised. Second, it provides a legal out for the controller. When responding to an emergency, a controller has a bit more leeway to reduce separation standards that otherwise would be inflexible.

Without question, declaring an emergency should be an option only used as a last resort and, to be sure, doing so ups the ante with respect to any follow-up questioning, but under certain conditions it may be the only available choice. Any time a pilot feels there is justification to use his emergency authority in order to deviate from a controller's instructions, he should do so without any hesitation or worry about what will follow later on. Horror stories circulate about what the FAA has done to pilots who, for legitimate reasons, have violated some regulations during the course of an emergency. But I know from experience that the controllers and other FAA officials who work with pilots on a daily basis are only concerned with ensuring that whatever risks existed were either eliminated or reduced to the maximum extent possible.

The odds are that anyone involved with an emergency situation will understand what was done and, more important, why it was done. Even in the unlikely event that a pilot should run across one of those narrow-minded, ill-informed individuals who does not understand what it is like in the real world, it is still better to have to deal with him than not to be able to deal at all.

When to Follow the Plan

Now it is time to explore the other side of the coin. While there are situations in which it is not only appropriate to question or refuse an ATC instruction but also essential to maintaining a safe flight environment, there are just as many times when it is inappropriate, unsafe, and unprofessional to do so. There are a few pilots who will question and argue about everything from why an approach sequence was determined as it was to why every procedure in existence cannot be altered to accommodate their individual wants. While it is true that neither pilots nor controllers usually lacks self-confidence and boldness, most understand that the exercise of self-control is essential to keeping communications on an even keel. No one wants to have some comment made in haste come back to haunt them at the least opportune time. Since every transmission made by pilots and controllers to one another is recorded for posterity or fourteen days, whichever comes first, if there is an incident that needs further investigation, posterity comes first and it hangs around until the situation is resolved.

One way to determine whether discretion is the better part of valor or the only old pilot is a bold pilot is to decide if what you want to say represents a need or a want. If the discussion with the controller involves communicating something that is necessary for safety, boldness wins hands down. If, on the other hand, questioning the controller about something is done to feed an ego or to work the system to an individual advantage at the possible expense of others, restraint should be the choice. The fact is that our air traffic system has been developed to efficiently accommodate as many pilots as possible. While each of us cannot always be number one to take off or land, most of us receive the best available service most of the time.

Contrary to what some may think, when a controller is directing six or seven pilots as they fly through her area, that controller is usually in a better position to determine what will be most efficient for each pilot. That is not so because the controller has super powers, but rather because either from the vantage point of looking at a radarscope or through a tower window, she is afforded a perspective that enables her to develop a more objective view of the entire traffic picture. That bird's eye view is one seldom seen by pilots but it is the tool that allows for the most efficient use of the surrounding airspace.

Consequently, what seems reasonably arguable to a pilot ends up being denied by a controller. Not because it might make life easier and shorten that pilot's time in the air, but because by doing so it unnecessarily delays three or four other pilots. Rather than look at how one pilot would most benefit from a request, controllers look at how to most equitably spread out whatever delays must occur among as many pilots as possible, thereby minimizing the total delay to each one. On an individual basis, that fact may not appease the pilot who has to bear the brunt of the refusal, but in the overall scheme of his flying life it means that more often than not he will be the recipient of more efficient service.

If that is not enough reason to avoid arguing on the frequency and if the fact that it is unprofessional to do so doesn't diminish the desire, then add to those the issue that needlessly tying up a frequency can become unsafe very quickly. Whenever the air traffic in a given area is heavy, time available on any frequency is at a premium. If someone decides to tie up one of those frequencies just to make a personal statement about the quality of air traffic service, the chances are good that some other pilot might unnecessarily be placed in a hazardous situation simply because he could not break in on the meaningless conversation.

Controllers likewise are expected to adhere to the same standards of self-restraint by which pilots operate. It does little good for all the pilots on a frequency to maintain their professionalism if there is a controller constantly shooting off her mouth about one thing or another at the other end of the mike. In just such circumstances in the past, a well-placed word or two regarding professionalism diplomatically spoken by a pilot over the air has worked wonders at quieting the irritating perpetrator. If that doesn't work, making a note of the time and the frequency on which the controller did her ranting and then phoning in a complaint to the facility is worth the effort.

Remember, everything controllers say is recorded too. Regardless of who has a complaint, the place to have it answered is on the ground.

Fortunately, most of the time there is mutual respect and cooperation between pilots and controllers. In those occasional situations where a difference of opinion develops, the final say, of course, ultimately goes to the person who is right.

Emergency Situations: When I Need Them

AIR TRAFFIC CONTROLLERS are a lot like police officers: they don't seem to be around when you need them, but make one mistake … . When a pilot mistakenly enters Class B airspace without a clearance, out of the woodwork come two or three controllers just waiting to nail the errant aviator. But when that same pilot gets into a situation where a little help from the ground would be welcome, none can be found. In reality, finding a controller to help in an emergency situation is probably one of the easiest pieces of the puzzle to locate. It is how to use that help that is not always as easy to discern.

There are any number of ways that controllers can assist pilots who are faced with unexpected problems in the air, and we will look at some of those options. But, at the outset, what every pilot needs to recognize and accept is that when any emergency pops its head into the cockpit, the only person who can directly affect the outcome is the one sitting behind the controls. While that may seem obvious, all too often inexperienced pilots look to someone else (often the controller) to solve a problem that can only be remedied in the air.

Pilots seem to go through a natural progression as their flying experience develops. In the beginning, most novices are glad to hear a voice from the ground just about all the time, but especially whenever they run into some unforeseen problem. The feeling of just being connected to someone on solid ground seems to help. As their experience increases and their confidence builds with each passing hour, those voices from below that used to be considered welcome company in the cockpit often turn into intrusions in their private little world. By then, flying an airplane has become second nature and having someone else trying to tell them anything about how to do it is an insult. Becoming a more self-assured and independent pilot is one of the goals we all strive toward, but keep in mind that if the time ever comes when outside help would again be comforting, don't let pride stand in the way of asking for it.

Fortunately, thanks to the increased reliability of today's modern airplanes and thanks to advances such as improved weather reporting capabilities, the chances are excellent that most pilots will never need a controller for anything more than the routine contact that is a part of everyday flying. Mechanical failures, which used to be a common occurrence, have become the exception rather than the rule. Other advances in communication and navigation equipment have made the problem of maintaining good situational awareness much easier. All pilots train for a variety of emergency situations, but thankfully most of us will never have to use that training when we fly.

Before we all get lulled into a state of complacency, remember that Murphy's Law still lives. If something can go wrong, it will and often at the most inopportune time. Occasionally, the unexpected includes something for which we have not trained or something that was never even considered possible. As pilots we need to think about as many different scenarios as possible and we need to know what controllers and others outside the airplane can do to help us. Even the most experienced pilots need to play the *What-If* game on a daily basis.

Trying to explore every conceivable situation that could befall a pilot easily could fill several volumes and, to a certain degree, is outside of the scope of this book. Laying a framework from which pilots can begin to explore and better understand how the air traffic system in general and controllers in particular can most effectively assist pilots who are faced with the unusual or unexpected is both more relevant and less daunting to attempt.

What Constitutes an Emergency

Exactly what constitutes an emergency depends upon a host of variables, many of which cannot be laid out in black and white. The Pilot/Controller Glossary in the *Aeronautical Information Manual* (AIM) doesn't provide much assistance with respect to the definition. It states simply that an emergency is "a distress or an urgency condition." To one pilot, flying into a cloud easily could be deemed an emergency, to another it's not a problem. One corporate pilot I knew who was transporting several high-level executives from his company on a single-pilot flight determined that his desperate need to use the bathroom facilities combined with his inability to leave the cockpit indeed created an emergency situation. An emergency then, like beauty, is in the eye of the beholder.

It seems that for each individual pilot, what would be considered an emergency does not have to do so much with a particular set of conditions or circumstances, but rather how those factors might alter the successful conclusion to a flight. Over my years of participating in and watching pilots and controllers deal with various unusual situations, one thing that has become clear to me is that an emergency is as much a state of mind as it is a set of conditions. Exactly what that mindset is can determine how successfully a pilot will cope with her dilemma.

One of the first steps in creating the proper mindset is to accept that sometimes bad things happen to even the best-prepared and educated pilots. Many college-age students possess an incredibly strong sense of invulnerability. They tend to think bad things will not happen to them and if they do the results will not really hurt. As an instructor I emphasize to all my students that a pilot must mentally prepare herself ahead of time for the likelihood of an unexpected or emergency situation. That way it will be easier to deal with one if and when it arises.

As part of that mental preparation and to increase the opportunity for a successful outcome to any emergency, every pilot needs to convince herself that much of the success will depend almost entirely upon her taking control of the circumstances. Taking control means that a pilot has to put aside any hesitation she may have about talking to controllers, directing controllers, or allowing anything else to interfere with her decision-making process. In any emergency a pilot not only has to maintain control of her airplane but also, to whatever extent possible, she has to control the surrounding conditions that may affect her safety.

On the other side of the partnership, controllers can and often do play an integral role in working with pilots who are faced with emergencies. In those instances, it is not unusual for a controller to be just as busy as the pilot. Additionally, controllers know that their mental preparation and their approach to assisting pilots often play into helping them develop and maintain the most effective mindset for dealing with the situation.

At no time did that become more apparent to me than when I was faced with assisting a pilot who had run out of fuel. Just as he was about to leave my airspace on a nighttime instrument flight, the pilot informed me both of his engines had quit due to fuel starvation. In the ensuing minutes, as calmly as my pounding heart would allow, I directed him to the closest airport, provided information on runway direction and length, and advised him regarding the procedure for turning on the runway lights. Through it all his demeanor remained as seemingly unaffected as mine. On relatively short final he asked me for the field elevation; information I did not readily possess. For whatever reason, when I finally found and transmitted the figures to him, my voice cracked slightly in the process. Even more unsettling than my loss of composure was his reply offered in an equally shaky voice. That night I learned firsthand that, whether or not it should be so, pilots who are faced with a highly stressful situation often depend upon controllers to help them keep the peace. Fortunately most controllers know this and bring it to the forefront of their minds when the need arises.

One of the other basic tenets to which both pilots and controllers should adhere when working with an emergency situation is, do not do anything to make an already difficult situation worse. That tenet is often hard to adhere to, at least on the surface. No pilot or controller is intentionally going to do something to increase the level of difficulty or the workload in an already high-workload, high-stress situation, but each might do it unknowingly. Part of a pilot's gift to herself should be a promise to obtain the education needed to take her own counterproductive tendencies out of the picture. Another aspect of her learning is to recognize and learn how to prevent an otherwise well-meaning controller from adding fuel to the fire.

The best way for a pilot to keep the controller's feet firmly planted on the ground is for that pilot to take control of the situation from the air. Controllers have their own rules and regulations that affect how they react to particular emergency situations. While most often those procedures were developed to assist pilots in distress, occasionally they get in the way of higher priority duties. The problems are, first, that the controllers are obligated to follow the prescribed rules and regulations. Second, they may not be aware that the performance of their duties is having a negative impact on a pilot's ability to effectively deal with her own problems, unless the pilot so informs the controller.

During one instance when the crew of an air carrier reported an in-flight fire to the controller, the controller first did everything he could to expedite and direct the plane to the closest suitable airport. As he was required to do, the controller then went on to ask the crew a series of questions relating to fuel on board, the number of people on board, and so forth. After the third or fourth question the pilot responded that they were rather busy in the cockpit and the rest of the questions would have to wait until they landed. The controller was quite properly relieved of any additional requirements he might have been directed to fulfill and the air carrier crew was able to return to the job of flying.

The steps one should follow in emergencies are as follows. The first step is to let a controller know what the problem is. Fortunately, no matter where in the United States a pilot happens to be flying, it is almost a certainty that someone working within the air traffic system will be able to hear her and also will probably be able to see her on radar.

The next step is for a pilot to inform the controller what actions she will take. Then, if there is enough time to benefit from that controller's help, she should request whatever assistance she needs. The sooner a pilot can tell the controller her intentions, the sooner the controller can respond by alerting ground personnel, providing emergency vectors, or giving any other needed assistance. Controllers can help to make the system work to a pilot's advantage and help her gain the upper hand during an emergency, but the more time the controllers have to accomplish the job, the better the outcome will be.

When You Are Lost

The most common occurrence that might be classified as an emergency is getting lost. It is so common because it is just so easy to do. In many respects the old saying that applies to pilots who fly retractable gear aircraft and land them gear up is even truer for pilots who get lost: "There are those who have and there are those who will." Getting lost is not only the plight of the student pilot, there have been more than a few cases where highly experienced pilots have become *temporarily disoriented* and even one or two instances where scheduled air carriers ended up landing at the wrong airports. Neither the experience level of the pilot nor the amount of sophisticated equipment in the airplane guarantees immunity from this particular disease.

Interestingly though, the emergency part of getting lost has less to do with getting into the predicament and much more to do with how a pilot reacts once she recognizes the situation. In many ways it is a pilot's state of mind that first gets her into the position of being lost and in just as many ways it is her state of mind that prevents her from getting out of it.

What I am talking about can best be illustrated by an encounter I had with a student pilot one afternoon as I was working an approach control position. In a rather tense tone of voice this pilot contacted me with the following transmission: "Pittsburgh Approach, this is November 123, I am over Butler County Airport and I am lost." I checked my radarscope, saw a target over the named airport, issued the pilot a transponder code to squawk, and waited for the results. Sure enough, the lost student was exactly where he said he was. So, if he knew where he was, why was he lost?

It turned out that what this student pilot was really trying to communicate was the fact that he somehow had gotten away from his planned route of flight and did not know how to get from his newly discovered position to Beaver County Airport some fifteen to twenty miles away. Specifically, he knew where he was—over an airport he was not about to lose sight of—but relative to the rest of the world around him, he was completely befuddled. The bad news was that he had all the information he needed to find himself but he did not know how to use it. The good news was that he did the right thing and contacted me when he still had plenty of fuel left to stay airborne while we worked out a solution. In this case the solution was radar vectors and close monitoring until he reported his destination in sight.

Exactly when that student first began to lose his situational awareness and the reasons behind his failings are hard to say. Some of the more common reasons why pilots go astray can be as simple as forgetting to reset a heading indicator that has precessed, incorrectly tuning and/or identifying a VOR station, a change from the expected winds aloft, or simply failing to accurately hold a planned heading. Regardless of how someone gets to that place where he would rather not be, what he does when he arrives should be the first priority.

If any of the quick fixes from a pilot's own bag of trick do not solve the problem within a reasonable amount of time, the next step should be to seek outside assistance. Despite the repeated rejoinders from just about every pilot publication and department in the FAA urging early notification of their plight, too many lost pilots wait until their fuel supply has dwindled to an uncomfortably low level before they call for help. It is worth remembering that, as long as a pilot has enough fuel in her airplane to keep it flying for more than an hour or so, being lost will be more of an inconvenience than an emergency. It is only when time starts running out that the problem becomes serious.

If getting help from the outside world is one of the first priorities, then how can that best be accomplished? First, set aside the idea that the place to start is with the emergency frequency. If the loss of situational awareness occurs while you are communicating with an air traffic controller or a flight service specialist, let them know what has happened. That action may seem to be terribly obvious, but what is absolutely clear to more experienced pilots may not be so for beginners. A controller who is providing radar traffic advisories is only a transmission away from helping a pilot resolve the issue of being lost, if he knows there is a problem. Even a flight service specialist working without radar can get the process started or direct you to an appropriate frequency where someone else can join in the search. The point is, if you are already talking to someone, do not give up that connection unless or until you have a solid alternative to go to.

If you happen not to be communicating with anyone on the ground when you realize that what should look familiar does not, the next best step is to go back to the last ATC or flight service frequency on which you had been talking to someone—another good reason to write down every planned or assigned frequency in the expected sequence. There are a couple of reasons to go backward in time. First, the person with whom you had worked already will have some familiarity with where you were in the not-too-distant past, so he can rather quickly narrow down the search area. Second, even though it may have been twenty or thirty minutes since the previous communication ended, since most basic training aircraft travel at something less than the speed of light, you will most likely still be within range of their radios.

EMERGENCY FREQUENCY

If options one and two either do not fit the situation or yield no results after they have been tried, then it is time to tune in 121.5, the emergency frequency, and ask for some help. Using 121.5 does not doom a pilot to a lifetime of stigmatization as an idiot of the air nor does it represent the beginning of a long line of bureaucratic hurdles to living life as a normal, unencumbered pilot. In fact, using the frequency when there is legitimate concern, regardless of the reason, is an indication that good judgment preceded the decision.

The one thing that can be guaranteed is that when a pilot makes a request on 121.5, someone (quite possibly several someones) will answer the call. Except for a few instances, every FAA facility in the country monitors the frequency. In addition, a lot of private, professional, and military pilots also make it a habit to monitor the frequency whenever they are on a flight. In the unlikely event that someone does not immediately answer a transmission on 121.5, rather than get upset at the silence, be patient and try again in a few minutes. It is a virtual certainty that after one or two tries, there will be a response to your call.

The fact that so many people listen to the emergency frequency is the reason that it is not always the best place to start to request assistance. Depending upon your altitude, the terrain, and, if another pilot responds to your call, her aircraft's altitude, the person responding easily could be one hundred or two hundred miles away from you. While it may be comforting to know that at least someone is listening, it may take a bit longer to determine a more exact location for you. Still, 121.5 is a viable option and one you should use if the need arises.

After you find someone, the next step in the process is knowing what to say when you make that connection. You will need to have some answers for the questions that most likely will be asked. Regardless of who answers, some of the information they will need to help locate you includes (1) your last known position; (2) how long you have been flying since then; (3) what heading you were flying; (4) whether you recently checked your heading indicator against the compass; (5) whether you have VOR or GPS equipment in the airplane and understand how to use it; and finally and not so incidentally, (6) how much fuel you have left, preferably in time instead of gallons. Rather than having to think, compute, and talk all at the same time, the pilot who can gather and organize this information ahead of time can make the process of getting found much easier on everyone involved, most especially herself.

Now that you have completed the most difficult part, admitting to yourself that you are lost and initiating the request for help, it is time for the other folks involved to take on their share of the burden, finding you. The good news is that there are so many different ways to find a lost pilot, that at least one of them always can be guaranteed to work. Yet the one thing all the methods have in common is that each takes a certain amount of time to accomplish. The single most significant contribution a lost pilot can make to achieve a successful resolution to her situation is to provide those people trying to find her the time they need to do their jobs.

RADAR

If I had to guess what percentage of lost pilots find their way through the use of radar, my answer would be about 90 percent. Typically it takes very little effort on either the part of the pilot or the controller to get the job done. On any given day across the country, there are dozens of pilots who get lost, contact a radar controller, and get found, all in the course of a few minutes. With so many towers, approach control facilities, and en route centers with radar that blankets so much of the airspace, it is difficult to end up in an area without coverage.

In some respects, the overwhelming odds that some ATC facility will have radar coverage for the area in which a pilot became disoriented is what creates concern for many inexperienced pilots. They wonder if the controller with whom they have made contact belongs to the airspace in which they are, at least for the moment, aimlessly flying about. But the chances are excellent that if a controller can hear a pilot, he or another controller responsible for nearby or adjacent airspace will be able to identify and locate that pilot on the radarscope.

In virtually every area of the country at least two or three radar facilities, whether towers, approach controls, en route centers, or any combination thereof, have overlapping radar coverage in particular areas. It is common practice for a controller who is searching for a lost pilot to contact controllers in neighboring facilities to assist in the search. If the pilot happens to be flying in one of those areas of overlapping coverage, what one controller misses, another will most likely find. But even if a lost pilot is talking to one controller but flying completely out of his airspace, that coordination among the other controllers in the adjacent areas means that almost always she will be found in a matter of minutes.

As with any situation in which radar identification is the objective, a transponder-equipped aircraft makes the process easier. But even if a pilot happens to be flying a non-transponder-equipped aircraft when she gets lost, it again just becomes a matter of flying the headings as assigned by the controller. If after a few minutes the assigned headings do not jibe with anything the controller is seeing on his scope—as with the case of an incorrectly set heading indicator—the controller likely will just issue a series of turns given in degrees rather than turns to specific headings. For example, instead of telling a pilot to turn to a heading of 270 degrees the controller might say, "turn thirty degrees left."

Regardless of what method is used to radar identify an aircraft, once the process is completed the problem of being lost has been solved. But as with the student who knew where he was but little else, unless you are confident that the remainder of your journey can be completed uneventfully, do not be afraid to ask a controller for additional assistance. Although it is not that common, neither is it unheard of to get lost more than once in the same day. If things do not seem to be going according to plan, of which being lost might just be such an indicator, take advantage of all the assistance that is available. In the long run it saves everyone a lot of time.

Over the years, as VFR pilots have gone from occasionally talking to controllers and rarely working in a radar environment to making it a part of everyday flying, using that service as a means of finding their way has become a much easier and more natural reaction to solving their problems. Likewise, since so many radar controllers work with lost pilots at one time or another, they are both comfortable with and proficient in the ways of providing assistance to those pilots. Using radar to answer the age-old question of where am I is not the only solution to the problem but it is one no pilot ever should hesitate to use.

DIRECTION FINDING NETWORK

If for some reason radar does not do the trick or is not available, another equally efficient and successful method for finding lost pilots is the *Direction Finding Network* (DF Net). The beauty of the DF Net stems from its reliability and simplicity. The entire process depends upon using the signal from an aircraft's radio transmitter to establish a pilot's location.

The DF Net uses one or preferably more lines of position to determine the location of origin of the radio, and therefore the pilot. In a process similar to using two or more VOR signals to pinpoint where an airplane is, the DF Net, when activated, provides controllers and/or flight-service specialists a means by which they can determine an aircraft's bearing from each respective station. As with VOR signals, when the bearings from at least two stations are compared, the point at which they cross corresponds to the aircraft's location.

The ground equipment used consists of a small scope, similar in appearance to a radarscope with a compass rose encircling it. When a pilot keys her transmitter and is within range of the receiver on the ground, a single line appears on the scope. That line represents the aircraft's location relative to that receiver. For example if the line on the scope points to a bearing of 330 degrees, that indicates that the aircraft in question is northwest of the station. A second station might receive a bearing indication of 060 degrees. After plotting on a chart where those lines of position cross, a process that the ground personnel can accomplish, they can accurately determine a pilot's exact location. Even if only one station is used, at the very least, the controller or flight service specialist can advise a pilot how to get to that station and provide her with a known location from which to proceed.

To activate the DF Net you should place a call to flight service. That is not to say that an approach control or an en route center cannot get the ball rolling, but a flight service station, if it is not part of the DF Net for a given area, will have the most accurate information about what facilities are. In addition, the specialists at flight service can contact the various facilities that need to get involved without a pilot having to try a couple of different frequencies.

Once everyone is alerted, a specialist or a controller, if the pilot happens to have made her initial contact with an ATC facility, will advise a pilot to key her radio transmitter. They may ask her to count to ten and back, but actually talking into the mike is really not necessary. Just keying her transmitter will get the job done. The act of counting ensures the radio signal will be produced long enough to get an accurate and reliable indication from which to plot a location.

Although many DF Nets are set up to utilize one or more of the most commonly used air traffic control frequencies in an area, often a pilot will be advised to change to 121.5, the emergency frequency. The fact that the emergency frequency is used should not be cause for alarm. The only reason it is used is that since almost every ATC and flight service facility in the country share 121.5, its use reduces the coordination necessary to get everyone working from the same page. It also produces a much greater likelihood that at least two stations will be able to hear a pilot and, therefore, more accurately narrow down her position.

The *Direction Finding Network* has been around for a long time and its efficacy with respect to locating lost pilots has proven successful over and over again. Since the pilot, who already may be suffering a certain amount of anxiety, need do nothing more than key her microphone button, any added workload or stress that might be created with other methods is almost nonexistent when DF is used and the results are every bit as accurate as when radar is used. For many pilots over the years, DF has been a win-win situation.

PILOTAGE

Still another method by which lost pilots are often found is really just a variation on pilotage. Though this process is decidedly less scientific than the previous ones, it too has met with its share of successes over the years. The process consists of nothing more than a pilot describing what she sees out the window. But probably more than any of the other means by which lost pilots can be found, successful pilotage depends almost entirely on how accurately a pilot describes her surroundings.

If she happens to be lucky enough to get lost in the vicinity of Mt. Rushmore, for example, finding her should be a breeze. If she is not fortunate enough to be in proximity to some uniquely identifiable landmark or her perspective on what she sees is skewed, the process can take quite a bit longer. I once worked with a lost pilot who described one particular ground feature as a "little lake in front of him." The little lake turned out to be Lake Erie, a lake that on a day with less than stellar visibility occasionally keeps its opposite shore hidden. Add to that lesson the fact that it is not unheard of to be as much as one hundred to two hundred miles off course or the fact that one town in the Midwest with a train track running through it is like a dozen others and the process becomes a bit more difficult.

Pilotage does work, but the success of the outcome depends upon the objectivity of the person reporting the view and is almost always more time-consuming than other methods. It is okay to make it the method of choice but if after ten minutes or so of providing descriptions no tangible results are realized, the best advice is to ask for additional help. For reasons of which I am unsure, both controllers and other pilots who try to help a lost pilot find herself sometimes hang on to one method when it just does not provide the desired outcome. Too often the only results are a lot of time wasted and a pilot whose anxiety and alarm at the situation only heighten. Pilotage is always worth a try; just do not get locked into the idea that it is the only available solution.

SIGHTING BY AIRCRAFT

According to the controller's manual, one other way that may be used to help a lost pilot find her way is through sighting by another aircraft. That is, the problem may be resolved either by a controller vectoring one aircraft to the presumed location of another or by chance that a pilot flying in an area is both listening to a lost pilot and accidentally sees her in the air.

The only time I was involved with asking another pilot to help with a lost pilot was a sort of variation on sighting by another aircraft. Although I found the lost pilot on radar, a variety of factors combined to render him unable to use the information I gave him to return to the airport. Evidently this pilot had spent a lot of time trying to resolve the situation by himself. In the process he started to get low on fuel, had made so many twists and turns that he had little idea which way was up, and soon would face the unfamiliar task of flying after the sun went down. All those things combined to cause panic to linger just below the surface.

After more than a few minutes of trying various procedures unsuccessfully, I started to run out of ideas. Fortunately a pilot who had been listening to the ordeal on the frequency volunteered to lead the lost pilot home. After willingly accepting his offer, I vectored our rescuer to a position in front of the other pilot and pointed him out. After sighting what would turn out to be the lead aircraft, the relieved pilot dutifully and successfully followed him back to the airport and the story had a happy ending.

If we accept that, at one time or another, each of us who takes to the air on our own will become temporarily disoriented, then we can also accept that there are a lot of ways to bring resolution to the problem. We only have to ask in time for one of them to be implemented and carried out, with no strings attached. As long as we get found and proceed on our merry way without a major incident or accident occurring in the process, no lengthy explanations or reams of paperwork will follow the event. Getting lost is something that happens every day and helping a pilot find her way is equally uneventful to controllers and flight service specialists. It is just part of what they do, so should the need ever arise do not hesitate to give them the opportunity to do their jobs. It would be only foolhardy to let a relatively minor inconvenience turn into a major mishap.

When the Radio Dies

Those of us who have been flying for a few years can remember when general aviation aircraft radios left a lot to be desired. What those antiques known as "coffee grinders" lacked in ease of use and reliability they made up for in weight and bulkiness. Add to that the fact that the chances of always cranking in the correct frequency the first time were about as good as the chances that the person talking from the ground would actually be clear enough to understand.

Fortunately, today's general aviation pilots enjoy the use of sophisticated communications equipment with an incredibly strong history of reliability. In addition, with the exception of some of the most basic of training aircraft, most of the light planes that are flown with any regularity these days are equipped with dual communications radios. If for some reason the first one fails to work, a flip of the switch to the other usually resolves the problem. Also, more and more pilots are carrying a handheld transceiver in their flight bags just in case. The result of all these advances is, I suspect, that pilots feel protected against the complete inability to talk to anyone outside of their own little cocoon.

However, if there is any possibility that something can go wrong with any or all of the radios in an airplane (which is as much a probability as a possibility), knowing the proper way to deal with the problem can take the sting out of a potentially nasty situation and turn it into an exercise in confidence and discipline. If that is true, then when if ever is the loss of the ability to communicate an emergency? How do we, as pilots, know if it is an emergency and how do we act based upon the conclusions we reach?

The *AIM* provides as good a generalized approach to the subject as any I have seen:

> It is virtually impossible to provide regulations and procedures applicable to all possible situations associated with two-way radio communications failure. During two-way radio communications failure, when confronted by a situation not covered in the regulations, pilots are expected to exercise good judgment in whatever action they elect to take. Should the situation so dictate they should not be reluctant to use the emergency action contained in CFR Section 91.3(b).
>
> Whether two-way communications failure constitutes an emergency depends upon the circumstances, and in any event, it is a determination made by the pilot.

The amount of experience and expertise a pilot has and how often she has engaged in the mental gymnastics of the what-if game most likely will determine whether she views the comments from the AIM as appropriate to her pilot-in-command abilities or vague and lacking in direction. The AIM extract above is advising pilots to know the relevant existing regulations and, when regulations do not cover the situation, to make wise decisions and be careful. As always, a good decision at the end depends upon accurate and comprehensive knowledge at the beginning.

To begin with, when a VFR pilot loses her ability to communicate with people on the ground, seldom should that condition result in a serious or an emergency situation. The easiest solution to the problem is to locate an uncontrolled airport that is conveniently within reach and land there. The greatest concern in that instance should be that, since presumably every other pilot in the area who is capable of communicating on the correct *Common Traffic Advisory Frequency (CTAF)* is doing so, one who is not easily may be overlooked.

Although caution and diligence always should be exercised when operating into or out of an uncontrolled airport, both should be kicked up a notch when arriving unannounced. Since the pilot can't be heard, she needs to increase her chances of being seen. Turning on every light on the airplane prior to entering the traffic pattern can only increase the likelihood of being spotted. After that, it is just a matter of following normal procedures until clearing the active runway.

The specific airport a pilot opts to use after she has suffered a radio failure is entirely her choice to make, but consideration should be given to how much traffic is likely to be in the area and what repair facilities are available. If the most favored choice is, in fact, a controlled airport, the best option would be to first land at an uncontrolled airport and then try to make advanced arrangements before proceeding to the towered airport. Knowing when and from where a no-radio aircraft is arriving makes the process a lot easier on everyone involved.

When that is neither possible nor practical, you must look to the rules and procedures that exist. The first of those that ought to be implemented is to set the aircraft's transponder, if so equipped, to 7600, the lost communications code, *regardless of whether or not the airport is associated with a radar facility*. Even if the tower at the airport has neither radar nor an approach control facility located there, there still is a strong likelihood that some radar coverage exists. If that is true, when a controller notices the 7600 code on his radarscope, he will most likely notify the tower controller when the evidence suggests that the airport under his direction appears to be the destination of the aircraft involved. In any case, squawking 7600 cannot hurt and it can certainly help.

The second action is to *transmit in the blind*. That is, state your problem, state your intentions, and transmit continuous position reports under the assumption that, while your radio receiver may be inoperative, perhaps the transmitter is still working. If that is true, transmitting your intentions eliminates the element of surprise for the controllers and the other pilots in the area. This ought to be accomplished regardless of whether your destination is a controlled or an uncontrolled airport, but particularly when there is a control tower in operation.

With the previous two items completed, it is time to press onward. For airports that have no associated radar approach control, the procedures dictate that a pilot should remain outside of or above the Class D surface area until the direction and flow of traffic has been determined. That gives her an opportunity to determine the flow without actually getting in anyone's way, and to look for other traffic and decide how to fit in among the other airplanes. At this point it is critical to realize that, unless the tower controller has been alerted to the impending arrival by a radar controller somewhere, neither she nor the other pilots will be expecting an unknown aircraft to suddenly pop up in the area. Realistically, the person flying the no-radio airplane will be the one responsible for almost all the collision avoidance.

After having determined the traffic flow and traffic situation, the safest approach is to make a standard downwind entry into the pattern at pattern altitude. In the case of a receiver-only operation for which the tower controller either has been informed of the problem or has determined that your arrival is imminent, it becomes a matter of listening for and following his instructions. During the daytime, you will be asked to acknowledge receipt of the controller's transmissions by rocking your wings. At night the acknowledgment is made by flashing landing or navigation lights.

If nothing is working and your radios have become little more than expensive panel covers, it is time to start looking toward the tower for light gun signals. The light gun is an effective means of communicating instructions to a pilot in both daytime and nighttime conditions, but only if the pilot looks for the signal. A light gun produces an effective but very narrow beam of light when aimed at an airplane cockpit. It is neither so broad nor blinding that someone who is not consciously looking for it is likely to notice. Beyond that, the pilot is responsible for knowing what the various signs mean.

The most important signals are also the easiest to remember. Steady green means cleared to land. Steady red means give way to other aircraft and continue circling, and flashing red means that the airport is unsafe and a landing should not be attempted. It is best either to know what all the signals mean or to have that information readily available in the cockpit, but those three should at least keep most pilots out of serious trouble.

If, after very carefully looking for a light gun signal, a pilot concludes that none are being sent, it may be time to make the decision to invoke her emergency authority, but only with the clear understanding that in doing so she may bend or set aside some existing regulations. With respect to an unannounced aircraft arriving into a traffic pattern, the reality is that other pilots are not the only people who overlook an unexpected airplane; controllers often do the same thing. How likely it is that a controller will notice an unexpected airplane is inversely proportional to how restricted the airspace is in which it will be flying.

Much to my dismay, I was one of the people in the tower at Pittsburgh when a no-radio glider landed alongside of one of our primary arrival runways and went unnoticed until the pilot later called us on the phone. When he first described his predicament I thought it was a prank call. Only after checking his supposed landing site through the binoculars did I accept that he was telling the truth. The fact that none of the dozen or so subsequent arrivals made mention of the glider helped us to feel a bit less foolish, but it did not completely erase our embarrassment.

At any rate, for the pilot of a no-radio aircraft, if she has repeatedly looked for a light gun signal but has seen none, her options are either to land without a clearance, go around and re-enter the traffic pattern and hope for better luck the second time, or proceed to another airport and follow the recommended procedures there. In many instances, if a pilot has looked carefully for other traffic and has made every effort to ensure that the runway is clear of any aircraft or other obstructions, landing without a clearance may be the safest available option. Taking any action that possibly is in violation of an FAR is never an easy thing to do, but occasionally it is one of those unpleasant decisions that a pilot is required to make.

One communication method that deserves at least brief mention is the cell phone. I know of at least one instance (with many more suspected) in which a pilot who lost all power to his avionics and aircraft lights phoned the approach control at his destination to inform them of his problem and his arrival. While the FCC may have been less than happy with his choice, I suspect the controllers were only too happy to have answered the call. Good judgment and good decisions come in many different forms.

For the VFR pilot who finds herself faced with the loss of her radios while flying in Class B or C airspace, besides squawking 7600, her first action should be cautiously and nonabruptly leaving the airspace. When operating in the outskirts of the area or just passing through it, finding the quickest way out that also will keep a pilot out of the mix of arriving and departing traffic is likely to cause the least amount of disruption. If a pilot knows she already has been sequenced into her arrival slot, realistically she may be better off using the lost-communications procedures that have been developed for the instrument pilots. VFR pilots are not specifically covered by most of these regulations, but it is an area that, regardless of the vagueness of the applicability, may have to be considered.

When a pilot is flying in VFR conditions and her radios quit working, she gets some idea of what it must be like to be deaf. When the same situation occurs inside the cloud, blindness is added to the list of handicaps. It is a time when, almost above all else, the one thing a pilot wants to be certain of is that some controller somewhere knows where she is and has a reasonable idea of where she is going from there. Sitting in the cockpit with nothing but the sound of the engine to keep her company can be a bit unnerving. In addition to that, it is extremely easy to imagine that those controllers on the ground who moments earlier had been an integral part of her life, have suddenly forgotten that she ever existed. Fortunately, just the opposite is true. Since those controllers will have lost the capability to verbally confirm her actions, they will be very carefully monitoring her radar target while trying to anticipate her actions. If that pilot upholds her end of the pilot/controller partnership, she can be assured the controller or controllers involved with the situation will do the same.

For the instrument pilot, once a controller receives a 7600 transponder code, the wheels are put in motion to deal with the problem. For both the IFR pilot and the VFR pilot who had been receiving radar service, the first two items on a controller's to-do list probably will relate to an attempt to reestablish some form of communication. With the hope that the pilot's problem with her radios may only be the loss of her transmitting capability, the controller will take his turn at transmitting in the blind—something the pilot likewise always should try. The acknowledgment he will be looking for would then come from the aircraft's transponder. Something like "Mooney eight delta whiskey, if you hear me ident" is what a pilot likely would hear. If that works, the controller knows that a big part of the problem has been solved.

The second item deals with a pilot's navigation radios. Particularly if the controller knows that the pilot has been navigating toward a VOR, either within house or with the assistance of flight service, the controller will use the voice capability of that VOR to transmit instructions to her, again using a transponder reply as the means of acknowledgment. So, for a pilot, if her communications radios fail, her next step ought to be to listen over the closest or currently-in-use VOR for possible instructions. It is the next best thing to a full-blown conversation.

One of the next things a controller will do is to ensure that every other controller down the line knows that you will be entering his airspace and second that he also knows that you have lost your ability to communicate. For the instrument pilot that means that, but for the exceptions that shortly will be noted, she needs only to follow his clearance as issued and the controllers will follow through with their responsibilities by moving other traffic out of the way. For the VFR pilot who already had been directed to a position in the arrival sequence, though not specifically stated in the regulations, the best action to take would be to continue inbound to the airport and land on the previously assigned runway. In that case, because she is established in the sequence, her arrival should come as no surprise to the tower controller and a light gun landing authorization should be assured.

In a nonradar environment the controllers cannot see the transponder reply that alerts radar controllers to a pilot's loss of radios, but other factors will make her plight known to them. In the world of nonradar, compulsory reports by pilots are numerous and frequent. Any time a pilot misses even one of those required reports or does not respond to a single transmission from a controller, the hunt begins. In addition, if the nonradar area is underlying an area of radar coverage, in all likelihood the controller in whose airspace the 7600 code appears—reason to always use the code as conditions require—will alert the controller responsible for the aircraft. Before too long, the news will be out.

The requirements and responsibilities of the controller are really rather simple. Make sure every other controller who will or even might be involved with the no-radio aircraft knows about it well ahead of time. Make sure that every other aircraft that does or could represent a potential conflict for the incommunicado pilot is moved out of the way. It is the controller's responsibility to ensure a no-radio aircraft has clear sailing with respect to other traffic. It is the pilot's responsibility to follow the remaining procedures and regulations.

That being said, it is essential that pilots never assume that controllers know or understand the pilot's role in a lost communications situation. Controllers have to fulfill their own responsibilities and obligations, and they expect that pilots know and follow the rules that have been developed for them. That is not to suggest that unless a pilot is a walking encyclopedia of FARs she is in deep trouble, but when a pilot is unable to communicate with air traffic controllers, a critical safety net is lost. The overlapping responsibilities for safety that pilots and controllers share no longer exist. To the greatest extent possible, a pilot who is working without any assistance from the ground has to do just about everything right the first time. Controllers base their traffic separation procedures on the assumption that an instrument pilot knows what to do when her radios quit. Pilots have to know what to do to stay out of trouble with respect to all other aspects of their flight.

There are procedures that have been developed to keep pilots from hitting the ground or other obstructions. There are procedures that cover all of the normal circumstances that enable a pilot to navigate to her destination. And there are procedures a pilot can use to safely execute an approach and landing once she arrives there. The best a pilot can do is to develop a basic understanding and working knowledge of how to use each of them if or when her radios fail, and then exercise some common sense and good judgment when implementing them. The best controllers can do is to carefully monitor the pilot's actions and anticipate that she will fly what would be considered a normal flight profile.

Controllers may not be intimately familiar with all the regulations that govern a pilot's actions after she has experienced a radio failure, but they do have a sense of what should or should not happen during the course of a typical flight. How those controllers alter the flow of traffic around or away from a no-radio aircraft is based upon that understanding. Without question, any controller who is responsible for ensuring separation between a no-radio aircraft and his other traffic will provide a reasonable margin for error in case the pilot who is unable to communicate her intentions does something slightly unexpected. But that controller will also assume that he and that pilot share a baseline understanding of what is slightly unexpected as opposed to what is completely unanticipated. It is the responsibility of each pilot to ensure that such an assumption is a valid one.

For example, a controller may not know that a pilot who has lost her radios should fly the highest of three designated altitude possibilities or four route alternatives, but he has a clear expectation of what a pilot's actions should likely be at any given time. If the pilot is flying at an assigned altitude of 4,000 feet and ahead lies a mountain at 4,500 feet, the controller will anticipate that she will climb to a safe altitude and, therefore, he will move any conflicting traffic accordingly. Conversely, if the same pilot had been flying at 8,000 feet in the same area, the controller would not be anticipating any change in the aircraft's altitude. If a pilot were to unexpectedly make such a change, regardless of the reason, there would be a strong likelihood that the required safe separation between her aircraft and another might be lost. The procedures and regulations that govern a pilot's actions when dealing with the loss of her radios actually provide her with a logical, predictable path to follow. Whenever possible, staying on that path is the best assurance that everyone's expectations will be met.

Occasionally, though, a pilot who has lost her radios may find herself faced with a situation in which the regulations leave room for individual interpretation. One of the procedures laid out for pilots relates to how weather conditions should affect her decision-making process. It states, "If the failure occurs in VFR conditions, or if VFR conditions are encountered after the failure, each pilot shall continue the flight under VFR and land as soon as practicable."

That regulation, however, is not as hard and fast as it sounds. Suppose a pilot on an IFR clearance were flying in VFR conditions on top of an overcast layer when her radios fail. Sixty miles behind her there are no clouds, so a descent could be made in VFR conditions. Her original destination is only fifteen miles away, but the weather there is IFR. Should the pilot turn around and return to the VFR conditions or should she fly the instrument approach and land at her originally planned destination? The answer is that either solution would be legal.

Remember that the regulation states that a pilot should land as soon as *practicable*, not as soon as possible. A note accompanying that procedure states in part, "Pilots retain the prerogative of exercising their best judgment and are not required to land at an unauthorized airport, at an airport unsuitable for the type of aircraft flown, or to land only minutes short of their intended destination." Even with the mounds of regulations in existence, occasionally pilots are afforded the opportunity to make their own determination with respect to what is the best course of action to follow.

The point to remember is that a pilot should not and can not allow procedures that were developed for her welfare to become so restrictive that they actually cause her more harm than good. Different pilots faced with different circumstances are bound to react differently. The regulations allow for those differences. In spite of occasional interpretations to the contrary, none of the regulations by which pilots operate were developed to take the place of good judgment. As pilots we must never allow the expedience of regulatory compliance to take place at the expense of our personal responsibilities as pilots-in-command.

Whether we do our flying IFR or VFR, it is important to take the time to learn what to do when the radios quit working. For VFR pilots who often receive the same services as their IFR counterparts, it could mean solving the problem with much less confusion than might otherwise develop. For instrument pilots, it could mean the difference between having a confidence-inspiring experience and one that should have been cancelled before it ever got started.

One final point to remember is that, regardless of how a pilot handles an in-flight radio failure, if ATC had been at all involved with the flight when the failure occurred, upon landing she should call the closest air traffic or flight service facility and advise them of her safe arrival. I remember watching as a controller I worked with aged what seemed like ten years after an airplane he was controlling suddenly disappeared from his radarscope. It turned out that the pilot who had been operating on an instrument flight plan experienced a complete electrical failure en route. Since he had been flying in VFR conditions, he acted correctly and landed at the first suitable airport he found after the failure. His quick phone call after landing brought a huge sigh of relief from the entire radar room.

What Goes Up

I remember once asking the pilot of an air carrier flight that I had kept at a higher than usual altitude for a longer than usual period of time if he would be able to get down. In that deep gravelly voice that so often seemed to accompany airline pilots before women began to grace the cockpit he replied, "Son, I haven't left one up here yet." While the same comment repeated almost verbatim over the years led me to realize the originator of it probably had long since passed from the scene, its validity always will be there. Whether we like it or not, either at a time and place of our choosing or when the laws of physics overrule our intentions, any airplane we take from the ground eventually will return to it.

For the VFR pilot who has continued to experience her expected weather conditions, her return to earth is the culmination of a well-executed plan. But if her world of visual orientation has or is about to unexpectedly turn gray, life can get decidedly more interesting. Any time a VFR pilot is about to log some unexpected actual instrument time, there are a couple of basic premises she needs to keep in mind.

The first is that, nobody else is going to be able to do the flying for her, so keeping her aircraft under control is the single most critical priority. If that goes by the wayside, little else matters. The second point is that, depending upon a host of variables, there are some things that controllers can do to lessen the severity of the situation. Learning to control an airplane in instrument conditions is beyond the scope of this book. Learning how controllers can assist a pilot in distress, however, is worthy of some discussion.

Although controllers cannot get inside the cockpit and fly the airplane out of the problem, they can be a valuable resource for a VFR pilot who is in the midst of or is about to experience life inside the clouds, but only if they are aware of the situation. Putting aside fear of retribution or embarrassment and admitting that she needs help, for a pilot, should be second only to keeping the airplane under control. Gaining a better understanding of the kind of help that is available once the situation is out in the open can significantly simplify the decision-making process.

Many of the instances that involve VFR pilots who are about to encounter instrument conditions relate to getting caught on top of a cloud layer that unexpectedly closes in under them. Fortunately, this dilemma can be approached with a variety of workable solutions. The first is helping a pilot remove herself from the problem altogether.

Controllers have the ability to quickly gather a lot of information about weather conditions for a very broad area. Through a combination of pilot reports, various other air traffic controllers and flight service specialists, real-time weather information for almost the entire area that is within the range of her airplane can be provided for a pilot who is caught on top. The result is that frequently a pilot who thought a descent through the clouds was imminent ends up being able to fly to VFR conditions from where her flight can then continue.

When a descent in VFR conditions isn't in the cards, there are still a number of ways that controllers can assist a pilot. When an untrained pilot has to make a descent in instrument conditions, her objectives revolve around two considerations. The first is maintaining control of her plane, thereby preventing a situation that overstresses it. The second is assuring herself that VFR conditions will be reached well before terrain or obstructions interfere with her flight path.

With respect to the first consideration, a controller may not be able to grab the controls of the airplane, but he can help a pilot get into a position where any required maneuvering can be accomplished before she enters the clouds. For a variety of reasons, a straight gradual descent through the clouds is the safest way to get the job done.

In addition, if the airplane has retractable landing gear, the controller most likely will suggest that the pilot lower her gear prior to entering the clouds. That alone decreases the likelihood that the plane will accelerate beyond its never-exceed speed in the descent, which further reduces the chances that a pullout at the bottom will overstress the aircraft. It is similar to the situation when a person falls from the top of a five-story building. It isn't the fall that causes the damage; it's the sudden stop at the end.

Regarding the second point, again through the use of his network of resources, a controller can position a pilot in a location where she is all but guaranteed that her descent through the clouds will be completed at an altitude that is well above any solid objects on the ground. That valuable reassurance should enable a pilot to shift her concentration to where it belongs, that of flying the plane.

When a pilot ends up in the clouds before she is able to contact ATC for assistance, the element of surprise has a greater impact on how effectively each is able to contribute to a successful outcome, but as long as she keeps the plane flying, it is far from hopeless. Getting the airplane down in one piece will still be the sole responsibility of the pilot. Making sure that plane does not hit anything harder than the wispy vapor in the air is still the most valuable asset a controller can bring to the situation.

When the weather below is not cooperating and VFR conditions are nowhere to be found, an option that is available for either a VFR pilot trapped in the weather or an IFR pilot who has experienced instrument failure is the controller-assisted approach. In both circumstances, one of these approaches may be the easiest and safest way to get to a runway.

The first of these is the *Precision Approach Radar* or *PAR approach* and it easily can make one reminiscent of watching Jimmy Stewart being brought home on the *beam* through some of the worst weather imaginable. To fly the approach a pilot need only possess a working two-way radio and the ability to control her aircraft as directed by the controller. But it is important to remember that PAR approaches, though available for use by civilian aircraft, are only available at selected locations around the country, almost all of which are military installations.

A PAR approach is similar to an *ILS approach*. It is a precision approach that affords a pilot with both vertical and lateral electronic guidance to the runway. One of the main differences is that, instead of guidance being provided by localizer and glideslope needles in the aircraft, radar data from the ground provide the controller with the means to keep a pilot accurately aligned with the runway and in a proper descent to the ground.

Using one or sometimes two separate radarscopes, a controller is able to see an aircraft in both its lateral and vertical path as it progresses toward the runway. By issuing a pilot instructions in relation to her aircraft's position relative to an extended runway centerline and a glideslope that are depicted on the scope, he can accurately guide a pilot to within a couple of hundred feet of the runway threshold. When conditions are such that flying the plane requires a pilot's full concentration, a PAR approach may be the answer to her much-needed relief.

A more frequently, but equally effective controller-assisted approach is the *Airport Surveillance Radar* or *ASR approach*. Though not quite as precise as a PAR approach, an ASR approach can be conducted at most airports that have a radar approach control associated with them. The easiest way to describe an ASR approach is that it is similar to a localizer approach except that instead of following the information derived from the on-board localizer needle, a controller provides a pilot with guidance directions based upon the radar target location as displayed on his scope.

By reducing the usual range of airspace coverage on his radarscope to a much smaller range, the depicted runway centerline is displayed with much greater detail and accuracy. Through the process of continually issuing head-ings to a pilot, the controller is able to keep his aircraft target aligned with the runway. Add to that the capability to provide a pilot with accurate dis-tance information and, when requested, recommended minimum altitudes for each mile on final, and the ASR approach becomes a valuable alternative to a standard instrument approach to a runway. As with the PAR approach, when flying an ASR approach a pilot need only listen to the controller's instructions and fly her airplane accordingly to ensure a successful outcome.

In addition, a method of assistance that is sometimes used in conjunction with airport surveillance radar is the *No Gyro ASR approach*. Beyond all of the procedures that are used with a surveillance approach, should a pilot lose the use of her heading indicator or any other equipment that would make it difficult to fly a predetermined heading, the controller can provide an alter-native solution. Instead of issuing a pilot a specific heading to fly, the con-troller will advise her when to begin the turn and when to stop it. Using one or more timed standard-rate turns, a controller can watch a target's track on his radarscope, determine the number of degrees the ground track needs to be altered to produce the desired track, and then have a pilot start and stop her turn accordingly to achieve the desired results. The only on-board equip-ment besides a working radio that a pilot needs to conduct a No Gyro ASR approach, is a turn coordinator or turn-and-slip indicator. It may sound as though a pilot flying this type of an approach is coming home on the prover-bial wing and a prayer, but it is one that has been used often and with remarkable success.

When Time Is Running Out

Up to this point, everything we have looked at with respect to emergency sit-uations has been of the type that affords a pilot one of the greatest luxuries she could ask for—time. The nature of each potential problem was such that we could look at it carefully, analyze many of the available options, and, after careful deliberation, decide what was the best course of action to follow. Unfortunately, given the dynamic nature of flying, there are many instances in which the opportunity for developing a carefully thought out response is not available. When those situations arise pilots need to be able to react quickly in order to successfully resolve the issue. That is not to suggest that acting in haste without thinking about the consequences of our actions is very likely to produce an acceptable outcome. Rather, we should think about pos-sible solutions ahead of time.

Most pilots go through the drills for commonly anticipated emergency situations. Whether flying a single-engine aircraft or a twin, they religiously practice the steps to follow after an engine failure occurs. In-flight fires, unexpected icing conditions, and control malfunctions are also occurrences for which procedures, checklists, and practiced responses have been devel-oped in one form or another. While anything that contributes to a pilot's ability to act efficiently and effectively in the face of an unexpected threat to her safety and well-being is worth learning (and learning very well), sometimes a valuable resource is left out of the drills, and that is the controller.

PARTNERSHIP

The time to think about what controllers can or cannot do to help a pilot in the midst of a time-critical situation is not as it is developing, but ahead of time, when rational thought is more apt to be a planned event as opposed to a welcome surprise. What many pilots do not realize is that in an emergency situation there are often certain things that controllers can do to help reduce a pilot's workload thereby freeing up her available time for the newly introduced and, in all likelihood, unexpected priorities she is confronted with. There are also some steps that pilots can take in partnership with the controllers that can help them to avoid or minimize any added dangers that, rather than being unavoidable consequences of the problem, may be incidental sidebars to the main issue. Knowing what tasks can be altered, shared, or eliminated from a pilot's burden can have a positive impact on how successfully a problem is handled.

One of the best examples I ever saw with respect to how pilots and controllers working together can find success in a way that otherwise would have been impossible involved a military jet that was returning to Pittsburgh one evening after a routine training exercise. About thirty miles west of Pittsburgh, one of the two pilots observed that his partner's aircraft was shooting flames out of a place not meant for fire. After briefly discussing the risks associated with continuing inbound over a populated area, the pilot of the burning jet decided to eject.

One of the most obvious problems that confronted him was where to discard his plane. Saving himself only to have the flaming wreckage rain down upon an unsuspecting neighborhood did not seem like an option. He then asked the approach controller if he could advise him when he was nearing the Ohio River, planning to put the A-7 in the water. Using a video map on which the river was depicted, the controller informed the pilot that he indeed could give him an accurate indication of his relationship to the river. At the appointed time, the pilot evidently aimed the jet toward the river and abandoned ship.

The controller then marked the exact locations at which the pilot left the aircraft and where it then disappeared from the scope. During the course of the next thirty or forty minutes, several different aircraft were vectored to the spot of the pilot's departure and radio contact with the downed pilot finally was established. As the controller vectored a rescue helicopter to the vicinity, unable to hear the pilot directly, messages were relayed to him from the circling aircraft in an attempt to help the rescue crew pinpoint the pilot. After more than a few tense moments, the helicopter was able to land and later transport the pilot to a local hospital. The aircraft landed on the riverbank and, other than destroying some vegetation, did no other damage.

There were a lot of different factors that came together to contribute to a successful outcome that night, and luck or fate certainly was one of them.

But the fact that there were also a lot of people committed to making the best out of a very difficult situation had a tremendous influence on the results. As I thought about it afterward, it became clear to me just how important knowing what resources are available and how to most effectively employ them can be when an emergency arises.

Although that pilot decided that an off-airport landing was the most appropriate course of action, when an in-flight fire, an engine failure, or any other circumstance that requires an immediate descent for landing occurs, finding a suitable airport becomes one of the highest priorities. If a pilot is in contact with a radar controller, the most effective solution to the problem is to ask him to provide vectors to the closest available airport. Although the *Direct-to* feature on most GPS units can provide some of the same information, there are added advantages to working with a controller.

To begin with, a lot of the workload can be shifted from the cockpit to the controller. He can provide vectors, accurate distance and groundspeed information and he can often provide the guidance necessary to enable a pilot to properly align her aircraft with the closest runway, even before it is in sight. In instrument conditions, even when an approved approach is not available, controllers often can provide a pilot with crucial information regarding terrain and obstructions along the way.

If the chosen airport has a control tower, the radar controller will alert the controllers in the tower, and they will ensure that any and, if necessary, every runway is clear of traffic. Even the landing clearance will be relayed to a pilot by the radar controller. When an uncontrolled airport seems to be the best choice, requesting that the controller contact another pilot on his frequency to have that pilot use the appropriate traffic frequency at the airport to alert all other pilots to his situation can provide added assurance that no other aircraft will be in the way. The controller will also have available any information the pilot needs with respect to runway length, field lighting, or any other unique conditions that may exist.

OFF-AIRPORT LANDING

When there is no suitable airport within gliding distance, the decision becomes a matter of choosing the best available alternative, and here too controllers can help. Controllers are able to display most of the major highways in the area that may serve as an option, and they can also display cities and other more populated areas that should be avoided. Maybe most important, they can maintain communications with a pilot throughout all but the last few moments of the flight and mark the exact location the aircraft disappeared from the scope. If, in addition to the radar location, a pilot is able to give a description of her landing site to the controller while she is still in the air, it significantly improves his ability to direct others to the same place.

Pilots who are faced with an imminent off-airport landing but who are not in contact with a controller or anyone else can still take some steps to increase the chances that someone somewhere may be made aware of their situation. If the airplane is equipped with a transponder, one of the first things to do is to set 7700, the emergency code, into it. Any controller who observes an emergency code on his scope—which is all but impossible to miss—will track the associated radar target just as he would if he were in contact with the plane's pilot. When the target ceases to display a radar return, the controller will then take action to get some assistance to that location. That alone can significantly reduce the search area and, consequently, the time involved in finding a downed plane.

The next step a pilot can take to enhance her opportunity for rescue is to tune in 121.5, the emergency frequency, and use it for the remainder of her transmissions. Even if she cannot contact anyone on the frequency, she should provide an on-going narrative of the situation by transmitting in the blind. Even though there is no guarantee that anyone is receiving the information, by broadcasting what is happening, where she is, and where she will be landing, it opens the door for assistance that otherwise would not be available. It is not at all unusual for a controller or another pilot to hear the transmission even though the person making them is unable to receive any reply. In any case, it is always worth making the effort to try.

ENGINE FAILURE AT NIGHT

If a pilot ever experiences an engine failure at night, the procedure my first instructor offered over thirty years ago is as dear to my heart now as it was when first I heard it. Configure your airplane for best glide speed, align your aircraft into the wind, and, as may be best determined by who knows what means, decide upon the best possible landing site. Then, upon reaching an altitude of approximately two hundred to three hundred feet above the ground, turn on the landing light. If you like what you see, leave the light on. If not, turn it off as quickly as possible. Some long-held ideas are trite and meaningless; others carry the wisdom of the world in their words. You decide.

RUNNING OUT OF FUEL

One of the last situations that might require a pilot to take immediate action is one for which there seldom is a valid reason for allowing it to develop. Running out of fuel is something that always happens to that *other pilot*. The rest of us are just too wise to be caught with our fuel drains down. While the reasons that pilots exhaust their major source of energy and the psychology behind them are almost endless, before getting into the discussion of how a controller can help with the problem, there is one independent solution worth discussing.

The idea comes from a good friend and long-time flight instructor. That is, prior to every flight, calculate a *Wheels on the Ground (WOG) Time*. Based upon the amount of fuel on-board, the estimated rate of consumption, and the desired level of reserve fuel upon landing, determine how much time will elapse before the reserve needs to be tapped. Note the time of engine start and write down a time at which you must be on the ground. For example, if after all the calculations you determine that at 2:00 P.M. the allowable supply of fuel will have been exhausted, then twenty or thirty minutes prior to that, a suitable airport needs to be located. The WOG time essentially shifts the emphasis from a place to land to being a time to land, regardless of whether or not it is the originally planned destination. It is an easy effective way to make sure the wheels hit the runway long before the tanks run dry.

If the unthinkable ever happens to that other guy, and he is receiving services from an air traffic controller, the first and most important thing he can do is to advise that controller of his predicament at the first realization that a problem might be developing. I have been involved in and witnessed as a controller too many situations in which pilots who were low on fuel kept quiet with the hope that the fuel gauges were wrong, their calculations were wrong, or maybe divine intervention would somehow save the day. In a couple of those instances, it turned out that the gamble had some very high stakes.

To a controller, there are two classifications of low-fuel situations, and each means something different to him. The first is when a pilot advises the controller that she is in a *critical fuel* situation. What this declaration tells the controller is that, although the pilot is not currently in an emergency situation and she does have enough fuel to reach her destination, should any undue delay occur, everything could change in a hurry. In practice, what it most often results in is providing that pilot with the most expedient route to the airport that is *reasonably* available.

Pilots need to be very cautious when declaring critical fuel status to a controller. This is not because alarms will sound and the wrath of the bureaucrats will descend upon her, but because the result she is anticipating may not always be the one she gets. No controller will go out of his way to delay a pilot who is concerned about her fuel supply, but not every controller will disrupt other traffic to nonroutinely shorten a pilot's time in the air based upon the assertion that her fuel level is approaching critical. Why? Because to a controller, more often than not, critical fuel means that a pilot is getting close to using her legal reserve, but is not concerned with running out of fuel. If everyone else has to fly a ten-mile final that day, so too will the pilot who declares critical fuel. In the controller's mind that does not constitute an undue delay.

Consequently, if what a pilot is really thinking is that she may not have enough fuel to make it to the airport, the consequences be damned, what she needs to tell the controller is that she is running low on fuel and is declaring an emergency. One accident involving a foreign air carrier that ran out of fuel prior to reaching the airport was due at least in part to ineffectively communicating the seriousness of the problem to the controller, which was partially due to each party's different primary language. If a fuel supply is low enough to make a pilot question how long she will be able to stay airborne, she needs to emphatically inform the controller that she is declaring an emergency.

The controller will then make every effort to get that pilot to a suitable runway in the fastest way possible. He may offer an option of an alternative airport that is closer than the original destination or he may offer an alternate runway that is closer than the one originally assigned. Whatever the specific choices that a controller suggests to a pilot, each will include the understanding that any and all other traffic that might get in the way of her altered flight path will be moved out of the way. The only objective that will govern the controller's actions will be that of getting her to a runway without any delay at all. Maybe not divine intervention, but it is help that is available on demand.

All the Rest

Obviously, there are many more possible situations in which pilots may be forced to quickly develop a plan to deal with unexpected events. While it would be impossible to mention each one here, it is plausible for you to consider some of the more common events that befall many pilots as well as some of the more unusual circumstances. In the process of developing scenarios and action items to combat the challenges, it is worth thinking about how outside resources might contribute to a solution. Whether it is controllers, flight service specialists, other pilots, or even passengers, each might be able to bring a different perspective or some additional knowledge that could shed some new light on a seemingly old problem. And that could change the course of history, maybe in a small but nevertheless a very personal way.

Finally, for the relatively new pilots reading this, do not let all the discussions of what could happen dampen your flying spirits. The odds are good that you will enjoy an entire lifetime of flying without ever coming face-to-face with a serious emergency situation. If one does occur, having a good idea of how to handle it ahead of time is an excellent way to replace panic with patience and that alone can make all the difference in the world.

Radar and Radio Systems Failures: Whose Problem Is It?

WHENEVER YOU ARE out and about punching holes in the sky, something to keep in mind is that pilots are not the only ones who experience equipment problems. Be it in a tower, an approach control facility, or an en route center, controllers also have to deal with the occasional equipment malfunction. There is usually enough backup equipment to keep the controllers working, and the reliability of their equipment has greatly improved over the years, but every once in a while some unexpected event takes down a big chunk of a system. The real dilemma for pilots, other than the fact that both they and the controllers get caught by surprise, is the lack of any specific regulations that govern how pilots are supposed to respond to the problem. To a large degree, we are left to our own devices to make the best of a bad situation.

Regardless of the official position put forth by the FAA, the truth is that when an entire air traffic facility or even a major portion of one loses its radar or its radios, the confusion that exists when a similar event happens to a pilot is magnified many times over for the controllers. Instead of just one airplane being the object of a controller's attention, every one that is within her airspace represents a challenge. It is vitally important for pilots to (1) quickly recognize when the problem at hand is the controller's and not theirs, and (2) do everything within their power to reduce or eliminate the confusion that is likely to develop when things start to go wrong. One of the best ways to address the issue is to consider some of the consequences of a major equipment failure in an ATC facility and to develop some possible plans to deal with them. Rather than charging into the fray following some randomly selected path, we can fall back on more carefully thought out solutions.

Since specific regulations seldom address how pilots should react to equipment failures that occur on the ground, any solutions we consider will, at best, put us in the gray area of regulatory compliance and, at worst, put us on the other side of the fence altogether. But when the unexpected occurs, we need to make our decisions based upon what we determine will be the safest course of action. Like it or not, each of us has to look at the conditions as they exist and then individually decide what to do.

When Controllers Lose Their Radios

The best place to begin is to consider how traffic conditions will influence a pilot's decision to act when the controller he had been talking to suddenly falls silent—a most unusual occurrence regardless of the cause. If, for example, a VFR pilot is in the middle of a busy Class C area or in a similarly busy traffic pattern at an airport with a control tower when the controller's radios quit working, the best action is to get out of the area as quickly as possible.

When in a traffic pattern, staying close to the airport and circling while the controller tries to sort things out is not necessarily the best solution. Cautiously exiting the pattern and waiting things out at a location well outside the Class D airspace or at least temporarily finding another destination until the problem is resolved will greatly decrease the chances of trying to share the same piece of sky with someone else. The one exception might be, if a pilot is already established on final, as with the case when his radios quit (see Chapter 10), the safest course of action would be to continue inbound and look for a light gun signal.

If, prior to a controller losing her radios, communications on the frequency were sparse and a pilot had developed a good idea of what, if any, traffic is located nearby, leaving the area is not the only option to consider. More than what a pilot does, when a lot of traffic is not the major concern, how he executes his plan is the thing to consider. What has happened is that a controlled airport has become an uncontrolled airport temporarily, and for that regulations and procedures do exist. Using the tower frequency, pilots in the pattern and the airspace should begin broadcasting their positions and their intentions as if the tower did not exist and continue inbound with the hope that a fix will be found before too long. In either case, good judgment and a little common sense should guide the way.

The Impact of Weather Conditions

The next point to consider is how the existing weather conditions affect the actions a pilot will take. The VFR pilot typically has a great deal more flexibility to safely maneuver within or through the airspace in which he is flying. But the IFR pilot who is flying in VFR conditions, with the single exception of Class A airspace, can unilaterally choose to become a VFR pilot at any time. Even though the controller may not be able to hear his transmission, an IFR pilot can cancel his clearance, squawk 1200, the VFR code, and continue his chosen course of action as a VFR pilot. Whether that is always the wisest choice for the IFR pilot depends upon a number of variables, but it at least ought to be considered as an option.

One of his considerations should be that, as the airspace in which he is flying becomes more heavily populated, more restrictive in nature, and more complex in design, any time an IFR pilot can change to the world of visual flying and make further plans accordingly, it can reduce the confusion for the controller and increase his safety considerably. Once he joins the world of the VFR pilots though, other factors do come into play. Ironically, although VFR pilots have many more options than IFR pilots do when faced with a radio failure (regardless of whose radio quits working), the procedures that regulate those options are few and far between. Whereas instrument pilots can usually look to some FAR as a basis for any proposed action they might consider, VFR pilots often have to evaluate the situation and make a decision on their own. For pilots flying on instrument clearances, the choice then becomes whether to remain on that IFR clearance and operate within the more restrictive constraints of the related rules or cancel their clearance and move to the more uncertain but potentially safer world of VFR flight.

Take, for example, the situation of flying in Class B airspace when the controller's radios die. Generally speaking, a pilot operating on an instrument clearance might be expected to depart the Class B airspace and land as soon as practicable. Since no regulations specifically advise a VFR pilot to do the same thing, he could suddenly find himself in a no-man's land where he cannot get a clearance and cannot legally do anything without one.

How Extensive Is the Problem?

Being in Class B airspace without having a controller available to issue the necessary instructions can be a bit tricky for any pilot, IFR or VFR. Given that the situation certainly is possible, where do we begin to sort out the options? First we can find out if any other controller in the same facility has a working frequency. Although it can and has happened that all frequencies for one facility fail at the same time for the same reason, it is more common that only one or two controllers lose their frequencies. If a pilot happened to be working with an approach control facility when the controller's radios quit working and he had written down a number of the frequencies he planned to use, he could try to contact another controller on one of them, including ground control if all else failed. It may take a bit of extra explaining, but a controller working another position in the same facility eventually will be able to restore some order to the situation. If the pilot had not written down the frequencies, the *Airport Facility Directory* (A/FD) lists almost all of the available frequencies for a particular air traffic facility. Other pilots will probably be doing the same thing, so waiting patiently to talk with a controller who suddenly finds herself with a significantly increasing workload is essential for everyone involved.

When an entire tower or approach control facility or one or more sectors in a center loses its ability to communicate, the weather conditions in which a pilot is flying should be one of the primary factors he considers when evaluating his options. Staying VFR or, in the case of the IFR pilot, canceling his IFR clearance and remaining in VFR conditions again gives him increased flexibility, sometimes without the loss of efficiency. As in the case of the pilot's radios failing, if he knows he already was worked into the approach sequence and it was just a matter of waiting for his landing clearance, continuing inbound and looking for a light gun signal would be the best course of action. On the way in, looking for other planes whose pilots may not be sure of what to do is a priority that should move to the top of the list.

When the weather is below VFR and all the pilots in the airspace are there on instrument clearances, the traffic will be a bit more organized than when VFR aircraft are thrown into the mixture. However, the available options are fewer and seldom ideal. For the pilot caught in the middle of an instrument approach, it will be uncomfortable, but there are things he can do to reduce the risks, regardless of the path he chooses to take. To be sure, we are talking about a gray area, but a point to remember is that it was the controller not the pilots who suffered the communications failure. If a pilot knows whom he is following on the approach, there are a number of questions he can ask the pilot or pilots ahead that can ease the apprehension. With the increased use of GPS and instrument approaches coupled with *distance measuring equipment (DME)*, the question of where the lead aircraft is can be accurately answered. Other questions are how fast is he flying, what are the weather conditions he is in, and can he advise when he breaks out of the clouds?

If a pilot has been able to establish communications with the traffic ahead and behind him, and if he has decided that he can safely follow the one ahead and remain safely in front of the one behind, the most prudent course of action is to continue the approach. Before making a decision about what to do, remember that prior to communications failure, the approach sequence the controller established had to conform to certain criteria. The spacing of the aircraft in the sequence had to have been in compliance with required radar separation standards and would have to remain so all the way to the runway. In addition, that spacing also would have to be adequate enough to conform to the runway acceptance rate. That is, spacing should easily allow landing aircraft to clear the runway before any succeeding plane crosses the landing threshold. All of this should make a pilot's decision easier to make.

Regardless of whether the decision to continue is made by an IFR pilot or a VFR pilot, once it has been made extreme caution needs to be exercised. In addition to looking for errant aircraft, asking a preceding pilot to report clearing the runway should always be on a pilot's agenda, as should looking for a signal from the tower. If none is received and the runway appears clear, the whether or not to land decision rears its head. Getting on the ground and out of the way is greatly preferable to flying back into the world of the unknown.

Getting Out of the Way

If, in the pilot's judgment, his present course of action is fraught with more peril than he thinks is acceptable, one of the best ways to remove himself from the situation is to fly away from the approach course at a ninety-degree angle and at the lowest safe altitude, broadcasting his position and intentions before executing the maneuver. Any traffic that is flying on a downwind leg should be at a higher altitude, so the risk of getting in the way of those aircraft is greatly reduced. After leaving the bottlenecked area, as soon as possible pilots should attempt to contact the en route center controller whose airspace overlays the approach control area. That controller may not be able to immediately provide vectors to pilots in another controller's airspace, but often she can provide traffic advisories with respect to any planes in his immediate area. This may not be an ideal situation, but it is better than flying completely blind.

For pilots who are not lucky enough to be already established on the final approach course when the controller loses her communications, the options available to them may not be so easily discerned. Depending upon where in the Class B (or for that matter Class C) airspace they happen to be, either a delaying tactic within some portion of the airspace or a diversion out of it is probably the best way to handle the problem. Since they are still flying in airspace in which authorization from a controller is required prior to making any alterations in their flight paths, any changes pilots make obviously will be made without the requisite permission. But any action that reduces the complexity and the number of airplanes in airspace in which the controller cannot exercise any authority will be construed as an improvement.

When a pilot is flying under VFR rules in visual conditions, his safest move is to take the shortest path out of the Class B or C airspace that does not interfere with any of the normal approach or departure routes of the active runways at the primary airport. When operating close to either the ceiling or the floor (when it is not the surface) of the airspace, a pilot should respectively climb or descend out of it as quickly as possible, keeping in mind that other pilots may be doing the same thing. If caught somewhere in the middle of the lateral and/or vertical limits of Class B or C airspace, one of the safest ways to get out of it is to pick a reasonably close and uncommon altitude, such as 3,350 feet, and fly laterally toward the closest boundary that does not interfere with the routes previously mentioned.

When not already close to the floor or the ceiling of the Class B or C airspace, staying at one altitude and flying toward a boundary should be preferable to climbing or descending through many altitudes, whether operating as a VFR pilot or an IFR pilot flying in VFR conditions. With respect to the IFR pilots, the lost communications procedure relating to descending and landing if VFR conditions are encountered presumes that, since it was the pilot who lost his radios, a controller can move conflicting traffic out of his way if a descent is observed by the controller. Clearly, such is not the case when it is the controller who cannot talk to anyone.

Any time a pilot decides to pick one altitude and stay there until clear of the area, he greatly reduces the chances of getting in the way of another airplane. When he decides to climb or descend through two, three, or more frequently used or assigned altitudes, the odds that another airplane could be in the area significantly increase. Either way, a pilot has to stay on the alert for unexpected traffic, but the path of least resistance likely is also the one with the fewest airplanes.

For the instrument pilot who is looking out at the inside of a cloud when the controller quits talking to him, regardless of how he chooses to deal with the situation, his level of stress will most likely be a good bit higher than his VFR colleague's. Though it is not an ideal choice, one of the best things he can do is to pick an uncommon altitude and use that to stay as far away from the final approach area as possible. Although the departure area represents a hazard, most if not all departure traffic will be held on the ground until the frequency problem is resolved. So the greatest concentration of traffic usually will be in those segments immediately adjacent to the final approach courses to the primary airport.

In addition to avoiding as many airplanes as possible, the instrument pilot always has the other concern of avoiding whatever terrain or obstructions lay beneath his chosen flight path. With that in mind, after selecting a safe altitude, his attention should turn to flying a path that does not infringe upon the charted arrival and departure routes into or out of the airport. After the final approach area, the next highest concentration of aircraft will be along any of those routes. As soon as a pilot finds his yellow brick road, he should try to establish communications with an en route center controller and ask for traffic advisories and, whenever possible, vectors out of the area into a safer haven.

When a controller loses her ability to communicate with those for whom she is responsible, it is one of the most disruptive events that can occur, more so even than when she loses her radar. When the radar fails, there is always some form of backup available; when her radios quit working a controller loses all ability to keep the pilots under her direction out of potentially threatening situations. None of the suggested remedies to that problem are ideal options, but they do greatly reduce the risks.

However the individual chooses to work it out, the four points that should be considered are (1) operating as a VFR pilot whenever conditions permit, (2) getting out of the area in the most efficient and least disruptive way possible, (3) avoiding known congested areas and, above all else, (4) patiently and logically working with the resources that are available. Taking some kind of rational action is much better than flying around aimlessly with the hope that something or someone else will solve the problem for you.

When the Radar Goes Down

Whenever a critical component of a system fails, timing is everything. For the pilot of a light twin-engine aircraft, failure of the critical engine just after takeoff can be the first step down a long harrowing path to an occasionally uncertain outcome. The loss of that same engine at altitude during the en route portion of a flight may serve as a challenge that warrants a pilot's full attention, but seldom renders the situation uncontrollable. So it is with radar systems and the work of the air traffic controllers. At two o'clock in the morning under a clear, star-filled sky, if any of the components of a radar system cease to function, the event will attract everyone's attention, but the situation should be easily manageable. Let the same thing happen in a busy section of airspace with thunderstorms adding to the complexity of the problem, and suddenly everything is more problematic. More than anything else, the issue becomes one of capacity.

The use of radar to keep airplanes safely separated dictates just how many of those planes can be in one particular area at any one time. Since controllers may use lateral separation that is as little as the half mile or so afforded by target resolution up to the six-mile standard of certain wake turbulence separation requirements, they legally can put quite a few planes in a relatively confined area of the sky. If they lose the capability to use radar to keep their traffic separated, then they also lose the use of a great deal of airspace. What occurs, especially in those first few minutes after experiencing an unexpected radar outage, is that every controller whose airspace has been affected by the situation immediately must create a means for every airplane to transition to the separation standards as set forth in the nonradar requirements. Usually that requires the spacing between and among the aircraft in the area to be doubled or tripled. It doesn't take too much in the way of mental calculations to realize that if the airspace was already close to its capacity under the procedures that govern radar operations, the added constraints of the nonradar separation standards will push that capacity to the limit and sometimes beyond. How pilots respond to the situation determines how successful the outcome is. Any time a pilot hears a controller state something like "Radar contact lost, the system just went down," it is time to pay extremely close attention to everything that follows.

Options for VFR Pilots

For VFR pilots who had been receiving radar service from an en route center controller, that service is no longer available. The controller may just make a blanket transmission to all VFR pilots on the frequency restating that radar contact has been lost with each of them, they should squawk VFR and either monitor the frequency or just proceed on their own without ATC assistance. Regardless of which course a pilot chooses, the point to remember is that both the controller's time and time on the frequency will have become precious. During those times, questions to the controller should be eliminated, and even an acknowledgment of the controller's initial transmission is unwanted. When the radar fails, VFR pilots are the first to be left to their own devices not because they are any less important than IFR pilots, but because they legally and realistically have the flexibility to keep themselves out of trouble without having to rely on a controller for assistance.

When an unexpected radar outage occurs in a terminal environment, that is Class B or C airspace, even VFR pilots are likely to experience a significant impact and disruption to their flights. If the failure occurs when a VFR pilot is flying within Class C airspace, for all practical purposes the airspace ceases to exist. That doesn't mean that the area becomes a free-for-all where anything goes, but rather that extreme caution should be exercised.

For anyone flying within the Class C airspace whose continuance to the primary airport is not critically essential, the best advice is to cautiously and expeditiously leave the airspace until things settle down. For pilots outside of the area who have yet to cross the airspace boundary, staying on the outside is the most prudent course of action. For anyone else, as conditions permit, the controller will advise a pilot where and when to contact the controllers in the tower for authorization to continue to the airport. The reality is that until all of the instrument traffic in the area gets safely sorted out, VFR pilots will be put on hold.

Similarly, for VFR pilots who happen to get caught in Class B airspace when a radar failure occurs, the option of exiting the airspace as quickly and carefully as possible should be the first choice. Again, regardless of the official FAA position with respect to how effectively an air traffic facility is able to accommodate an unexpected loss of radar, the first fifteen or twenty minutes after the event occurs are likely to be the most critical. Staying in the area and adding to the complexity of the controllers' tasks under those circumstances is an unwise decision and an unnecessary burden.

The controllers' manual offers the following note with respect to dealing with VFR aircraft in Class B airspace following a radar outage: "Separation and sequencing for VFR aircraft is dependent upon radar. Efforts should be made to segregate VFR traffic from IFR traffic flows when a radar outage occurs." In practical terms, this says that since sequencing and separation for VFR aircraft stops when the radar does, the best controllers can do is develop some method to keep IFR and VFR aircraft from commingling. The most effective way to do that is to get as many VFR aircraft out of the Class B airspace as possible. If a VFR pilot devises his own plan to leave the airspace and communicates that plan to the controller, except in very rare instances, it will be graciously and quickly approved.

Radar Failure and the IFR Pilot

For a pilot flying on an instrument flight plan, when a radar outage occurs, the options are neither as simple nor as easily executable as for the VFR pilot.

For the pilot who is flying in VFR conditions and knows he can remain that way, canceling his instrument clearance offers a couple of advantages. If landing at an alternate airport is among his choices, getting there in a VFR aircraft will almost always be more efficient than trying to do so on an instrument clearance. Even if he is continuing to the primary airport, arranging to proceed there as a VFR aircraft can significantly speed up the process. The trade-off is that the assurance of IFR separation from other aircraft is lost, but when the weather is good, the gain greatly offsets the loss.

The instrument pilot who is flying in VFR conditions but knows that he will have to reenter the clouds to get to the airport really has only a couple of choices at his disposal. He can cancel his IFR clearance and go the way of the rest of the VFR pilots, that usually being out of the airspace altogether. He can cancel his clearance and negotiate a hold in VFR conditions within the airspace until the rest of the traffic gets into a manageable flow. At that point he can request a new instrument clearance to the airport. Or he can retain his original instrument clearance and follow whatever nonradar instructions he is given by the controller. Each option comes with its own set of advantages and disadvantages and it is up to the individual pilot to decide which outweighs which.

Remaining in VFR conditions and leaving the area carries with it a certain margin of safety. Looking for any traffic that might present a collision hazard is a valuable backup to the controller's efforts to do the same. Going to another airport as a result of that decision may not be an option. Holding somewhere VFR keeps the backup in place but may increase the flight time significantly. Transitioning to nonradar control places almost the entire burden of separation from other aircraft on the controller. It will also increase a pilot's time in the air but will enable him to continue to his original destination. Each of the three can be an acceptable choice, but if the last option is the one a pilot decides to use, it is important that he understand all the implications that accompany it.

To begin with, as a controller transitions her traffic from radar separation to the increased spacing dictated by nonradar standards, she may use some seemingly inefficient methods to accomplish the task. Some aircraft will be climbed or descended to a variety of different altitudes. Some will be directed to locations that are totally opposite to either their existing flight path or the direction of the airport. All will be given the highly detailed and restrictive routings that exist in the world of nonradar operations. At that point, a controller will give little or no thought to what is most direct or efficient for each pilot. Her instructions will be solely based upon what is the safest way to get all the traffic into a nonradar profile.

The pilot needs to be ready to significantly alter his course in response to his amended clearance. He should be ready to write down detailed routes that frequently include tracking one VOR radial to another or possibly flying DME arcs when necessary. He should be prepared to carry out the controller's instructions with a minimum of questioning and delay. At least temporarily, the time for vectors, direct routing, and flexibility has disappeared.

Accompanying the more restrictive procedures of the nonradar environment is the controller's inability to approve much in the way of a pilot's request to deviate from her instructions. Because nonradar separation is predicated upon having a means to accurately determine where each aircraft is at any given time, permitting a pilot to stray from his predetermined route is usually not an option. One of the results that a pilot should keep in mind is that, should he decide he needs to alter his course to avoid thunderstorms or any other unfavorable weather condition, the ease with which he will be able to fulfill that need is greatly reduced. Without question, a pilot always has the right to invoke his emergency authority, but doing so in the midst of a radar system failure is the last thing anyone needs. Prior thought and planning should reduce the chances of such a need arising and extreme discretion should be used before even considering throwing a monkey wrench into the plans. By today's standards, nonradar procedures are not the most efficient way to get pilots from one place to another, but they are both safe and reliable. If a pilot, by choice or necessity, decides to jump into the nonradar game, it may take him a while longer to get to his destination. However, he can rely on the fact that the means by which he moves forward will get him there safely.

Though it is fortunately a rare occurrence, an entire radar system—automation, primary radar, secondary radar, and antenna—can unexpectedly fail. A few years ago, most newspapers in New England carried a picture of the radar antenna that served Boston's Logan Airport lying useless on its side after a freak windstorm. A more common situation is the failure of one of the components of a radar system. Exactly how a particular failure will affect the pilots using the system depends upon which portion of the system is unavailable.

The loss of a primary radar system, that which utilizes the transmission and reflected return of energy, is actually the least disruptive to pilots. Much of today's air traffic control is based upon information derived from an aircraft's transponder reply, so as long as that signal is being received by a controller, the actual skin-paint radar target is seldom needed to keep aircraft safely separated.

What is important for pilots to realize is that, when a primary radar system does fail, the only targets displayed on a controller's radarscope will be those of aircraft that have working transponders. When such a failure occurs, controllers are required to transmit the following statement to pilots: "Primary radar out of service. Radar traffic advisories available on transponder aircraft only."

In Class B and C airspace where, but for the occasional exception, transponders are required for all aircraft, the loss of primary radar presents few problems for pilots or controllers. That combined with the fact that the vast majority of aircraft flying today are transponder equipped often makes the loss of a primary radar system all but transparent to pilots flying in the area. But any time a controller is using only secondary radar, the potential for a non-transponder-equipped aircraft to unexpectedly, and unbeknownst to the controller, become traffic for another pilot always exists. Whenever a pilot becomes aware of the fact that the primary radar for the area in which he is flying has failed, he should go on alert for the possibility of an undetected aircraft straying into his path.

When any other component of a system goes down, the only indication a pilot may receive with respect to the problem is some sense that the air traffic services he has come to expect just do not seem to be up to their normal level. Just as the entire system has a capacity level that is based upon fully functional equipment, each individual controller is capable of handling the normal amount of traffic only when she has all the necessary tools available to her. When one or more of the tools at her disposal fails to function properly, the resulting increase in workload often prevents a controller from taking under her direction the number of airplanes she normally would. The extent of the delays is dependent on how widespread the problem is.

For example, if in an approach control facility, the automated computer system quits working, two major consequences result. (1) All of the data blocks that are displayed in association with every aircraft a controller is directing disappear from his scope. In their stead are as many transponder returns as there are aircraft, but each is identical to the next. That results in the controller having to, first, concentrate more heavily on maintaining the identity of each individual target and, second, revert to referring to the flight progress strips to keep track of all the aircraft identifications, altitudes, and assigned speeds. (2) Without the capabilities afforded by automation, each handoff that a controller makes must be done manually instead of via the computer interface. What she was able to accomplish by the touch of a button she now has to do by verbally transferring all the required information relating to a particular airplane by means of an intercom line. This means that the controller has to become involved in more time-consuming tasks that further reduce the time she has available to concentrate on her primary responsibilities, safely and efficiently directing aircraft through her airspace.

Regardless of whether a pilot is even aware that some portion of the radar system has failed or if he is aware of the problem but uncertain of the consequences of the failure, he is still part of the solution. In almost every instance, the result for the controller will be an increased workload. Pilots can help to ease her burden by limiting the amount of additional services they request when all is not working properly. Under normal circumstances requests for weather information, pilot reports, or a change of routing, for example, are not unreasonable requests to make to a controller. But if that controller is already working to the fullest extent of her capabilities because of equipment problems, she has no reserve for the relevant but nonessential requests that pilots routinely make. Staying as aware as possible of the environment in which he is flying can make a significant difference to the controller with whom he is working. The increase in air traffic over the years has made it mandatory that controllers be provided with suitable equipment to allow them to keep pace with the traffic. When some of that equipment quits working, they do the best that they can with what is left.

It is worth noting that, for any given radar system in general or any one component in particular, there is almost always a backup that is available. Often the backup system comes on line automatically, other times it is available in very short order. Either way, the controllers have some tools available to minimize any disruptions caused by equipment failures.

Pilots too are now able to contribute valuable resources to situations that not so long ago had to be dealt with solely from the ground. With more and more aircraft being equipped with *Traffic Alert and Collision Avoidance Systems (TCAS)*, pilots can augment the controller's information (or lack of it in the case of radar failure) as a means of filling in the gaps when a critical component unexpectedly fails. TCAS alone can reduce the almost total dependence pilots have to place on controllers when flying in instrument conditions and it can be an extremely valuable backup to a controller's actions when part or all of a vital system quits working.

While equipment failures of any kind can create potentially serious situations and radar system failures are among the worst, the possibility of encountering one while flying should not become a reason to shy away from using the air traffic system. As long as pilots understand some of the problems that could occur and as long as they have some idea of how they can contribute to the solutions, everyone involved will be able to work together to resolve the situations that occur. Radar outages always create times when concern is prudent but panic is useless.

12

Approach Procedures: Shooting the Approach

EVEN IF YOU ARE A VFR PILOT who has not entertained any plans to join that segment of the aviation community that takes great delight in drilling holes in the clouds, it could be worth your while to learn some of the means by which they operate. A good bit of your time in the air will be spent sharing the sky with pilots who are flying on instrument clearances. Understanding the rules they play by and the more restrictive constraints under which they operate can provide you with valuable insight with respect to how you fit into the big picture. In addition, just because you are not now an instrument pilot does not mean you will never become one. Many pilots who swore they would never be able to fly on instruments are finding otherwise. Not only have they been able to master that seemingly obscure ability to stay upright in the clouds, but they have actually had a lot of fun in the process.

Instrument flying adds another dimension to our flying that we might otherwise never acquire. It improves our understanding of the power/performance relationship, which, in turn, improves our ability to more precisely control our aircraft. It enhances our ability to develop a more complete picture with respect to our overall situational awareness. And it increases our awareness of how to most effectively use and participate in the pilot/controller relationship. Even if we decide never to attack the clouds alone, the increased breadth of knowledge and understanding gained from acquiring that instrument rating could be well worth the time and effort.

If, after thinking about it, you decide that you are one of those pilots who is only going to fly when the sky is blue, it still will not hurt to learn some of the basic concepts that keep instrument pilots out of trouble. Many of the same principles they use can be applied to VFR flying as well. For example, whether flying via published airways or on a direct route, the wise instrument pilots establish a minimum safe altitude for each portion of their route. Though the charts they use to determine what those altitudes will be more readily display the pertinent information they need than do those used in VFR flying, with a little bit of study and probing, pilots who fly visually can create their own lowest acceptable altitude. While that may seem less of an issue for pilots who are always supposed to be able to see the ground long before it becomes a hazard, more than a few collisions with Mother Earth have occurred in weather that was legally VFR.

Although all instrument flying is both challenging and rewarding, in many respects, flying an instrument approach is when it all comes together. It is the one time when a pilot gets the opportunity to use just about everything she has learned in the course of her instrument training. In addition, most of the instrument approach procedures embody many of the principles that are so integral to instrument flying in general. As a result, as we explore some of the instrument approach procedures and methods in particular, we begin to comprehend more about instrument flying in general. Finally, the instrument approach is supposed to be the routine culmination of an equally routine but satisfying excursion into the air. Most of the time that is how it ends, but statistics show that, for a variety of reasons, the instrument approach also seems to carry with it a series of inherent traps for the unwary pilot. Many of those traps can be hazardous for both the VFR and the IFR pilot.

One such trap relates directly to the pilot/controller relationship. In spite of the fact that a great deal of effort has been expended by a lot of people, one of the main problems that befalls pilots who are or are about to conduct an instrument approach is that they fail to completely understand what the controllers are saying and how those instructions relate to their responsibilities as pilots. Most of the standard phraseology and instructions that should present little opportunity for misunderstanding by pilots instead have lulled some of them into a false sense of security and, therefore, into some potentially dangerous situations. Part of the problem stems from the fact that similar instructions occasionally are imbued with subtle differences that alter how they should be followed. It is vitally important that both pilots and controllers make a concentrated effort to resolve those misunderstandings before they become accidents.

Any time a pilot is flying on an instrument clearance, and especially when she is flying in actual instrument conditions, it is important to know whether she is flying in a radar or a nonradar environment. Complicating that issue is the fact that often it is possible to flip back and forth from one to the other several times during a given flight. It is very possible to depart a satellite airport in nonradar conditions, become established in a radar environment, and then revert to the nonradar world upon beginning an approach to another satellite airport.

Depending upon what type of air traffic separation is being used—radar or nonradar—certain responsibilities are exchanged between the pilot and the controller and certain safeguards are eliminated altogether. It is essential that pilots and controllers have a clear understanding of what each is supposed to be doing in every instance and clear expectations regarding their changing roles as each particular phase of flight is encountered. But often that is where the confusion begins to develop.

A good place to begin the discussion is in relation to understanding the most common instances in which a pilot, at least for some period of time, will be flying in a nonradar environment. Because radar, like VHF transmissions, is line-of-sight, as pilots get farther and farther away from a radar antenna site at the lower altitudes, the likelihood of ending up in a nonradar situation greatly increases. Pilots departing from or flying into airports that are at the outer edges of an approach control's airspace will very often spend the beginning or the end of their trip in a nonradar environment. If mountainous terrain or other obstructions shield the radar signal from an airport, even airports closer to the antenna will be outside of the coverage area.

If instead of an approach control facility, an en route center is responsible for the airspace above an airport, the chances that the area immediately adjacent to the airport will be below the radar transmissions are even greater still. The centers use long-range radar more suited to covering larger areas of airspace, but only at altitudes usually higher than three thousand feet above the ground. Below those altitudes, pilots can be almost certain that they will be flying without the advantages of radar.

Another obvious clue that a pilot is about to embark upon an exercise in nonradar control is a controller telling a pilot, "Radar contact lost" or "Radar services terminated." Even those sometimes can lead to confusion for less experienced pilots. Once when I was flying with a student on an instrument flight plan, because of the loss of one radar site, the controller advised us that our radar service was terminated. The student's response to me was, "He can't do that, we're IFR." Being so used to flying under radar control, my student somehow made the connection that anyone flying IFR had to stay under radar control.

He quickly learned some of the other indicators that radar was no longer available. He had to begin calculating time estimates to the various compulsory-reporting points along our route and he had to copy down some rather lengthy and detailed route amendments that included an altitude crossing restriction at one location. With the exception of crossing restrictions, which can apply in either venue, the remainder of the alterations we experienced were directly the result of having transitioned to a nonradar environment.

Entering Radar

Whenever a pilot enters or re-enters the world of radar the controller will say the words, "Radar contact." Experienced pilots listen carefully for that phrase and if they do not hear it at what they determine to be the appropriate time, they frequently ask the controller for confirmation. Being a somewhat experienced pilot, when just that situation occurred a while ago, I asked the controller if he had us in radar contact. In a somewhat irritated voice he replied, "I gave you that right after you departed." Although I did not think that senility had yet taken over my senses, I got what I wanted and wrote his attitude off to having a bad day.

A less obvious but easily discernable means of detecting radar control is when a controller gives a pilot a heading to fly with the rejoinder, "vectors for… ." Although some controllers have tried to issue nonradar vectors as part of a desperation effort to salvage a compromising situation, it cannot be done without radar. Additionally, direct routing that does not include specific VOR radials or published airways almost always occurs only in a radar environment. Since controllers can see the aircraft targets on their scopes, they are less concerned with requiring pilots to confine their flights to narrowly defined corridors.

Having gained some understanding of when controllers will use radar and nonradar separation and having discovered ways to determine which is being used at any given time, the next point to consider is why knowing the difference is so important. One of the most important reasons to know whether a pilot is flying in a radar or a nonradar environment is directly related to what the use of radar brings to the table.

Radar Benefits

The most significant benefit radar provides for pilots is the safety net it affords them. Because controllers can watch the progress of an aircraft and immediately assess the accuracy of its flight path, a pilot who begins to stray in the wrong direction can be alerted to the fact. Because controllers can monitor an aircraft's altitude, particularly when it is flying in close proximity to the ground, they likewise can advise a pilot anytime her altitude goes below the minimum safe altitude. Add to that the fact that a controller using radar becomes a second set of eyes for pilots who are looking for any traffic in their area, and the list of safety backups provided by radar just gets longer.

When we consider that most of the time in most areas of the United States pilots have grown accustomed to the advantages of having radar services available, we also begin to understand why the lack of it can have an adverse effect on pilots' safety. Being used to flying in a radar environment, it becomes very easy to take for granted the many safeguards that radar affords us. When we do occasionally fly without its benefits, we often forget that there is no longer someone looking over our shoulder to help us correct our mistakes.

When it comes time to fly an instrument approach, all of those considerations regarding how the controllers are carrying out their responsibilities take on an even greater importance for pilots. As a pilot's airplane gets progressively closer to the ground, the margin for error becomes increasingly smaller. For the pilot who is executing an instrument approach in an area of nonradar control, the responsibility for maintaining both legal and safe terrain clearance and the correct flight path shifts entirely to the pilot. There is no way for a controller to be able to ensure that she will stay at or above the minimum altitudes prescribed for each phase of the approach or that she will fly the procedure as depicted. Every pilot has to recognize that it is her job and her job only to accurately fly the approach.

The only way to accomplish that is to have a thorough and complete understanding of the *Instrument Approach Procedures (IAP)*, which are on the individual charts associated with each approach. Each chart effectively provides pilots with the means to transition from the en route segment to the approach phase, properly align her aircraft inbound on the final approach course, and then safely descend on the approach to the point where she will either continue and land or execute a missed approach. All of which can and is accomplished without any navigational assistance from ATC. But because there are no controllers to offer any form of backup assistance, each approach has to be flown correctly the first time.

At the other end of the spectrum, while flying an approach with radar assistance offsets some of the disadvantages of executing one in a nonradar environment, doing so creates other ambiguities that are unique to the process. Radar service frequently relieves pilots of a lot of work and some of the responsibility for ensuring that they will always maintain proper and safe terrain clearance, but it replaces that work with another kind of mental responsibility and awareness. In certain instances pilots are responsible for ensuring that they fly at the correct altitude for the particular phase of the approach. In other seemingly similar situations, the controllers accept that responsibility.

If that is not confusing enough, even after pilots receive what may seem like an endless array of vectors, and even though the controllers are responsible for ensuring that the vectoring is accomplished in conjunction with an associated safe altitude, it is the pilot's job always to be the safety backup. Although GPS and the moving maps that are associated with many of the units greatly enhance a pilot's ability to maintain her situational awareness in the face of repeated vectors, with or without that electronic assistance, it is a pilot's responsibility to always know where she is. If, for example, a radio failure should occur at any time, a pilot has to be able to untangle the vectors and know where she is and what is a safe altitude for that area. That is just one of the reasons why receiving radar assistance can lead to a dangerously false sense of security.

Another is that, in the world of radar, sometimes pilots are bound to follow the rules relating to radar control and at other times they must abide by the procedures as laid out in the IAPs, even though they are still receiving radar assistance. The determining factor with respect to which way the winds will blow on this issue is directly related to whether or not a pilot is flying on a published route or portion of an approach and whether or not she *will remain on that published path*.

The reasoning behind the policy is actually fairly logical. Any time a pilot is flying on a published airway, transition route, or approach, she has instrument charts available that provide all the essential altitude information for each phase of the flight. Because that information is so readily available and accessible to her, as long as a pilot is at or above the depicted altitude associated with her location, any additional altitude limitations imposed on her by a controller are unnecessary. Regardless of whether a pilot is ten or a hundred miles from the airport, as long as she stays on those published routes she will always be able to determine the appropriate altitudes to fly along the way. Consequently, in the absence of a controller's authorization to descend to a lower altitude, the responsibility to adhere to those published altitudes rests solely with the pilot.

Only when a controller takes a pilot off of a published airway or transition route and initiates vectors for an approach does that controller become responsible for ensuring that the pilot remains at a safe altitude until she is reestablished on another published route—usually the final approach course. While it is easy and, in fact, mandatory for a pilot to have a general idea of her location when she is being vectored, it is almost impossible for her to determine exactly where she is at any given moment. Add to that the fact that it is often possible for a controller to vector a pilot at the *Minimum Vectoring Altitude (MVA)*, an altitude that is almost always lower than any associated published altitude, and it becomes virtually impossible for any pilot to continually know what altitude constitutes a safe altitude for a given area. Under normal circumstances it is the controller's responsibility to ensure a pilot is always flying at a safe altitude, but in the catch-all world of pilot-in-command responsibilities, it remains the pilot's job to ensure the controller never makes a mistake. Rest assured, however rarely it happens, controllers do make that mistake.

When the abnormal occurs as when either a pilot or a controller loses his ability to communicate, every pilot has to be ready immediately to reassume the job of maintaining a safe altitude on the way back to a published route. Fortunately, in the case of a pilot who is being vectored for an approach, there is an available reference pilots can use to quickly determine a safe altitude for the area in which they are flying.

Either in the heading section of the Jeppesen approach charts or on the plan view section of the government charts, there is a small circle within which are altitudes known as the *Minimum Sector Altitudes (MSA)*. Although there can be as many as four different MSAs noted on a particular chart, the altitude depicted within each sector guarantees, in that sector, at least one-thousand-foot clearance from any obstacle within twenty-five miles of the navigational aid named above the circle. When the protected area is less than twenty-five miles, that too will be noted. If more than one altitude is depicted and a pilot is unsure of which sector she is in, the best solution is to climb to the highest altitude shown. But it is important to remember that an MSA exists for emergency use only. It will provide a pilot with a much-needed obstacle clearance altitude when no other is available, but it may not assure that she will be able to receive adequate navigational signal reception.

As long as a pilot has a good foundation of knowledge and as long as she stays alert for the possible traps in the language, radar control need not create unnecessary confusion. When a pilot is cleared for an approach with an altitude restriction, that restriction remains in effect until she is on a published portion of the approach. When a pilot is cleared for an approach without a restriction it means that, first, she is on a published route or portion of the approach and, second, she can only descend to the lowest published altitude related to that portion of the approach where she is *presently located*. That is, the absence of an altitude restriction does not necessarily mean that a pilot immediately may descend to the final or even the initial approach altitude.

Any altitude restriction issued by a controller in conjunction with an instrument approach is *only* required when he takes a pilot off of a published route and provides her with vectors to the final approach course. Then, the restriction issued in conjunction with the approach clearance only applies until a pilot intercepts the course. At that point, a pilot again is expected to comply with all published altitudes for the remainder of the approach.

As a brief aside, it is worth noting that the approach phase of a flight is not the only time during which certain responsibilities are exchanged between pilot and controller. Whenever a pilot is flying en route on a published airway and a controller takes her off of that route and begins vectoring her, that controller also assumes the responsibility for assuring the aircraft stays at an altitude that complies with all legal terrain and obstruction clearance requirements.

If, however, a pilot either files for a direct route that does not utilize published airways or requests direct off-airway routing once airborne, it is her responsibility to ensure she stays at or above the minimum altitude required for IFR operations. FAR 91.177(a)(2) basically requires that, if a published airway or other applicable minimum altitude is not prescribed for the area in which she will be flying, essentially a pilot has to create her own airway and determine an appropriate altitude to fly that is one thousand feet—two thousand feet in designated mountainous terrain—above the highest obstacle 4 NM either side of the course to be flown. The person who initiates the action that will take a pilot off of a published route—pilot or controller—determines who is responsible for ensuring an appropriate altitude is flown.

Any time a pilot flies at a minimum safe altitude, any margin for error that exists is significantly reduced. As a result, it is also a time when being unsure of a controller's instructions or clearance could create a potentially serious problem. If ever the time arises when something just does not seem right, rather than risking the safety of her flight, a pilot always should ask for clarification of the instructions. It is worth taking as much time as is necessary to make every flight and every approach as safe as possible.

Visual Approaches

Whenever the weather conditions are conducive, flying a visual approach can be one of the most efficient methods for a pilot operating on an instrument clearance to get to her destination airport. Because the procedures associated with a visual approach are an uncommon mix of the rules that pertain to both VFR and IFR operations, occasional misunderstandings can occur with respect to who is responsible for what. The place to begin to unravel the confusion is with the explanation offered in the controllers' manual. It says, "A visual approach is an ATC authorization for an aircraft on an IFR flight plan to proceed visually to the airport of intended landing; it is not an instrument approach procedure. Also, there is no missed approach segment. An aircraft unable to complete a visual approach shall be handled as any go-around and appropriate separation must be provided."

Rather than being some type of instrument procedure, a visual approach is nothing more than a means for a pilot flying on an instrument clearance to get to an airport by using visual flight rules. Once an IFR pilot has been cleared for a visual approach, all the flexibility and limitations that are integral components of the rules that govern flight for VFR pilots now pertain to her flight as well. For the instrument pilot to safely conduct the approach, she needs to have a solid understanding of all the applicable rules and requirements.

RULES AND REQUIREMENTS

The first requirement is that the weather at the destination airport must be VFR. If official weather reporting is available at a pilot's destination then the ceiling must be at least a thousand feet and the visibility must be at least three miles, with no exceptions. Sometimes a pilot may want to dispute the accuracy of the weather as officially reported, but if it is less than one thousand and three, the controller's hands are tied. He cannot, under any circumstance, clear a pilot for a visual approach.

At airports where weather reporting is not available, the pilot requesting a visual approach becomes the weather observer. In fact, to a controller, the very act of a pilot requesting a visual approach indicates that she is in VFR conditions and she will remain so for the duration of her approach and landing at the airport. If that is not the case and, for example, a pilot will need to descend below a cloud layer before she will encounter the VFR conditions, she should advise the controller of her situation and that she will let him know when the approach clearance can be accepted. It is one of those rare instances when a pilot gets to have the first and the last word on the subject. The controller is just there to make it all legal.

The next condition that must exist before a pilot may be cleared for a visual approach is that she must have the airport and/or the traffic she is following to the airport in sight but *not necessarily both in every instance*. In the situation where there is no preceding traffic, then clearly all that is required is for the pilot to have the airport or the runway in sight at an airport with an operating control tower, or just the airport in sight when it is uncontrolled, and she may be cleared for the approach. The distinction between controlled versus uncontrolled airports is significant. In almost every instance, when a pilot is flying into a controlled airport, she will be cleared for a visual approach to a specific runway. When she is flying into an uncontrolled airport, she will be cleared for a visual approach to the airport under the assumption that the pilot will then conform to the existing flow of traffic and make her own runway selection accordingly.

When a pilot will be following traffic to an airport, one of two situations must exist. The first is that she has to have the traffic in sight and she must be able to follow it to the airport, all the while maintaining her own separation from it. The second is that, when she does not have the preceding traffic in sight, the controller must ensure that the required radar separation will exist either until the following pilot sees the lead aircraft or until the first plane has landed.

For example, if the controller points out a Boeing 737 you are to follow to the airport and you report seeing the aircraft, he will instruct you to follow it and then clear you for a visual approach. It then becomes your responsibility to maintain a safe distance behind the aircraft, taking into account wake turbulence avoidance and the runway acceptance capacity. If you ever become unsure about whether you have the right aircraft in sight, or if you lose visual contact with it, advise the controller immediately. To ignore the problem in the hope that visual contact will be regained might only cause a bad situation to turn worse.

Alternatively, if the aircraft you are following is six miles ahead, you do not see it but you couldn't catch it if you were flying a Lear Jet, the controller may advise you of the traffic and clear you for the visual approach regardless. By doing so, he is implying that he is taking responsibility for ensuring the required separation will exist. The important point to consider is that, in the first situation, the pilot is responsible for her own separation, not the controller.

A twist that can further complicate the issue is the situation in which a pilot sees the traffic she is following, but she does not have the airport in sight. The assumption is that, since she is following a pilot who does have the airport in sight, sooner or later she eventually will see the airport. That assumes that the lead pilot has the correct airport in sight. In the case of a 737, that is probably a safe assumption. Nevertheless, it is not a 100 percent guarantee. If a pilot does not see her traffic, then she must have the airport in sight before she will be cleared for the visual approach.

EXPECTATIONS

Having met all the requirements and understood the responsibilities associated with them, you need to fully understand the expectations placed upon a pilot executing a visual approach. Although not actually an expectation, every pilot needs to realize that acceptance of a visual approach *does not* constitute the cancellation of her instrument clearance. She may be expected to function as a VFR pilot, but if or when the need arises to return to instrument conditions, the authorization to do so remains in existence until either she cancels her clearance or she lands at an airport with an operating control tower. With that comes the understanding that controllers are, therefore, required to continue to provide a pilot with the required separation from other aircraft.

So, once a pilot is cleared for a visual approach, for all intents and purposes she becomes a VFR pilot. Maintaining appropriate clearance from the clouds, ground, and obstructions becomes her responsibility. Determining the exact course to fly to the airport also falls within a pilot's discretion, as does altitude management. If at any point or for any reason a pilot decides that she cannot comply with all the requirements, it is her responsibility to advise the controller and request an alternate clearance. All of her choices need to fall within the realm of logic and reason. Just as a VFR pilot is not expected to make unannounced drastic alterations to her path to the airport, neither is the instrument pilot on a visual approach. Finally, as with the VFR pilot, if a pilot has to abort her landing attempt, there is no ready missed-approach procedure to follow. That, too, has to be worked out with the appropriate controller.

VECTORS FOR THE VISUAL APPROACH

One final oddity relating to visual approaches has to do with when a controller may initiate vectors for the approach as opposed to when a pilot may request one. Before a controller may initiate vectors for a visual approach—assign heading to fly specifically for the purpose of issuing a visual approach—the ceiling has to be at least five hundred feet above his minimum vectoring altitude and the visibility must be at least three miles. Since ceilings are reported in feet above ground (AGL) and vectoring altitudes are based upon mean sea level (MSL), some converting is in order. For example, let's assume that the field elevation at Rangoon International is 1,000 feet MSL, and the minimum vectoring altitude is 2,000 feet MSL. That also means that the MVA is 1,000 feet AGL. Consequently, even if Rangoon were reporting VFR conditions with a 1,000-foot ceiling, the official ceiling would have to be at least 1,500 feet before a controller could initiate vectors for a visual approach.

Fortunately, the reason is easier to understand than the preceding calculations. Since, upon accepting a visual approach clearance, a pilot must adhere to the VFR cloud clearance requirements, and since the MVA is the lowest altitude a controller may assign, it follows that a pilot flying at the MVA must be at least five hundred feet below the clouds if both she and the controller are to be able to meet their respective responsibilities. If the controller had assigned an altitude that put the pilot closer than five hundred feet to the cloud bases and then issued the visual approach clearance, upon accepting it, the pilot already would have violated her requirements. The underlying reasoning is that a controller should not be permitted to initiate an action that puts a pilot in a compromising position.

There is, however, a loophole any pilot can use should the appropriate situation arise. Any time a pilot is being vectored for an instrument approach, and she is able to meet all of the requirements that go along with requesting a visual approach, she may do so even if the ceiling is below what the controller needs to initiate vectors for it. The assumption is that, upon accepting the approach clearance, a pilot will descend to an altitude that meets the cloud clearance requirements. Not so incidentally, that altitude will be below the MVA and, therefore, may be selected by the pilot but not assigned by the controller. The whole thing may seem like an exercise in futility, but knowing the rules and how to apply them in his favor may make it worth a pilot's efforts.

When it is properly utilized, a visual approach can save a pilot a lot of time and money without compromising her safety. The most important thing to remember is that many of the responsibilities that normally reside with the controller during an instrument approach shift to the pilot flying a visual approach. For those pilots who know and understand all the irregularities and quirks of the visual approach, flying one should solve more problems than it creates.

Contact Approaches

A contact approach is similar to a visual approach, only different. I suspect that there have been many times when a pilot who really wanted a contact approach, either because of a lack of knowledge and understanding or because of restrictions placed upon her by her employer, ended up asking for a visual approach. Unfortunately, the two are not interchangeable. A contact approach carries with it certain responsibilities expected of the pilot that are decidedly different from those that accompany flying a visual approach. It is important that any pilot who requests a contact approach understand those differences and how they might affect her execution of the approach.

To begin with, any time a pilot wants to fly a contact approach, she must ask for it using its exact name. Many a pilot has told a controller that she has the airport in sight or she would like to proceed visually or any other number of variations on the same theme, but none of those will open the gate to the approach. Second, although not quite the same as with Special VFR, the reported ground visibility at the airport must be at least one statute mile and the pilot must have at least one mile flight visibility and the reasonable expectation that it will not drop below that anywhere along the route to the airport. In addition, she must be able to remain clear of the clouds as she maneuvers to her destination. Finally, with the approach clearance, the controller will issue an altitude restriction stated as "at or below" a designated altitude. Since ATC is required to provide approved separation between the aircraft cleared for the approach and all other IFR and Special VFR aircraft, limiting the pilot's ceiling while still allowing a degree of flexibility regarding the altitude she chooses to fly accomplishes the task.

Where a contact approach begins to differ from Special VFR is with an added requirement that, as stated in the controllers' manual, "A standard or special instrument approach procedure has been published and is functioning for the airport of intended landing." The reason for the additional restriction is that, in the event a pilot is not able to complete her journey using the methods employed with a contact approach, she must have some alternately approved means by which she can continue her flight to the airport.

Once a pilot is cleared for the approach, what does it mean? It means that she may leave any published route or assigned heading and, using the available visual ground references for navigation, she may plot her own course to the airport. It also permits her to descend and take any other reasonable action necessary to maintain her situational awareness and also to remain clear of the clouds. Additionally, once a pilot begins her own navigation toward the airport, all responsibility for maintaining a legal altitude with respect to the ground and any obstructions along the way rests entirely with the pilot. Since the approach is almost completely based upon a pilot using ground references to find the airport, realistically it follows that only pilots who are familiar with a particular area should request the approach. But it is always up to the pilot to make that decision.

It should be understood that, as with Special VFR, a contact approach places a pilot in the position of having to fly visually in an area of very marginal weather. Any time the conditions deteriorate beyond what is acceptable, she needs to inform the controller of the situation and take alternate actions to ensure her safety is never compromised. Because a contact approach is imprecise at best, controllers will always provide more than minimum spacing between the aircraft on the approach and any other nearby traffic. But if a pilot should unexpectedly start to execute some wild unusual maneuvers to avoid some weather, the extra room she had been afforded could get used up in a hurry. It is another instance of a little common sense going a long way.

When a pilot has confidence in her own ability and is familiar with her immediate surroundings, a contact approach can be a useful alternative. But the option to use it always has to be exercised with extreme caution. Two of the most important points to remember are (1) never hesitate to ask for an alternate clearance if conditions turn out to be worse than expected, and (2) save yourself and the controllers a lot of unnecessary frustration by asking for the approach by its correct name. It is a contact approach, not a visual approach.

Shooting Any Approach

Flying on instruments, particularly in conjunction with an instrument approach, can be an exciting and challenging way for a pilot to exercise her ability and skills. Besides the obvious advantage of improving any pilot's all-around flying ability, being able to fly an instrument approach can become the difference between having an expensive toy and owning an extremely useful means of transportation.

Rather than intending to explore all variety of approaches, this chapter reviewed the unusual ones, particularly as they relate to the pilot/controller partnership. If we can begin to understand and acknowledge that little, if anything, in the world of instrument flying is as black and white as the regulations suggest at first glance, we can continue to examine every instrument approach in light of a new perspective. Only when a pilot becomes as familiar with her approach charts as she is with the menu at her favorite pub will the surprises be eliminated. Just about everything a pilot will ever need for a routine approach can be found somewhere on the charts. When additional help is needed, the controllers often can provide that added assistance. Do not shy away from those controllers; learn to use their training and expertise to add safety and enjoyment to all your flying.

13

Takeoff and Landing Shortcuts: Let Them Work for You

UNFORTUNATELY, THE DAYS WE CAN spend flying around aimlessly just for the sheer joy of experiencing life in the air are either significantly limited or are gone completely. As is true with many other pleasurable pastimes, the rising costs involved with flying have reached the point where many of the unnecessary expenses that used to be acceptable, if not welcome, can no longer be tolerated. Compounding the problem of increased costs is the fact that we also have to contend on a daily basis with an air traffic system that has been pushed to its limits.

We often end up flying our advanced, efficient airplanes into airports that for one reason or another might be described as being ten or fifteen years behind the times. So, we often end up flying airplanes that effectively employ their technological advances only during the en route portions of our trips. When we near our destination the scene is frequently one of airspace congestion and an airport that has reached or exceeded its capacity. Not long ago I spent twenty-five minutes sitting at the runway waiting to depart from a reliever airport in New England that was far from the major airport it was meant to relieve.

The message here is not meant to place blame because the issues are many and complex. My goal is to look at the resulting consequences. Every time an airplane sits on the ground waiting to depart or holds in the air awaiting a position in the landing sequence, it adds up to an unwelcome and expensive depletion of fuel. Although they are not the ultimate solution to the problem, there are a few ways we can take maximum advantage of our National Airspace System and the controllers who administer it as it exists today.

Unused Runways

Any time a pilot uses an airport that has more than one runway, particularly when all of the runways are not being used for arrivals or departures, he easily can hasten his arrival or departure by requesting the use of one of the inactive runways. Since runway length is seldom a major concern for most light-plane pilots, the determining factor in selecting a runway is opting for the one that is most closely aligned with the wind. In acknowledgment of the validity of that preference, the controllers' manual states: "Except where a 'runway use' program is in effect, use the runway most nearly aligned with the wind when 5 knots or more."

What that means for pilots is that, whenever the winds are five knots or greater, the controllers are required to assign the runway that affords pilots the most favorable conditions for takeoff and landing. But when the wind conditions are not extreme (a subjective term for which each pilot must make his own determination), wind direction alone does not have to be the deciding factor. Since quite a few pilots learned to fly at airports where there were only two choices regarding which runway to use, the chances are excellent that, very early in their careers, they learned to accept and compensate for the effects that crosswinds have on their airplanes as they arrive or depart. Using a runway where the wind does not exceed either their own abilities or the stated crosswind components of their airplanes presents a manageable challenge for them.

If that is the case, why are air traffic controllers so hesitant to offer a pilot the use of another runway just because of the crosswind associated with it? The main reason is that the regulations by which they are bound do not permit them to make the offer. Should a controller take it upon herself to do otherwise and an incident or an accident results, she will have put herself in the unenviable position of being a possible contributor to the situation. The sad reality is that many of the constraints that affect both pilots and controllers are the direct result of past litigation, irrespective of whether those results actually have a positive impact on safety.

But legal issues aside, the more important reason why controllers do not offer pilots runways with wind conditions that are beyond the limits as set forth in their regulations relates to a valid concern. There is really no way that a controller can accurately determine if an individual pilot is capable of handling a given set of conditions. Although more experienced pilots know enough to refuse any instruction or clearance they believe is unsafe, some of our newer friends in the air have a strong tendency to assume that controllers somehow have an innate sense of all things possible. As with a child who, over time, sees his parents wisdom diminish to zero as he approaches his teenage years, belief in the all-knowing controllers likewise disappears as the flying hours accumulate.

Fortunately, there is an easy way to get around all the red tape that surrounds runway selection. As pilot-in-command, anytime a pilot would like to exercise the option of using a runway other than the one that had been assigned by ATC, he need only make his request known to the controller. If the actual winds at the airport do not present a hazardous situation for him and he would like to expedite his arrival or departure with a lesser used runway, he should ask for the authorization to use whatever runway will result in the least delay. Since one of the guiding principles by which controllers operate is that the sooner an airplane moves out of their area the sooner another can take its place, a request that aligns itself with that principle, traffic permitting, often will be granted. In addition, since the pilot is the one who initiates the request, it frees the controller from the decision-making responsibility that rightly belongs in the cockpit.

It is worth remembering that the best-laid plans occasionally do go awry. If a decision that seemed wise on a five-mile final turns out to be more than a pilot cares to tackle as the full impact of that decision becomes more apparent closer to the airport, it would be wise to reevaluate the situation. When a pilot ends up flying sideways on short final in an attempt to remain aligned with the runway, in spite of any protestations by the controller, it is never too late to go around and get back in line with everyone else. It's not the most pleasant of options maybe, but expedience should never override safety.

Runway Use Programs

Another consideration relating to the issue of which runway to use is the runway use program. At certain airports, a *Runway Use* program may determine which runway or runways are considered the active runways. Taking into account noise-sensitive areas that abut an airport, certain runways are designated to be preferred whenever conditions are conducive to their use. Consequently, even though another available runway may be more closely aligned with the wind, pilots will be assigned to the one that creates the least noise impact on an area.

However, if a pilot makes the decision that using a runway other than the preferred one is in his best interest, he should make his wishes known to the controllers. A note in the controllers' manual that relates to the issue clearly states: "If in the interest of safety a runway different from that specified is preferred, the pilot is expected to advise ATC accordingly. ATC will honor such requests and advise pilots when the requested runway is noise sensitive." Such a decision may or may not save a pilot time, but in that instance time should not be the deciding factor.

Similarly, there are times when a controller may assign a runway in the interest of saving time for everyone even when her decision may not be in the best interest of everyone involved. After having spent a pleasant afternoon with a friend as we chased around the area in his plane searching for the elusively perfect $1.00 hamburger, I ended up flying the leg back to his home base. As we approach the airport the ATIS gave the wind as coming from 170 degrees at 17 knots gusting to 26 knots. Since runway 17 was the active, I was not overly concerned with the wind. When we contacted the tower controller, we learned that in an apparent effort to avoid having to slow the aircraft behind us, he had reassigned us to runway 24. Not being crazy about the idea of tackling the existing crosswind unnecessarily, I rogered the controller's instructions and asked him for a wind check. After a momentary silence he replied with the same winds and, "Continue inbound for runway 17, keep your speed up as long as possible." Had my question not accomplished the desired results I would have taken the next step, but sometimes any of us can get lucky.

When it works to everyone's advantage, using a runway other than the active is an easy way to make the most efficient use of an airport. More often than not, controllers welcome a pilot's request to use a different runway. It is always wise, however, to be prepared for the occasion when a controller may have to deny a pilot's plea. Though occasionally it will be because of noise restrictions, more frequently it will be because granting one pilot's request would unfairly delay several others. Regardless of the reason, rarely will any controller get upset with a pilot just for asking. Any time there is a chance that a pilot can save himself some time without degrading safety, it is worth taking the time to ask.

Intersection Departures

There is an old saying in aviation, "Two of the most useless things for a pilot are sky above and runway behind him." With that thought in mind, the topic of runway intersection departures nevertheless deserves some consideration. No one can dispute the fact that always using the entire length of a runway could someday mean the difference between having a ready-made backup available instead of using the cross-town boulevard as a last ditch effort, as it were, for landing. It is something that every pilot should consider before requesting or accepting an intersection departure.

The majority of general aviation pilots do their everyday flying out of airports with runways that range in length from 2,500 to about 5,000 feet and no one considers it unsafe. Rather than taxiing his single-engine Cessna, Piper or whatever a mile and a half out of his way to use all of a 10,000-foot runway, a pilot easily could opt for one of the intersections along the way and still have over 5,000 feet of runway left at his disposal. Since using an intersection for departure can be an effective timesaving option, it makes sense to consider it carefully. Regardless of which path he chooses, it is a choice that each pilot should make for himself. Even when a controller instructs a pilot to plan the use of an intersection, that pilot always has the right to refuse the instruction and opt for the full length of the runway.

In addition, there are some circumstances in which using an intersection actually could cause a pilot to waste more time than he saves. Because of the wake-turbulence-avoidance procedures that controllers are required to adhere to, any time a jet or any aircraft weighing 12,500 pounds or more departs from the end of the runway, there is a three-minute delay that is instituted for a small aircraft waiting to take off from any intersection along the runway. The reasoning is that three minutes is thought to be enough time for the damaging effects of wake turbulence to dissipate. But for the pilot who is trying to get out of a busy airport that is heavily populated by large jet aircraft, it is worth remembering that before the three-minute delay caused by one departure has passed, the next jet will have already rolled as well. If there is a long line of large aircraft departing from the end of the runway, a pilot at an intersection could experience a rather lengthy delay. Before asking for or accepting an intersection, it is a good idea to ask the ground controller what the overall picture looks like.

Most of the time when the tower controller's response to a pilot's request for takeoff clearance is "Hold for wake turbulence," the pilot has the option of waiving the three-minute delay that otherwise would be imposed upon him for using the intersection. But this is another one of those times when someone who is requesting to exercise the waiver needs to be very specific in his request. Simply stating that he is ready for takeoff will not do it. Instead, the pilot has to say something to the effect of "I am requesting to deviate from the required three-minute interval." That lets the controller know that he is familiar with the regulation and that he is willing to assume all responsibility for handling any unfavorable conditions that might be encountered as a result of wake turbulence.

Keep in mind, though, even when a pilot decides to accept the entire three-minute delay, he should never mislead himself into thinking that it represents a guarantee that all of the wake turbulence will have dissipated. Any time a pilot takes off or lands behind a large aircraft, the possibility of an encounter with wake turbulence exists, regardless of how long the delay is. It is impossible for anyone to know for sure when there will be the disturbed air remnants from a previous aircraft. The best defense against the effects is good decision-making skills, prudent use of wake-turbulence-avoidance procedures, and always being prepared for a possible encounter.

There are some situations when, regardless of a pilot's request, the controller will not authorize waiving the three-minute delay. Any time a heavy jet or a Boeing 757 takes off from the end of the runway, a pilot waiting to depart from an intersection will be required to wait the entire three minutes and the reasoning is well founded. Any encounter with wake turbulence, but particularly one that occurs just after takeoff or just before landing, can become a handful for any pilot. But that generated by a heavy jet can be too much to overcome even for the most experienced pilots. No pilot should be in so much of a hurry that he would be willing to risk an unnecessary encounter with such an elusive element.

Since most of the airports frequented by most general aviation pilots are not normally graced with an abundance of large airplanes, heavy or otherwise, an intersection departure can be an extremely effective way for a pilot to reduce his time spent on the ground. After carefully considering all the factors, if he decides the ensuing takeoff will be safe to make, no one will question his decision. And that is one of the best parts about an intersection departure. The choice of whether or not to make one always belongs to the person sitting in the cockpit.

VFR for the IFR Pilot

Though not really a takeoff shortcut, there is an option that can be used by a pilot operating on an instrument clearance that occasionally can allow him to get up and out more quickly than might otherwise be the case. Often one of the best times to use it is shortly after takeoff. The problem, however, is that both experienced pilots and controllers are unfamiliar and, as a result, uncomfortable with the procedure. It is, simply, the option for a pilot on an IFR flight plan to conduct a *VFR climb/descent*. The matching authorization from the controller is an instruction to either "maintain VFR conditions" or "climb/descend VFR." Both the procedure and the invocation of its use are easily accomplished, but understanding each partner's responsibilities takes a bit more thought.

The easiest way to explain the procedure is by way of an example. Suppose you have just departed an airport on an IFR clearance but you are flying in VFR conditions. The departure controller has restricted you to an altitude lower than that which you requested because of inbound IFR traffic that is at a higher altitude but still some distance away from you. The departure controller issued you an altitude restriction not because she was concerned about a possible collision, but because she was not sure the required radar separation between your aircraft and the other would exist as you passed through the other's altitude. She advises you of the traffic but you do not see it, so visual separation cannot be applied. You are, however, sure that you can maintain VFR conditions and, should the other aircraft become a factor, you know that you will be able to see and avoid it. You request a VFR climb through the conflicting altitude. The controller authorizes the climb.

A request by a pilot for a VFR climb/descent temporarily cancels a pilot's IFR clearance and, in so doing, also temporarily relieves the controller of the responsibility to provide approved IFR separation for his aircraft. Usually a limitation will be included with the controller's authorization so that both pilot and controller will have a clear understanding with respect to when the VFR operation will be terminated. In the case of a VFR climb, the controller might state, "Climb VFR between 5,000 and 7,000 feet." Even though nothing specifically is stated with respect to a pilot's IFR clearance, *for all ATC purposes*, during that period when the aircraft hits 5,000 feet until it leaves 7,000 feet, the aircraft is a VFR aircraft. After he reaches 7,000 feet, a pilot automatically reverts to his IFR clearance and life goes on as usual.

Most of the confusion with the procedure stems from the fact that it is not used very often. Consequently, many pilots are unaware of its existence and just as many controllers, whenever such a request is made, quickly have to research the issue before they are comfortable with relinquishing their responsibility to provide the otherwise required IFR separation for the pilot.

While on occasion a request for a VFR climb/descent can be a safe, efficient, and effective means to get a pilot where he wants to go, the request also eliminates some of the safeguards inherent in an instrument clearance. A pilot who asks for one is making the assumption that he will always be able to see and avoid traffic that might become a potential hazard for him. As VFR pilots, we do that every time we fly and the results bear out the efficacy of the procedure. As long as a pilot (who occasionally also must convince the controller of the legality of the procedure) understands the entirety of his responsibilities with respect to a VFR climb/descent, the procedure can be one more tool to use when the conditions are right.

Fit Yourself In

At every airport that has a moderate or greater amount of traffic, there are procedures that have been developed to most effectively move that traffic through the airspace. Although each approach control that serves a particular airport has its own unique variations on the methods they use to keep airplanes apart, there are some general characteristics of airspace structure that most have in common. If a pilot can gain some understanding of what they are, he can use that knowledge to learn how to more efficiently maneuver throughout the myriad parcels of airspace that make up any one approach control area.

DESIGN OBJECTIVES

Every approach control area has been designed with two major objectives in mind. The first is to create procedures that, to the greatest extent possible, eliminate the need to have opposite direction traffic utilizing the same airways or routes. The result of that objective is that most approach control airspace has been designed using a method called *Corner Post Arrival Gates*. That simply means that all instrument arrivals enter the airspace over one of four equidistant points, referred to as gates, from the airport, usually located at what could be considered the four corners of the airspace. In between each gate is a *Departure Corridor*, where not surprisingly all instrument departures exit the approach control airspace. The result is that, by design, arrival aircraft and departure aircraft are seldom placed in a situation where they are headed at one another, thereby significantly reducing the possibility that an error by a pilot or a controller will result in a catastrophic event.

The second major design objective by which approach control airspace is created is to segregate high-performance aircraft from those that constitute the majority of the general aviation fleet. Most of the time this separation is accomplished by using different altitudes to keep the various groupings of aircraft away from one another. Again not surprisingly, high-performance aircraft use the higher altitudes as much as possible and the rest of the traffic is relegated to the lower strata of airspace.

While this method works well from the perspective of the controllers and the pilots of the faster traffic, many of today's general aviation aircraft do not fit into one category or the other. More and more light planes are capable of operating at altitudes that even a few years ago were all but impossible to attain, but frequently their climb performance on the way up and their speed once they get there still remain somewhat incompatible with the high-performance aircraft that dominate the domain. All of which, at least to a certain degree, is prelude to the issue that many light-plane pilots are now faced with, how to use the airspace structure in combination with their aircraft's performance to their best advantage. It should also be noted that, in almost every instance, the situations and conditions that affect light-plane pilots flying on instrument clearances have a similar impact on VFR pilots operating in Class B or C airspace.

The easiest way to explain the concepts involved is with an illustration. Although ideally the paths of arrival and departure aircraft should never cross, realistically that is not the case. When their paths do intersect, controllers usually keep the airplanes separated from one another by using different altitudes. Normally inbound aircraft are restricted to using two or three different altitudes as they approach the airport. Departures are then either restricted to a lower altitude until they are beyond the arrival routes or are kept away from the arrival routes—usually in a pie-shaped sector of airspace—until they have climbed above the arrivals, at which time they are turned on course. The decision of whether to keep a pilot below the inbound traffic or climb it in the airspace immediately adjacent to the departure end of the runway relies heavily upon a pilot's final requested altitude as one of the determining factors.

The pilot's decision then becomes, Do I go high or low? When a pilot files for a high altitude (usually being eight thousand feet or above), he will probably be instructed to follow the procedures designed for the high-performance aircraft and he will be climbed before he is turned. While it may take a jet only four or five miles to reach an altitude above the inbound traffic, a lesser performing aircraft may end up flying an additional ten miles or more before it reaches the same requisite altitude. Whereas, when a pilot files for a lower altitude, often the method of choice is to keep him at a lower altitude until he has crossed the arrival route and then climb him to his requested altitude. The result is that the pilot at the lower altitude gets turned to his requested course sooner than his counterpart who is flying higher. This prompts the question, can a pilot ever get all of what he wants without having to compromise altitude efficiency for flight-path efficiency?

Fortunately, the answer is yes, at least sometimes. A pilot cannot be expected to know exactly what will work best at every different airport throughout the country, but he does have a means to get some of the questions answered before he leaves the ground. Usually when a pilot will be departing an airport that is within Class B or C airspace, regardless of whether the flight will be IFR or VFR, the place to begin the research is with the controller who is working clearance delivery. Since she is the person who either issues an instrument clearance to an IFR pilot or similarly compiled instructions to a VFR pilot, she can be instrumental in a pilot's decision-making process.

Rather than asking the controller, "What happens if I do this or what happens if I do that?" it is easier and more effective to present the situation to her and then let her offer the solution. Just provide the controller with your destination or direction of flight and requested altitude (which for the instrument pilot she will already have) and ask her to suggest what she thinks will be the most effective method to use to get on course the soonest. If it turns out that the most efficient altitude or course suggested is not the one a pilot wants, a little bit of negotiating is in order. If, for example, a pilot would like a higher final altitude than what is offered, he could agree to using a lower one initially with the understanding that, at some reasonable point along the line, he will be assigned the higher requested altitude.

Controllers know the procedures at their respective airports very well, so they know ahead of time what will or will not work. Most pilots will be pleasantly surprised at the cooperation of the controllers and the results of their mutual efforts with respect to helping them to more effectively use the existing procedures to their advantage. Besides helping a pilot get on course as quickly as possible, working to get the most out of the system can considerably ease a controller's workload. It is another one of those instances when everyone involved comes out ahead.

Another point to keep in mind when traveling through approach control airspace either en route to a satellite airport within the area or heading to points beyond is that sometimes the least disruptive path to take is directly over the primary airport. Whenever a pilot is flying at a high enough altitude, usually four thousand or five thousand feet above the ground, the one area that is seldom occupied by arrivals or departures is overhead the airport. The departures have yet to climb to that altitude and the arrivals have descended well below it. Whereas, pilots who are flying at lower altitudes frequently can expect to be vectored fifteen or twenty miles out of their way in an effort to keep them out of the mix of traffic using the primary airport. Even though a relatively small altitude change could save significant time, controllers are reluctant to initiate an instruction to make him do other than what he originally requested. But when a pilot offers to accept a more efficient alternative, controllers will almost always be happy to accommodate his request.

Remaining Flexible

One of the last points every pilot should consider is that he needs to remain as flexible as possible and he needs to communicate his willingness to consider alternative options to controllers whenever the potential exists to more efficiently utilize the airspace in which he is flying. Simply advising a controller on initial contact that, given his route or destination, he will accept any suggestions with respect to the best way to get where he wants to go can provide some very positive results. For example, if a pilot wants to land at a satellite airport that is relatively close to the primary airport, he could discuss whether staying at a higher altitude and making a more rapid descent after clearing the main airport is possible. Such a plan, though unlikely to be initiated by a controller, could save a pilot substantial time and energy, but first he has to say something.

The air traffic system has its limitations, but sometimes they are not as severe as many pilots perceive them to be. Whenever you have the opportunity to ask controllers about the procedures and possible shortcuts that can make flying through their airspace more efficient, you can get the most out of every minute in the air. When you go to an unfamiliar area, do not hesitate to take advantage of the controllers' knowledge and training. Most of the time they are more than willing to help, but sometimes they have to be asked.

One of the best ways to learn when shortcuts may be available and how best to utilize them is to train yourself to look for alternate options every time you fly. Plan ahead and take the time to think about the different ways you might be able to fly through an area. Look at some of the airways that are likely to be heavily traveled, look at the runway configurations and try to determine what the arrival and departure routes might be, and finally put all that information together and try to envision the overall traffic flow for a particular piece of the sky. You may not always come up with the right answers, but even the process of asking the questions will expand your thought processes to include more options than you might have thought possible.

Dealing with Errors: Oops! I Goofed

HUMAN ERROR—like it or not, we are stuck with the problem. Almost every aviation accident study conducted in recent years resulted in the same conclusion. In one form or another, human error was overwhelmingly the reason most of the accidents happened and no pilot, regardless of age, knowledge, training, or experience is immune from the problem. For new or inexperienced pilots it probably comes as no surprise that making mistakes goes with the territory of learning to fly. The truth is that sometimes it is no fun to be a beginner, but there is just no other way to start. While none of us can do anything about our inherently human propensity to sometimes get it wrong, we can take some steps toward getting it right more often or, at the very least, recognizing earlier when everything is not as it should be.

For most pilots, the place to begin is by accepting the fact that the mistakes they make, particularly as they relate to working within the air traffic system, are frequently embarrassing, rarely life threatening, and almost never new and innovative. As was mentioned many pages ago, most of the rules, regulations, and procedures that exist within the framework of the air traffic system have been developed to create a system that is error tolerant as opposed to error free. Most often, the only expectation for perfection lies within a pilot's mind, and unfortunately it is also the one that can be the most difficult to overcome.

Each pilot should take some comfort in knowing that every other pilot who has gone before her has added a list of blunders to the pages of aviation history. There have been many times when pilots have taken the most basic rules of air traffic control and bent and twisted them beyond all recognition, this pilot included. Any pilot who has ever talked to an air traffic controller can look back into her sordid past and come up with at least a couple of times when she would be reluctant to admit that she was the pilot-in-command.

Some of the more famous (or infamous, as the case may be) incidents that have marred the past of even our most highly revered aviators include landing at one airport while talking to the controllers at another one; landing at an airport just to find out where you are; reporting your position as ten miles east when, in fact, you were ten miles west (one of our most popular options); taking off or landing on the wrong runway; flying through an area without the required clearance; making an unauthorized descent through the clouds; taking off or landing on a taxiway by mistake; and just about anything else imaginable. Both pilots and controllers have an uncanny ability to take just about any situation, regardless of how simple it may seem, and turn it into a complex series of events that can tax even the most imaginative of thinkers.

The best way to deal with errors is to prevent them in the first place. Of the volumes of aviation literature in existence today, dozens of them are dedicated to just that—teaching pilots how to avoid many of the mistakes of the past. In that regard, nothing can take the place of a sound educational program and a solid foundation of knowledge with respect to the world in which a pilot will be living. There are just no acceptable shortcuts around the learning process.

But even the best programs in the world cannot teach a pilot everything she needs to know about everything that she will encounter. Even if they could, no pilot can guarantee that she will do everything correctly all of the time. But that doesn't mean the problem is unsolvable. There are a few simple steps every pilot can take to minimize those times when she is about to stray down the wrong path. The first is for a pilot to continuously check to determine if her perception of reality matches what is actually happening, and that can be accomplished by asking herself a few basic questions.

With respect to working with controllers, the beginning question should be, Is the instruction or information the controller just gave me the one that I was expecting? The next should be, Is the instruction I just received logical, does it make sense given my present flight condition? A third should be, Can I follow the instructions I just received without compromising the safety of my flight in any way? Finally, one of the most important questions is, Does all information confirm that I can safely continue? If all of the answers to the questions are yes, then everything is in order. But if the answer to any one of them is no, additional probing into the situation is necessary before taking any additional actions.

For example, assume you are a VFR pilot inbound to an airport within Class C airspace and you are already receiving vectors for the approach sequence. The next instruction the controller issues, without any explanation, is a turn away from the airport and a climb that may put you into the clouds. A review of the four questions above reveals that none of them could be answered yes, yet countless pilots faced with similar circumstances have faithfully and blindly followed similar instructions in similar situations. All of which leads us to the inevitable conclusion that air traffic controllers, being humans too, are subject to the same faults and limitations that haunt everyone else in the aviation community, in spite of what a few controllers would have us believe.

On their side of the ledger go things like providing a series of perfect vectors to the wrong airport; issuing instructions meant for one pilot to another; controlling a VFR pilot as though he were on an IFR clearance; instructing a pilot to turn left instead of right; clearing a pilot for takeoff or landing on an occupied runway; and anything else imaginable. But just being aware that controllers, too, make mistakes can be one of the first significant steps in preventing similar situations from occurring in the future.

Another simple way to prevent a misunderstood or confusing situation from developing into a full-blown error is to first recognize the warning signs and second, if the issue cannot be resolved within the cockpit, ask for assistance. The time to take action is whenever that first twinge of apprehension arises from somewhere within our mind. If something, however elusive, seems to be out of order, rather than waiting for clarification or for some divine power to make things right, accept the feeling as a wakeup call to do something. One of the easiest steps to take to resolve a budding dilemma is to ask a controller for help. Although none of us likes to admit that we are not all-knowing and all-seeing, the sooner a controller can be advised of a potential problem, the easier it will be for him to help a pilot resolve the issue at hand.

Consider a couple of the more common mistakes that pilots make and how they easily can be avoided just by asking for a little assistance. It is very easy, for example, for a pilot who is flying into an unfamiliar airport to suddenly become confused with respect to which runway is the correct one or even whether she is actually in right or left traffic. Often experienced pilots, some of whom have no doubt suffered through such an experience, preempt the problem by asking for "vectors to the final approach course" long before it becomes an issue. But often too many more plod along waiting for the light to dawn on the darkness of their confusion. Rather than create a potentially dangerous situation by landing on the wrong runway, it is far better for a pilot to admit her confusion and request some assistance. When the controller replies with something to the effect of "It's the longest runway and the approach end is just across the river," what was, moments before, a confusing maze of concrete can instantly become crystal clear.

In another example, if a controller asks a pilot for her distance from the airport but she hasn't the vaguest idea what it is (not an ideal situation but it happens), rather than make up an answer she should try to provide whatever honest answer best explains her position. "I don't know my exact distance but I am passing over downtown" is highly preferable to a fictitious "ten miles." The controller asked the question for a reason. In the world of air traffic control, with respect to safety the truth never hurts no matter how silly the answer might seem at the time.

Admitting the Problem

When prevention does not do the trick, and a pilot or a controller recognizes that he has made a mistake, the next most important item on the agenda must be to admit that a problem has occurred. Very early in my career as an air traffic controller one of the veterans who was training me offered the advice that, whenever I made a mistake and he assured me I would, the best thing to do was to admit it to the pilot and go on from there. Without exception, that bit of wisdom served me extremely well both as a controller and as a pilot. I learned that the only mistake that could be considered a stupid one was the mistake made by someone who was foolish enough not to admit that he made it. Even if the initial error happened to go unnoticed, which it usually doesn't, what started as a minor oversight can end up setting the stage for a developing nightmare.

But sometimes, as strange as it might seem, admitting to ourselves that we've made a mistake is sometimes harder than confessing our transgression to someone else. Whether it is fear of embarrassment or the fear of uncovering a heretofore hidden fatal flaw in our character or the anticipated admonishment by someone in authority or still some other psychologically based foundation, we can only guess. The problem is that allowing it to get in the way of resolving the issue only compounds the error.

When the time comes that a pilot realizes she has made a mistake, she needs to draw upon her mental discipline and work with what is left. Instead of getting caught in the trap of worrying about what others might think or what the consequences of her actions might be, she needs to pick up the pieces and continue to fly the airplane. Any time a pilot or a controller lets a mistake bother him, he may be opening the door to a barrage of needless and preventable emotions that easily could signal the beginning of a vicious and never-ending cycle of events.

Although I have conveniently erased my own reactions to unpleasant happenings from my consciousness, I recall having witnessed more than a few ruminations by pilots and controllers I had been training after they had strayed from the straight-and-narrow. In one particular situation wherein I was training a developmental controller during a busy approach session, he issued an incorrect instruction to a pilot that all too quickly put her nose-to-nose with an airplane not all that far away. After a few tense moments of awaiting the correction that never came, I stepped in and resolved the issue. In our later debriefing when I asked why he did not fix a problem that he clearly had noticed, he replied that he was so upset with himself for making the mistake in the first place that he could not think of an acceptable solution. Neither a pilot nor a controller can afford the luxury of spending time addressing his emotional condition in the midst of a dynamic time-critical situation. That needs to wait for the post-flight or position-relief debriefing.

What then are the possible consequences for a pilot who admits to a controller that she has made a mistake? Realistically, since controllers are in fact human, pilots need to be ready to expect and accept the full gamut of human emotions and responses. More often than not, pilots are pleasantly surprised by how controllers react. Very early in their training controllers are taught to understand that mistakes will be made and dealing with them is as much a part of their job as anything else. Believe it or not, the vast majority of controllers are sincere, dedicated people who enjoy working with and helping pilots as much as possible.

That is not to suggest, however, that a pilot will never run across some bozo who neither knows the difference between an elevator and an aileron nor cares. There continues to be a small number of controllers who have done just about everything possible to discredit their colleagues and their profession, but the rare encounter with one of them should not be reason to fear the rest. Neither should it ever be the reason a pilot abdicates her responsibility to ensure the safety of her aircraft. Instead, she needs to conscientiously and judiciously exercise that responsibility at all times and if that means politely but firmly telling a controller to back off, then so be it. Then, when she gets on the ground, taking the time to follow up the incident with a formal complaint to the appropriate facility can be the most effective measure to prevent similar situations from occurring in the future.

Occasionally, even the most patient controllers can and do get upset or frustrated with a pilot and their consternation likewise sometimes becomes blatantly evident on the frequency. Although it can happen for any number of reasons, usually it occurs when a pilot makes an ill-timed mistake that creates the potential for putting herself and possibly others in a hazardous situation. Although more of an explanation than a justification, occasionally it is all but impossible to stay cool and calm when a pilot unexpectedly does something to unnecessarily increase the risk of an accident or an incident, regardless of how unintentional her actions may have been. When certain events begin to unfold, a lot of things can happen very quickly and many of them can do so with decidedly unfavorable consequences. Even though displaying his ire may not be the best way for a controller to handle a problem, pilots who have mistakenly acted incorrectly need to accept an occasional sharp comment from controllers as they go through the learning process. It is usually easy to distinguish the controller who is reacting to one unsettling event from the congenital grump who dislikes everyone in general. Sometimes, discretion really is the better part of valor.

Someone Else's Error

Sometimes the tide turns and rather than a pilot having to be concerned with her own mistake she has to first, recognize when a controller has erred and second, decide what is the best way to deal with the situation. As was mentioned earlier, controllers make their share of bona fide blunders but, as often as not, it is other controllers rather than pilots who detect these mistakes and correct them. For the most part, the air traffic system and the procedures by which it operates have been set up with a series of checks and balances. A mistake that goes unnoticed by one controller frequently comes to the attention of another member of the team and is often resolved before any pilot is even aware of it. But sometimes, a pilot has to become the last line of defense in preventing an unsafe situation from developing.

When the time comes to successfully fulfill her responsibility as a safety backup to the air traffic system, each pilot needs to develop a mindset in which monitoring a controller's actions, detecting his errors, and exposing those errors to the light of day is part of her job. Rather than being an extraneous task that is best left to someone else, staying alert to the possibility of a controller mistake falls within the responsibilities of every pilot. Consequently, understanding why controllers make mistakes, when they are most likely to occur, and how to recognize the origins of a good idea gone bad is essential if a pilot is to effectively exercise that responsibility.

Though certainly every controller has his share of daily mishaps, the majority of the more noticeable mistakes can be attributed to developmental controllers who are still undergoing training. Much like a student pilot who has an instructor sitting in the right seat, a controller who is still being trained is under the constant and direct supervision of a fully rated controller who is ready and able to instantly take over the position if conditions begin to get out of hand. As part of their instructional process, these new controllers have to be able to make and correct their own errors if they are to progress along the learning curve. Pilots who find themselves the subjects of these experiences need to remember that, just as being a good pilot does not come overnight, neither does being a good controller. It may not always be fun, but as long as safety is not an issue, a little patience and understanding can go a long way toward helping novice controllers reach the end of their training road.

When the mistake carries with it the potential to do more than just create a temporary inconvenience for a pilot, it is an entirely different ballgame. Whether it is someone in training or a full-performance-level controller (the determination of which is not a pilot's responsibility to make), when a controller gives a pilot an instruction that she knows is either wrong or was given to the wrong pilot, she needs to advise that controller immediately. There is no reason to be hesitant about letting a controller know he made a mistake. First of all, it is the pilot not the controller who will be most directly affected by that error. To be truthful, controllers expect that they will be victims of their own mental lapses every so often, and they actually rely on pilots to bring those moments to their attention. Everyone involved has a very real stake in the results.

A controller is capable of making a mistake at any time, and while pilots should constantly be on the alert for that possibility, there are particular times when any controller will be more apt to err. It is fair to assume that as a controller's workload increases, the chance of doing something wrong almost always increases proportionally. Part of that reason is just a numbers game. As he makes more transmissions to more pilots, he simply has more opportunities to give an incorrect instruction. But it is also a matter of what a controller cannot do while he is talking to pilots. Every moment a controller spends talking to a pilot on the frequency is one less moment he has to think about what he has said and what he will say next. An error made that he might have detected, given the time to briefly reflect on his work, is much more likely to go unnoticed when he is busy. So every pilot needs to stay especially alert as the traffic gets heavier.

One of the best indicators a pilot can use to recognize when a controller is getting into a very high workload situation and one that will, therefore, increase the chances that he will make a mistake is when the frequency of his on-the-air corrections also increases. Whenever pilots start to hear a controller say something to the effect of, "One delta whiskey descend and maintain four thousand, *correction* descend and maintain three thousand," that is an error corrected. When those corrections become the rule rather than the exception, pilots need to pay very close attention to what is happening. That controller has started to spend more time just attending to the moment's traffic and less time thinking about the big picture. It does not happen all that often but when it does, many times it is the pilots who have to fill in the missing pieces of the puzzle.

Though many of the more common errors that controllers make are, in most instances, relatively harmless, any time a pilot detects one she nonetheless needs to bring it to their attention. Every so often one of those seemingly harmless mistakes can signal the beginning of a much bigger problem. As an example, when many controllers get busy, one of the things that occurs is transposing aircraft call signs. Cessna 23 Tango becomes Cessna 32 Tango. But when that happens, as much as she might not want to bother an already busy controller with what seems a trivial correction, a pilot needs to verify that the instruction that was issued with the transposed call sign was in fact meant for her. The day she does not verify it will be the day that there actually is a 32 Tango on the frequency and the downward spiral will begin. Likewise, if a controller calls your Bonanza an Arrow, take the time to correct him. Should a controller ever become bothered or defensive with respect to being corrected, which is unlikely but possible, don't worry about it. It is much better to offend someone than it is to let an error go uncorrected. Besides, it's your job to do it.

One of the most common errors that befalls a more inexperienced controller but one that can also afflict any of them at any time is when a controller instructs a pilot to turn in one direction when he actually wanted her to turn in the other. While it is one that can quickly turn a safe situation unsafe, fortunately it is also one that is easy to catch. In the normal course of events, a controller will almost always instruct a pilot to turn to a new heading in the direction that will result in the shortest turn. For example, if the plane's heading was 090 degrees and the controller wanted the pilot to turn it to a heading of 360 degrees, he would issue a left turn. If for some reason he did want the pilot to make a turn the long way around the compass, that controller should always emphasize that point one way or another. But, in the absence of that emphasis, any time a pilot is issued a heading that seems unusual or is unexpected, she should ask for verification.

One other fairly common mistake that controllers make may seem like little more than a nuisance to a pilot, but it can create a potentially hazardous situation for the unwary. For some controllers, issuing traffic with reference to the clock positions can be just about as difficult to master as processing the information is for pilots. But when a controller advises a pilot that she has traffic at 3 o'clock eastbound (that would indicate to a pilot that the traffic had already passed her location) it is time for a pilot to start looking for that traffic at her 9 o'clock position. Most assuredly, that is where the traffic will be. No controller is going to waste his or a pilot's time by issuing traffic that could not possibly be a matter of importance.

Regardless of the particular situation, when a pilot suspects that the controller has issued her an instruction that is either wrong or does not make any sense, one of the best ways to resolve the issue is to ask for verification as she repeats the instruction back to the controller. If, for example, the controller transmits, "Turn left heading three four zero," but a pilot believes a right turn is in order, the response should be, "Verify a left (emphasis on left) turn heading three four zero?" For some reason, it is much more likely that a controller will catch his mistake when he hears his same instruction repeated back to him by someone else. It is very similar to someone trying to proofread his own writing. The expectation of what was meant is so strong that the realization of what was actually said becomes almost irrelevant. It is as if a different voice saying the same thing alerts a different part of the brain, a portion that might not otherwise be alerted were the controller to just repeat the same thing he originally said a second time.

Achieving Error Tolerance

Finally, it is essential to realize that who makes the mistake or who makes more mistakes, pilots or controllers, is not the issue of concern. On any given day, each of us will contribute our share of errors to the process of working with one another. Two things are vitally important for every pilot and controller: first, expecting that neither will perform perfectly all of the time; and second, concentrating on reducing, minimizing the effect of, or eliminating as many of the errors as possible. If the air traffic system is to continue to be truly error tolerant, then everyone involved with it needs to learn how to best compensate for those errors when they are committed.

Most of us are neither better nor worse than those who have gone before or those who will follow. Although most of the nonhuman components in the aviation world have had their reliability dramatically increase over the years, the human element, however central to the overall success of aviation, still exhibits many of its frailties. All too often, a little bit of knowledge and a lot of plain luck can be the difference between making just the right decision at just the right time and getting caught up in circumstances that seem to conspire against us regardless of what we do. When a situation unexpectedly turns sour, any time wasted on deciding who is at fault would be much more wisely spent on finding resolution to the problem. To err is human; to fix the mistake is the job of every pilot and controller in the field.

15

The Pilot/Controller Partnership: Some Final Thoughts

WHEN I WAS FIRST APPROACHED to write this new edition of *The Air Traffic System, A Commonsense Guide*, some of the initial enthusiasm I felt quickly was replaced by an equal share of reluctance. Although I continued to work with the ATC system on a regular basis over the years, it was as a pilot not a controller. I became familiar with all of the changes that directly affected pilots—airspace, weather reporting formats, GPS, and so on—but I had not worked as a controller for quite a while. As a college professor who daily taught air traffic control students in both the classroom and the radar simulation lab, I kept up-to-date on all the latest regulations and procedures that affected how controllers did their jobs, but I was no longer one of them. So I wondered whether I would be able to convey the most important principles and concepts by which they abided to the pilots who most needed the information.

I began my research by talking to controllers in the field and visiting a busy approach control/tower facility and a likewise busy en route center. While the air traffic system finally did catch up to the technology of the twentieth century—albeit in the twenty-first century—what I quickly realized was that all of the procedures and methods of controlling traffic with which I was familiar were still being used, exactly as they had been fifteen years before. In some instances the radarscopes were new and improved, traffic management computers and the staff to operate them had replaced negotiating via an intercom, and the availability of real-time weather information had taken a quantum leap forward during my absence. But the real heart of the controller's job, talking with and working with pilots, had remained surprisingly but comfortably familiar. What likewise remained unchanged were the pilot/controller partnership and its vital importance as the most essential component of the air traffic system.

It is the people, not the massive arrays of equipment, who make our aviation system the most efficient and safest in the world. Without pilots, controllers would be out of a job. But it should also be obvious that if we are to keep all of today's pilots flying their respective airplanes with that degree of efficiency and safety that they have come to expect, the services of the air traffic controllers are essential and integral to that goal. If it ever was, it is no longer a one-sided system; we all need each other to survive and to do that most effectively every pilot and every controller needs to continue to foster an atmosphere of mutual respect and cooperation.

As trivial as it might sound, the single most effective way for a pilot to get the very best out of the air traffic system and the controllers who staff it is to treat each and every one of those controllers with kindness and courtesy. If for no other reason, there are a couple of very compelling (however self-serving they also may be) factors to consider when working within the pilot/controller partnership. The first is that controllers either consciously or unconsciously assess every pilot with whom they come in contact. The totality of that assessment is based solely upon the communications they have with that pilot. It is not just what a pilot says that helps them to determine his level of competence and cooperative nature, but how he says it. If a pilot seems to be congenial, relaxed, and in tune with the ways of the aviation world, most controllers react favorably. If another pilot strikes the controllers as being angry, argumentative, and displeased with just about every instruction he receives, most controller will, at least to some degree, respond in kind. It is not so much that the reactions of the controllers are intentional but rather that they are just human nature.

Being so one-dimensional, a controller's assessment of a pilot will be inaccurate at times. Some pilots are always more outgoing than others even though each is both willing and competent to work cooperatively with controllers. Some are more serious-minded and businesslike and equate any other demeanor with being unprofessional. And even the best of us may have some outside influences that can cause us to be less considerate than we otherwise might be. But however validly or mistakenly a controller appraises a pilot, her resulting determination gets thrown into the mix when she works a pilot into her traffic flow.

When one of the college's flight instructors was leaving to embark upon his career as a line pilot for a regional airline, I reminded him of my thoughts with respect to getting the most out of the air traffic system. About a year later he returned for a visit and enthusiastically reported that my advice to him had proved to be well founded. He said that in return for his consistently pleasant demeanor on the frequencies, almost every controller he worked with went out of his way to afford him the best possible service, at times, almost to his embarrassment. What he learned only after a while and what some pilots never seem to grasp is that controllers do recognize the voices of pilots with whom they work repeatedly. Whether or not that turns out to be a good thing almost entirely depends upon the pilot.

When that recognition turns out to be more of a bad thing, most controllers will likewise react accordingly. Except for the occasional idiot who lives in the darkest recesses of some ATC facilities, no controller will ever intentionally delay a pilot simply because he is lacking in the basics of human relations. But, on almost a minute-by-minute basis, one of the things that controllers do is cast the tie-breaking vote in an air traffic conflict. That is, whenever two airplanes are heading for the same piece of the sky at the same time, it becomes the responsibility of the controller to take some kind of action to ensure that only one gets there first. All things being equal, if the decision is between letting happy-pilot get there first or allowing grumpy-pilot to have his way, it is not too difficult to guess which way the coin will fall. The truth is that how we say something is every bit as important as what we say.

None of this is meant to suggest that pilots do not have legitimate occasion to be displeased with one aspect or another of the air traffic system or its controllers. There will undoubtedly be those times when a pilot believes that the system that was meant to serve him is instead pledging its allegiance to someone else. But more often than not, when a pilot complains about the system to a controller he is venting his ire to the wrong person. Controllers have no more power to change a set of regulated traffic procedures than pilots have to change their company's noise-abatement procedures. Whenever a situation arises in which things do not seem to be going as smoothly as they should, each of us should take a moment to think before we express our displeasure on the frequency. Is it the individual controller who is causing the problem or is it a policy or procedure that seems to be blocking the way to a more efficient flight? If the answer is the latter, raising the issue with someone who has no power to change the system really is an exercise in futility.

Still, there are bound to be those times when one thing or another starts to go awry. When that happens there likely will be words exchanged in the heat of the moment that result in an unpleasant confrontation. Basic human nature combined with real and legitimate concerns on both sides of the fence make those times inevitable. Add to that the fact that aviation tends to attract some very independent, free-spirited individuals and it all adds up to a recipe for a few outspoken conversations. But if each of us can make a conscious effort to exercise as much restraint as possible, the results usually will be much more favorable for everyone involved.

One of the best ways to acquire an attitude of willing cooperation is to learn as much as possible about the other person's role in the pilot/controller partnership. Over the years, I have had the good fortune to wear the hats of student pilot, pilot, flight instructor, air traffic controller, and collegiate educator for both flight and air traffic students. One of the results of playing those various roles has been that I have had numerous opportunities to expose pilots and controllers of almost every experience level to the other side of the partnership. Almost without exception, as each began to learn more about the other's tasks and responsibilities and the amount of education and skill it takes to successfully fulfill their duties, they came away with a much greater appreciation and respect for their partners.

Through the use of some very advanced and realistic radar and tower simulation equipment, many pilots have been able to experience, firsthand, what it is like to be responsible for directing traffic through their assigned airspace. In the process they begin to grasp the concept that controlling air traffic is based more on dealing with countless variables and the effects those variables have on exercising good judgment than it is on applying the rules and regulations. They learn that when a controller vectors an airplane there is not a precise mathematical formula to derive the correct heading. Rather, the answer comes from a variety of factors that must be considered. A controller has to keep in mind things such as the winds aloft at various altitudes, other weather conditions, the individuality of each pilot, the type of aircraft he is flying, and a host of other variables. Each of these considerations, regardless of how subtle or obscure any one of them might be, continually must be taken into account because each is an integral component of the process of safely controlling airplanes.

Controllers spend anywhere from two to four years in the various stages of training that lead to becoming fully rated controllers. But when the formal training ends, the real learning begins. On average, it takes most controllers at least another year or two of working traffic by themselves before they become truly seasoned and capable of handling anything that may come their way. Prior to that they know the fundamentals, they know how to handle the usual, and some of the unusual situations that occur, and they know how to ask for help when it is needed. But the personal confidence and judgment required to take on anything pilots may throw their way comes only with the passage of time. For a pilot who can have the opportunity, one hour spent vectoring airplanes on a simulator can do more to convince him what a controller's job is like than a thousand pages of words could ever do.

Controllers, on the other hand, need to understand and experience what it is like to be a pilot-in-command. For more than a few controllers who are also pilots, gaining a different perspective is much less of an issue. Many of them are as addicted to flying as the most active full-time pilots and they often can be found at their local airports eagerly readying for their next leap into the air. But even some of the others who are not pilots occasionally get the opportunity to ride along with a friend and experience some of what goes on in the cockpit. Although riding along with someone else who is doing all of the work can never be a substitute for flying solo and bearing all the responsibility that goes with the territory alone, it is still an opportunity worth taking. Otherwise, when controllers do not frequently associate themselves with the world of the pilot, it is easy to become detached from that other real world.

There is a natural tendency for controllers to forget that when a pilot asks for a different altitude because of icing or turbulence or he asks for a different heading around some nasty looking clouds, there is often a sense of urgency that has prompted the request. It is not that controllers are oblivious to a pilot's request or unconcerned with his situation, but the sense of immediacy that the pilot may be feeling is hard to recall when the controller hearing it is sitting comfortably in a quiet, motionless radar room. The best solution to the problem is for pilots to take every opportunity they can to get those ground-loving controllers into the air. It used to be commonplace for general aviation pilots to ask if there were any controllers at the airport who wanted to go along for a ride any time they had an extra seat available. In many areas that practice seems to have fallen by the wayside, but it is one of the easiest ways to remind controllers that there are actually real people inside those little targets they watch every day.

Impact of September 11, 2001

Unfortunately for everyone in the aviation community, what used to be as easy as picking up a telephone is now next to impossible. While there is not much that can be said or anything that has not already been said, it is almost impossible to write about the world of aviation without making some mention of the incredibly terrible events of September 11, 2001. In more ways than pilots might ever have imagined, since that day changes to the ways in which both pilots and controllers do business occur on almost a daily basis. None more profoundly affect the pilot/controller partnership than the restrictions that significantly hamper the ability of each to interact with the other.

Through the Wings Program and a number of other worthwhile pilot-controller forums, the FAA is making a significant effort to offer pilots a series of events at which they and controllers can get together to discuss problems and differing opinions relating to situations that occur within the air traffic system. Controllers get to hear firsthand some of the specific complaints that pilots have and they, in turn, get the opportunity to more fully explain why certain procedures exist. Though neither side may walk away completely convinced that the other's position should be the prevailing one, everyone usually gains a greater appreciation for the genuine concern exhibited by all of the participants.

Unfortunately, many of the opportunities that used to occur to visit one another's place of work have all but disappeared. In a strange and sad twist of irony, it is now easier for a traveler to traverse the city of Berlin than it is for a pilot to gain access to an air traffic facility, or for a controller to ride along in the cockpit of an airliner, both of which used to be commonplace. The new reality is that each is first seen as a threat to the other and only if and when that threat is replaced by the assurance of good intentions are pilots and controllers allowed to experience each other's worlds. However real the threat to our national security is, the loss of easy access to the cockpits and the air traffic facilities for controllers and pilots is an equally significant loss for the pilot/controller partnership.

Another consequence of the September 11 events is that pilots, controllers, and flight service specialists have been forced to deal with *Temporary Flight Restrictions (TFR)* in unprecedented numbers. Sometimes on a daily basis, dozens of TFRs around the country appear, disappear, and then reappear almost without warning. As a result of their transgressions, a few pilots who ventured into those forbidden areas were afforded the opportunity to get more up close and personal with military fighter escorts than they might have cared to. But TFRs are another airspace restriction we all will have to live with for at least the foreseeable future.

But there are other changes under way that suggest the ways in which pilots and controllers work with one another will likewise be different. The already existing TCAS equipment available for the higher-end aircraft has shifted some of the ability to electronically see traffic from what was once the private domain of the controllers to the cockpit where it can be more readily accessed. That in turn has given pilots the added ability to more directly affect their own safety. While a few controllers may see TCAS as an erosion to their authority, the vast majority see it for what it is, an essential backup to air traffic control. Before long, similar capabilities undoubtedly will work their way into the cockpits of most general aviation airplanes, thereby offering the promise of increased safety for every pilot.

Even that is just the beginning. Free Flight, a concept by which pilots determine their individual flight paths based upon weather and other traffic information, all of which is available in the cockpit, is already being tested in certain areas and likewise promises to alter the ways in which pilot and controller work together. Rather than directly controlling each aircraft, the job of the controller may evolve into more of a monitoring role, stepping in only when it is absolutely necessary. In addition, it is not unlikely that in the future the entire architecture of the air traffic system and the radar systems that serve it will both change dramatically. The possibilities truly are endless.

But, whether for better or worse—a debate for which there likewise may be no end—as each change is made, as each new piece of technology is added to our aviation system, and as the resulting automation continues to increase, the roles of the pilots and the controllers and how they work together also will take on new and different dimensions. It seems that how far they will be removed from the foreground will depend upon who is designing that new architecture.

For those charged with shaping the future of air travel, they would be well served to keep in mind those events of September 11, 2001. As the events themselves were a never-before-experienced disaster of almost unimaginable proportions, the response to them, which was of historical proportions, also covered ground that had yet to be trod upon. At an unknown yet potentially great risk to themselves, pilots and air traffic controllers around the country and around the world undertook the massive effort to safely land in a matter of hours every airplane that was either within or bound for the United States. Although anyone who was in any way involved in the world of aviation likely will never forget the unsettling silence that was the result of those efforts, nowhere is there a more powerful example of the strength and value of the pilot/controller relationship than in the events of that day.

Whatever else may be changing in the world of aviation, the good news is that the quality of the people who inhabit that world is not. Whether it is the pilots or the controllers, the determination and dedication with which they approach their respective roles seem only to have increased over the years. As each continues to explore and understand the other's contributions to the goals of improved safety and increased efficiency, the appreciation they share for their mutually dependent partnership can only get better.